Earth 2012-33

Oracles of the Sea

Praise for the Earth 2012-33 Series

The Earth 2012-33 Series will speak to hearts around the world. It will quicken the Awakening in many people who have tried to make sense of similar experiences. It will bring relief to those of us who have pictured a negative future. It will help others realize the potential that is being birthed within us all in this extraordinary time. After working closely with Dr. Aurora Juliana Ariel on this project and personally experiencing TheQuest, I am excited to see the powerful ramifications this book will have on people around the world. —*Jack Canfield, Author of Success Principles and Co-Author of the Chicken Soup For The Soul Series*

This inspiring, prophetic book speaks to a Soul Awakening that if embraced, can take humanity through a quantum leap into a future Eden that has forever lived as a vision within the hearts of humanity. —*John Gray, Author of Men Are From Mars, Women Are From Venus*

A clarion call to consciousness awakening to itself, Earth 2012-33 books quicken spiritual unfolding by lovingly guiding you through one of the most difficult and transformative periods in human history. —*Leonard Laskow, M.D., Author of Healing With Love*

This book rises to the heights of poetry, unveiling a majesty of human potential like a torch in the morning light. It adds its brilliance to what is silently arising all around us. —*Jonathan Kolber*

This book will guide you inward to remember your truth and why you were born at this glorious moment in time! —*Jared Rosen, Author of The Flip: Turn Your World Around, and Inner Security And Infinite Wealth*

This powerful, practical book will guide you through one of the most challenging periods in our collective history. Read it please! —*Harold H. Bloomfield, M.D., NY Times bestselling author of 19 books.*

In this exciting book you are immediately transformed by Aurora's passionate wisdom and captivated in a fascinating wake-up call to humankind. This masterpiece is a must to read! —*Karina Schelde, Author of Soul Voice*

This book is filled with love, clarity, and reverence... a breath of Light and air. It is a wonderful offering! Truly Inspiring! What a gift! It is food for the soul. —*Allan Cohen, Author of 20 books including The Dragon Doesn't Live Here Anymore*

In the book, Earth 2012-33: The Ultimate Quest, Aurora Juliana Ariel graces us with the wisdom and inspiration of her clear channel to Spirit. The truths that we hear in her writing are echoes of the free, expansive and Radiant Being that is the Eternal Self. We are fortunate to have pure souls like Aurora on this planet to remind us of who we really are. Her book is a great gift for those who would travel the path of spiritual transcendence, awakening and its abiding peace. —*Kamala Allen, PhD, Author of A Woman's Guide to Opening A Man's Heart.*

This book is so full of light! Our collective objective as spiritual beings is to increase the vibratory rate of all whom we come in contact with and to those whom we reach out to. The energy field this comprehensive body of work emits is very empowering and humanity will benefit greatly from it. In a world shrouded in darkness, it will help to light the way to peace, love and understanding. —*Bruce Robert Travis, Author of My Past Life As Jesus: An Autobiography Of Two Lifetimes*

Aurora's work goes directly to the core issues that humanity needs to address in order to shift into the new paradigm. Her experience and insights into the evolution of the soul shines a healing light and balm into areas of the human psyche that need healing, transmutation, and release. Her techniques for clearing and raising our frequencies to accelerate our process of Self-Mastery and Ascension are most effective and transforming. —*Aeoliah, Composer, Author, Reiki Master*

This inspirational book (Earth 2012-33: The Ultimate Quest), will help give you guidance and inner peace in a world filled with so many adversities, Dr. Ariel will bring balance to your world through her writings. —*Mariah Napenthe Brown, owner of Da Kitchen Restaurants, and daughter of Dr. Ariel*

Words cannot adequately express the wisdom, majesty and beauty of the inspired information in this book. As I read the uplifting and empowering words, I "feel" how important it is that this wondrous message be distributed far and wide to awaken and empower the millions of people that have been waiting for these words all their lives. It is sacred work! Humanity is at a time of ripeness for this awakening. This book of spiritual teaching and encouragement can help facilitate this awakening. This exquisitely beautiful work will truly enlighten the world. —*Sharon Huffman, Contributing Author of Ten Traits of Highly Effective Teachers; and Chicken Soup For the Soul*

This exquisitely crafted body of knowledge is a profound embrace of the spiritual history of humanity, offering insights into the power of TheQuest to conquer all obstacles, returning us quickly to the joyful expression of our Divine Nature. The triumphant arrival of the long-awaited Violet Race is celebrated as we traverse the Divine Romance of the journey of our hearts through time. The story of The Great Adventure is our true story, for we are the Heroes of the new Heaven on Earth. For all who wish to undertake the challenge of this time of transformation, this book is a guide and a blessing! —*Mirra Rose, Internationally renowned Spiritual Teacher and Healer*

I have just read Aurora Ariel's book Earth 2012-33: The Ultimate Quest. I got a spiritual uplift from reading the content and a reminder that "my world" is determined by myself and the Inner Aspects within me. I thank Dr. Ariel for her boldness, in writing, in life in general and her views of spirituality in Today's world. Her technique of looking within ourself to unlock our subconscious patterns that hold us back from being who we really are - our full potential - is unique. It shows me that my existence is determined by me and the inner aspects within me. I also appreciate what Aurora shares about her own struggles & triumphs, her boldness in writing and in Life. Thank you, Aurora for being yourself. —*Chris Brown in AZ*

The Earth 2012-33 Series of books have brought me hope and tools I can use to further change my life. Tools for awakening, uncovering, and healing my Shadow Self. The books call to me, challenging me to heal my lifetimes of shadows and seek to fully enter my rightful Authentic Self. This allows me to meet my full potential face to face, by using Miracles of The Quest. —*Linda Camarata, LPN, Phoenix, Arizona*

An uplifting beautifully written book, with much more than prophecies and predictions, Earth 2012-33, The Ultimate Quest, reminds us of our mission, our destiny, and most importantly, that the world needs us. —*Marci Winters, editor for the Maui Vision magazine, writer, screenwriter, director, and producer.*

2012 is prophesied by many to be the end of the World, but what does it mean on a spiritual level? Earth 2012-33: The Ultimate Quest - How to Find Peace in a World of Chaos encourages readers to embark on a personal quest to push themselves to find inner peace. With many ideas fresh and new to readers throughout, the Earth 2012-33 series, would be excellent reading for anyone who feels like their lives are at the end times, and thinks it could be better. —*Midwest Book Review (Oregon, WI USA) (also posted on Amazon.com). Gave a 5 Star rating.*

Congratulations and thank you for sharing these wonderful discoveries with us – it reads like a very precious spiritual guide and such insightful journey into the realm of the soul and psyche. I wish you great success – it vibrates like a bestseller! —*Marius Michael George, Artist*

I have read Aurora's first book in the Earth 2012-33 Series. My opinion? It is amazing, it is a treasure, it is true, and it works. If there is one book you should INVEST your time and energy (your pearls) in learning for the times in which we live, it is in Earth 2012:The Ultimate Quest. Aurora is a great writer because the book is easy to read and understand. This is what a great write can do. I can't wait to read her next, newest book. And her music... is Heaven on Earth. Skip the Latte this week and get her book and CD. —*Dorlon Peckham*

Earth 2012-33: The Ultimate Quest winning a Visionary Award (COVR) is so exciting!! Your book is so revolutionary and such a blessing to the planet. —*Bernadette Jean Marie, Health Practitioner, Ojai, California*

Hello from Australia. I am reading your amazing book, Earth 2012-33: The Ultimate Quest. I love it! There is something about you. I went looking in this shop for something I wasn't sure what for, and your book made me buy it. The pieces fell into place as I began to read. I needed to know about TheQuest. —*Zoey Loizou, Melbourne, Australia*

First of all, let me thank YOU for your book. In the body of literature out there dealing with 2012 and transformation, your book is an important contribution. (I have read more than a few.) I bought Earth 2012-33: The Ultimate Quest because it offers a way to find out what part of me stands in the way of bringing out my Authentic Self. (I have not done any psychotherapy or other such work other than one past life regression. I do share the characteristics of Violet Persons.) After a successful career in the corporate world for many years, I find myself on my own going where I know not. I sense that if I can connect with the 'Divine Within', I can get past the paralysis I find myself in. I like your book because: Your writing style is approachable and candid. The chapters are short and well organized. This makes it easy to not only comprehend the information the first time through, but it is easy to go back and find information again to bring it all together. It is also fun to re-read many times to assimilate the information! Your book is both personal and global, approaching the galactic. These are necessary perspectives to keep together in our minds and hearts in these times. I sense that your book is giving me a 'shovel' with which to dig into my inner world and see what is there, and perhaps, construct a tunnel of light to where darkness now resides. Thank you again, Aurora, for your book and your gifts of communication! - *Chuck Wright, Chesapeake, Virginia*

I finally have your book, Earth 2012-33: The Ultimate Quest and can't put it down. Part 1 defined my life to a T. You must have been through so much. So far, I have gotten to the Art of Self Counseling and am reading the 7 Steps. From the first few chapters, I realize that this book is going to affect my life! One day soon, I will be writing you about the results. As recently as this morning, I see events and behavioral patterns repeating themselves in my life and am ready to make an improvement. I would write more, but am too anxious to continue reading! Bless you! —*Annie Drake, Sales Associate, Costa Rica*

Barnes and Noble customer review: July 17, 2008 - Rated: 5 Stars - Such a wonderful piece of work. I am eager to see more from this writer.

I was visiting a small book store one day, looking at the many shelves of books and their titles. Searching for words that could possibly lead me to find meaning for the turmoil in my life, I was drawn to Earth 2012-33: The Ultimate Quest, How to Find Peace in a World of Chaos even though I was more familiar with the other authors. As I began reading the book, I got this rock solid feeling. Like when you know everything is going to be all right. The words spoke to me of gentleness and kindness, no blame, so simple to follow. I was amazed, and reread several chapters at once before putting the book down. As life returned to my normal chaos, I would pick up the book and reread several chapters finding comfort. I slept with this book on my bed for weeks, awakening in the middle of the night to read yet again and find comfort. This went on for six months when I realized I wanted to not only change my life but help others find a way to change their lives also. Not having much confidence in myself, I mustered energy to contact Dr. Ariel and thought, "Why not?" Sending off a note inquiring about the one year Counselor Certification Course, I am happy to say I am now a student of TheQuest with Dr. Ariel. I am excited about the rewards that are received through The Quest Counselor program. It is that feeling that I can handle my life with seven simple steps. This program gives to the individual tools to take with you forever, wherever, whenever you are in need of assistance. You can do this for yourself! We can help our loved ones with these simple steps. TheQuest is a gift to humanity. Thanks Dr. Ariel for sharing your program of insight into the human psyche, and giving us a way to heal and help others. —*Linda Camarata, LPN, Phoenix, Arizona*

Earth 2012-33: The Ultimate Quest has two major themes. First, is the precarious situation that exists in our world today as we approach the year 2012, or the end of the Mayan calendar and what this could mean for the Earth and all life upon it. More specifically, Dr. Ariel believes the fate of the world is in our hands and that we can create or, re create true Heaven on Earth, and avoid all the negative doomsday scenarios that seem to be encroaching on our lives at an increasing rate. How we can do this brings us to the second theme which is TheQuest. TheQuest is a unique form of psychotherapy that Dr. Ariel has created that allows us to swiftly identify and change all negative programs we have absorbed into our sub-conscious, the very same programs that are responsible for the dire state of the world at this time. With this therapy, one can go back and change negative programs or patterns that were handed down from our ancestors, thus reversing much damage that has been done.

What's even more exciting is that she offers TheQuest as a self healing system, which can be easily learned and practiced without having to pay a therapist huge amounts of money. Dr. Ariel goes into both these themes with great depth and understanding, leaving the reader (or me at least) thoroughly convinced and motivated. I especially appreciated the book's positive outlook and creative solutions to the "doomsday scenarios" we are so easily led to believe are approaching in the near future. Without ignoring the negative possibilities we are facing, she kept a powerful positive outlook and offered much to think about and do in the face of our dire situation.

EARTH 2012-33: The Ultimate Quest spoke to me in many ways, voicing things that I had long felt but never was really able to access in a book that I have been trying to write on similar topics. I found reading it to be a powerful, inspiring experience. I certainly learned a lot of things of great value and many changes will result in my life as a direct result of reading this book. I wanted to delve deeper into TheQuest experience, so I went to the website given in the book and called a phone number there. Low and behold I found myself talking to the author herself in Hawaii, and by the time I hung up I had committed to a two year study with her, that I have embarked upon and am certain will be a life changing experience for me. I would say for certain that the first book in the Earth 2012-33 series had a huge impact. I have recommended the bok to several people. I tell people it is a book that can change your life, a must for anyone who is at all concerned about the fate of the Earth and the human race. It is fresh and new, easy to read and very convincing.... And, Dr. Ariel is there to back up her work 100 percent. —*Tanager Kastner, Vermont*

Thank you and Namaste with all my heart and awareness for the passion and commitment and insight and tools and love you bring to life itself and to me and to us at such a timely and receptive moment, through your study and your experiential wisdom and your book with "A way through" the darkness into the joyous light, right here, right now, and soon everywhere. —*Wendy Singleton, Maui, Hawaii*

I got your book today. Started reading it. Very beautifully done in all of its aspects. I am very inspired by what your intentionality is for our beautiful Earth bubble and its "Asleep At The Wheel' human doings!!! —*Daveed Cusack, Marin, California*

Yesterday I sat in a quiet place to settle into an uninterrupted read of Earth 2012-33: The Ultimate Quest. I bawled my eyes out within the first couple of chapters ... WOW. Very effective in reaching the 'higher self' within each being. The medicine of this book is in the reading. It gave me strength to write a letter to my ex husband and reach out in the spirit of

Ho'oponopono. Let's see if it works magic. It's an honor, really, to know you and play a small part in global transformation. Sending you love and light and heartfelt support. —*Tara Grace, Realtor*

I read your book last night and it's GREAT! The writing is graceful and transparent and it's a flowing balance of useful techniques, personal stories, academic research and profound social commentary. An amazing amount for one book, presented in a way that isn't at all overwhelming or crowded. I'm so proud of you! I agree that there are those of us who came here to spearhead an evolutionary leap in humankind and it's an honor to support each other as we navigate through the insanity of human life to do that. —*Vajra, M.A., Founder and Director of Diamond Light Center for Spiritual Awakening*

We love your book so much! It's interesting that the word that surfaces in my mind when I think of you is proud! Your synthesis of so many good things plus your own evolved additions and stories makes for a very nourishing elixir. —*Tomas and Dr. Joan Heartfield, authors of Romancing the Beloved. Co-Creators of Conversations That Matter, Opening to Love Ceremonies, and Romancing the Beloved*

I am truly grateful for this book. I found its contents fascinating. I highly recommend it to the many friends I know. —*Ronald Cole, Astrologer*

Earth 2012-33: The Ultimate Quest... I am absolutely blown away! I don't know if I've ever seen anything quite like this! I can't wait to continue this beautiful piece of work of yours. What a fabulous job! —*Jody Mack, Real Estate Broker, Aspen, Colorado*

Powerful book!!! Salute to success! —*Bruce BecVar, recording artist, composer, multi-instrumentalist*

You deserve so much credit for all you have put into this effort. It is a beautiful thing. The cover is beautiful, you are beautiful, and I know the book, the music, all the multimedia projects will be a huge success. It has been a pleasure to see this whole venture come into reality. —*Bill Mollring*

Congratulations, love the cover! You are on the right path. It has to be a defining moment – I am so happy for you! — *Arben Kryeziu*

Congratulations! What a beautiful cover and how exciting to be bringing out your life's work. Thank you for sharing it with us. With much Aloha! —*Neto and Barbara, recording artists*

Wow! This is unreal! —*Mimi Hu, Levin & Hu, CPA Firm*

Oh, sweet mystic, congratulations. Your persistence in the face of all obstacles is in itself a tribute to the human spirit and dream potential. My full admiration goes out to you. I am so very blessed by the knowledge of your courage and perseverance. Peace as the main topic will trigger folks in turmoil from all types of people.. it will transcend the boundaries folks put up to new age... old to young, all religions.. smart move! — *DJ Martinovich*

This is beautiful! The book design is elegant, your words profound. Congratulations! You created a great cover, and with such powerful high praise your presentation looks like an "Oprah must read". You should be ecstatic! —*Mark Mackay, Artist*

Oh my God! Everything looks amazing! The book cover is stunning! Its perfect. Beyond my imagination! —*Aradeus Daffin, Aurora's youngest son*

Earth 2012-33: Time of the Awakening Soul is about awakening to our Authentic Selves. I learned so many things about my self from reading this book. First and foremost, I realized I identified with all 22 signatures of the Violet Soul. I reread the chapter on the 22 Master Qualities several times. I now sense I am unique, and not the odd one out in the family.

There is a family of Violet Souls that I belong to. I don't have to know them personally, but I do know we are persons of extraordinary potential. We cross paths every day and are joining together to save the planet. We are having visions, and we are carrying out our visions to create a new way to live together in a world of peace, with extraordinary potential. The words of this book confirms for me, when we walk our own path to assist this Awakening for the survival of humanity, we are becoming more aware of our own true potential. We are finding peace, healing our psyche as we shake off the Shadow Self and are coming into our Authentic Selves. —*Linda Camarata, LPN, Phoenix, Arizona*

Healing, Inspired Music, Books & Audio CDs

By #1 Bestselling Award Winning Author, Aurora Juliana Ariel, PhD

Earth 2012-33: The Ultimate Quest - Vol 1
How To Find Peace In a World of Chaos

Earth 2012-33: Time of the Awakening Soul - Vol 2
How Millions of People Are Changing Our Future

Earth 2012-33: The Violet Age - Vol 3
A Return to Eden, The Regenesis that is Birthing a New World

Earth 2012-33: Oracles of the Sea - Vol 4
The Human Dolphin Connection

TheQuest Self Healing System
TheQuest book, Healing Journal, and 7 Step CD

The Indwelling Spirit
An Illumined Pathway to Freedom, Enlightenment and Peace

Sacred Knowledge Collection CDs
Exploring the Afterlife; The Soul's Journey; Journey Into the Future

Healing Music For An Awakening World CDs
12 Healing Music Journeys by Aurora, Bruce BecVar & Krystofer

The Healing Power of Love CDs
7 Divine Healing Transmissions

Renaissance of Grace
Aurora's World Music CD with Bruce BecVar

Gypsy Soul, Heart of Passion
Gypsy World Music CD by Bruce BecVar & Aurora

River of Gold
New Age Music CD by Bruce BecVar and Aurora

AVAILABLE IN BOOK & MUSIC STORES WORLDWIDE

A New Frontier In Multimedia Arts
Inspired Music, Books, & Films

Publisher: AEOS, Inc.
PO Box 433, Malibu, California 90265
Ph: 310-591-8799 Fax: 413-521-8799
Email: Info@AEOS.ws
Website: http://www.AEOS.ws

Cover Art "Guardians of the Grail" **by** Andrew Annenberg
http://www.AndrewAnnenberg.com
Art Direction and Cover Design by Aurora Juliana Ariel
Master Interior Design by Kareen Ross
Bio Photos by Monique Feil & Carl Studna
Dolphin Picture by Ted Roe
Edit by Michael Holwell

Printed in the USA

FIRST EDITION
Library of Congress
ISBN 978-0-9847571-8-3

Dedication

I dedicate this offering
To Awakening Souls worldwide
In gratitude and awe of the Majesty and Grace
Of the Cetacean Nations,
Whose alchemical and healing gifts are helping
Inspire us to nobler heights and
Conscious Stewardship of the Earth

* * * * * * *

An Invitation

Come Awakening Souls
Live in the Glorious New Paradigm with us
Where Heaven knows its fulfillment on Earth
Sing, dance, let Joy lead you onward
Let starry skies and brilliant sunsets
Fill your minds with Deep Contentment
Keep you simple, in Deep Quiet
Keep you Openhearted, Joyful
Laughter, Play, Divine Orchestrations
Brilliant Symphonies, Sacred Events
This is the life we call you to, humanity
The life that knows Joy in every breath

- The Dolphins

Acknowledgments

With the deepest gratitude
I acknowledge and thank...

The many incredible teachers who have shed light on my pathway, too numerous to name.

The dolphins. for the spectacular journey I was taken on as you invited me into your world, showered me with gifts, and reawakened my child-like wonder in the Magic of Life. Thank you for inspiring this book and for initiating the Earth 2012-33 series. I am deeply grateful for the honor of being chosen to bring your message to the world, so that people everywhere will know of your Great Offering to humanity at this time.

Jack Canfield, for your sage advice on the Earth 2012-33 series, willingness to come on board as co-author to help steward this project (though Life had its own plan), and your help with choosing the initial stories for this book.

Joe Sugarman, Tara Grace, and Marc Ivey for your support of AEOS and my Life's Work.

My beautiful children, Mariah, Araphiel, Gabriel, and Aradeus, for your love, support, and unwavering belief in me.

Andrew Annenberg for providing your gorgeous cover art, 'Guardians of the Grail.'

Ted Roe, for the dolphin picture that is gracing the entry into the 7 parts.

Everyone who shared their inspiring stories in this book, including Teresa Hill, Joe Noonan, Ilona Selke, Rytwin Lee, Marla Maples, Pamela Polland, Nancy Smyth Myers, Jason Cressey, Catherine Espinoza, Bennie Kante, Cecily Miller, Lily Townsend, Judith Greenwood, John Kahele, Paul Doty, Matisha, Shivani Goodman PhD, Kiki Corbin, Paulette Chang, Paul Overman, Emerald Starr, Shanta Hartzell, Takara, Rona Smith, Cindy Brower, Mirra Rose, Trish Regan, Robert Frey, Ted Roe, Daniel McCulloch, Morning Star Black, Paula Peterson, Linda Chambers, Susan

Thompson, Doug Hackett, Donna Waugh Campbell, Becky Stambaugh, Jiah Miesel, Mark Mackay, Lois Hootz, Sylvie Tannesen, and Karina Ashana. Your stories have been an important addition to this treatise on the Human Dolphin connection.

Michael Holwell, for opening your beautiful home in Hawaii to me while I completed this book, and for lending your incredible proof reading skills, excellent cacao products from your Completely Different Chocolate Company (my favorite: Kona Coffee Dark), and filling my off time with magical adventures, dolphins encounters, Full Moon Total Lunar Eclipse at 5 am, trek to the Volcano and more, which we both joyously shared.

Elizabeth Lutz and Bernadette Vazquez of my Sacred Healing Circle, for your support and loving presence in my life.

My dearest friends, Bernadette and Chester Jagiello, Arya Bruce BecVar, Melea Moir, Susan Saltz, Sirah Vettese, Landon Fey, Teresa Hill, and the many others who have graced my life with your loving presence. Your love and support has meant everything to me.

Contents

Part Five: Interventions and Protection

Part Six: Telepathic Communications

Part Seven: Divine Destiny

Addendum:

Introduction

The stories in this book are true. As miraculous as they may seem, they are written by credible people whose lives have been greatly impacted by dolphin encounters worldwide. Reading this book with an open mind can expand your awareness to the infinite wonders many are experiencing in this time. This is the mystical side of our present day planetary equation, a doorway that is open to each one of us.

To protect the sacred lands and bays dolphins frequent, I've chosen to keep specific locations nameless. When and if you are called into the dolphin world, they will find you and you them... just as they are now touching your life through this book. Perhaps the MAGIC is just beginning, or maybe you are a veteran of dolphin encounters. Either way, this book will initiate you into the next level of your awakening.

The human dolphin connection is an important thread being woven into the tapestry of this significant time, with its portent to raise humanity into a whole new way of living and being that could birth a New World.

Each book in the Earth 2012-33 series has been an important piece to the puzzle in our present planetary equation. It is not only exciting, it is life changing. The second you begin reading, hearing, or seeing something about dolphins, they magically enter your world. If you have not experienced this yet, just be open. It's only a matter of time!

The dolphins have been present since the inception of the Earth 2012-33 series. In fact, it was the dolphins who initiated it. I tell that amazing story in chapter two of Part One.

Powerful allies at this historical time in Earth history, the rash of dolphin encounters taking place worldwide are far reaching. Dolphins have become major contributors in the awakening that is advancing the soul evolution of the planet. Facilitating a dramatic shift in the consciousness of humanity, it is as if they hold alchemical keys to transforming us back to our original innocence, no matter what trials or tribulations we've endured or how long we've departed from our once joyous nature. Restored to our innate childlike wonder, we enter the Miracle Consciousness and live a Miraculous Life. This is the gift the dolphins are offering humanity at this time.

A Quick Recap...

In the first book of the Earth 2012-33 series, *Earth 2012-33: The Ultimate Quest*, How to Find Peace in a World of Chaos, I spoke of the glorious time we are in as we reach what is perhaps Earth's most epic moment in history on our journey through the Gateway of 2012-33. I revealed the signs of the times, the portent in the skies, and the prophetic wisdom of the Elders, as Earth Inhabitants are being prepared at inner levels to make the Shift of the Ages. A serious body of work in the voice of the pioneering doctor, healer, scientist, humanitarian, mystic and futurist, I lay out the cause of suffering creating the dire potentials before us and a cure in the psychological healing system I developed called TheQuest.

In the second book of the series, *Earth 2012-33: Time of the Awakening Soul, How Millions Are Changing Our Future*, I unveiled the mystical connection inspiring Violet People in their mission to birth a New World. I bring an understanding of the Violet Person and lay out their 22 master qualities. These Violet qualities are presently shared by millions of Awakening Souls worldwide. Take the test to see if you are a Violet.

Violet Soul influence has greatly impacted our world since the 60's, when a host of positive planetary movements launched New Archetypes for the New Millennium, setting the stage for an enlightened era prophesied by Elders of many nations. Woven throughout the book are extraordinary stories written by Violet People

In the third book of the series, *Earth 2012-33: The Violet Age, A Return to Eden,* I continue the Earth 2012-33 saga with mystical stories to inspire the souls of humanity and their own awakening. There are many phenomena inspiring the Violet Movement, awakening humanity to play its unique role in transforming the planet.

In this fourth book of the series, the MAGIC continues. Please write me and let me know what you think about this book, and if the dolphins have brought magic into your life.

Part One

Mystery & Magic

Magic

O, Beloved
Feel the Magic of our Presence with you
as we glide through the turquoise waters of the Earth
playing with the Joyous Awakening of your True Spirit
We have called you and you have come.
We bring the Magic of Life abundantly,
magnificently to the shores of your reality.
You dwell for a time in our Realms.
We show you the Peace that is lived in Joy and the
Wondrousness of Life you must be reawakened to
for it is the Forgotten Knowledge.
O, Glorious Ones
We see your True Radiance
Shining forth from the Cave of self,
that long lost treasure you must now divine
And in finding this lost part of you,
learn once again to live it fully.
For it has been a long time on Earth
Since you danced with us in our waters
and knew the Blessed Union we once shared,
when you were Divine because you knew you were
and so lived a Sacred Life that befits a Divine One.
You have lost the dance, Beloved!
As you come into our waters
You find the Dance of Life again.
As you drink deeply of this most sacred experience,
the Magic of our Presence is bequeathed to you.

- The Dolphins

CHAPTER ONE

Extraordinary Encounters

For the past thirty three years, dolphin interactions with humans have increased dramatically resulting in a host of miraculous stories that include extraordinary encounters, mystical experiences, profound visions, telepathic communications, unexpected healings, life changes, inner transformations, and spiritual awakenings. Amazingly, these experiences are similar to events recorded at the advent of the Golden Age in Greece.

Dolphin encounters were said to be a part of Greek history at a time when profound changes in consciousness moved its people into a Renaissance that birthed a Golden Age. Through present-time dolphin encounters, we are seeing a similar pattern and with it, a definite piece to the puzzle of our present day Earth experience.

This worldwide phenomenon speaks to this critical time in Earth's history. The message the dolphins bring is, humanity must awaken and take their place as conscious stewards of the Earth, restoring balance to the ecological fabric of our world. Thus, awakened from normal lives and from diverse backgrounds and belief systems, the thousands of individuals who are experiencing these encounters with the dolphins share a common bond and responsibility.

Individuals who have experienced spiritual, as well as physical healings from the dolphins first hand are telling extraordinary stories. After swimming with dolphins, people say they feel more alive and carefree. They may unexpectedly find they have a deeper sense of fulfillment. Many find a renewed purpose and focus in their lives, have their dreams reawakened and in some cases fulfilled.

All types of physical ailments have literally disappeared from swimming with dolphins, while many tell of increased vitality and stamina. Dramatic changes are witnessed in children who are neurologically impaired. Excruciating pain is relieved in cases where it could not be diminished by our most powerful drugs.

The Dolphin Phenomenon takes us around the world to the many sites where extraordinary encounters with the dolphins are ongoing. From Australia's Monkey Mia, where generations of dolphins seem to be doing their own study of humanity, to the pink river dolphins of the Amazon in South America, spinner and bottlenose dolphins from the remote shores of Hawaii and the Caribbean, to encounters in Australia, New Zealand, Costa Rica, Europe, the Middle East, Indonesia, Russia, and Asia, individuals weave their extraordinary stories into a magical tapestry that has distinct common threads.

In these encounters with dolphins, people are becoming more conscious of their higher spiritual potentials. Many speak of experiencing ecstatic feelings of joy and a deeper sense of peace. Countless individuals worldwide have been inspired into personal missions on behalf of the cetaceans and our planet, others to bring forth inspired music, art, books and films. Still others are laying the groundwork for a Golden Age, bringing forth New Archetypes for the New Millennium. Encounters with dolphins have completely changed their lives.

The stories in this book are filled with magic and mystery, ushering us into a mystical world that speaks to this important time in history where humanity is undergoing a profound awakening. Inspired by the dolphins, we are called out of ordinary lives to explore our own extraordinary potential as conscious spiritual beings having a 3D virtual human experience. Heartwarming stories fill this book, mystical adventures that reveal the treasured experiences of those whose lives have been transformed by dolphins.

It is this heightened attunement with the Divine within us, within nature, and within all of life that has opened the gateways to the Golden Ages throughout history. It is what beckons us now as we embrace the potentials that await us in this New Millennium. Weaving the threads of this phenomenon from its most ancient historical significance into the present, we find we are moving into a future that may yet be our most Glorious Age.

CHAPTER TWO

An Unexpected Destiny

It was the dolphins who brought me into a greater awareness of the Awakening. While I had seen the signs of this glorious time in people I met across the Earth, there was one facet of the Awakening that I still wasn't completely aware of. It was the different phenomena that were contributing to the Great Awakening, the knowledge of which birthed the Earth 2012-33 series. How the dolphins called me to this project still amazes me to this day.

1994 was one of the busiest times of my life. I was producing a weekly one hour prime time TV show in Hawaii called Quest For Truth, showcasing advances in every field, including topics on health, healing, spirituality, and the mystical traditions of the world's religions. I was flying into LA from Hawaii once a month for my M.A. degree program in Psychology at the University of Santa Monica (USM), while completing my B.A. in Hawaii.

I had four children with two teens going off at the same time and had become the sole support of our family. On top of all of that, I was heading a global Earth Vision Center project, which kept me traveling back and forth to LA every six weeks and to other parts of the world. To say the least, I was not looking for another project.

It all started one evening at a Fourth of July party at my home in Kailua. A man arrived who I had not seen in two years. He was so completely changed I had to ask, "What happened to you?" I was astounded by the dramatic difference in this individual. When I asked him what had taken place, he said it had all started when he swam with the dolphins.

From that moment on, a heart that had been closed from so much pain was opened and he began to relate to others in a whole new way. He felt a deep inner peace and renewed connection with Spirit. Now he was following his intuition and was open, loving, sharing his truth and fulfilling his destiny, writing a spiritual screenplay. Where before he had related to others from a purely intellectual level, now he poured his heart into every word. The healing the dolphins had transmitted had completely changed his life. This was definitely not the person I remembered. I had heard people were swimming with dolphins out in Makua on the far side of the island, but I didn't know anything about it. Could this man have had his life direction this changed by dolphins? I was amazed. He was a completely different person on a higher destiny path.

Moments later we were off to see the fireworks at the beach. Stepping out the door, he turned to me, his voice echoing beneath a star filled sky, *"You have to go swim with the dolphins!"* The words reverberated through me as if a trumpet had sounded, while a powerful current of energy ran through my body from head to toe. In that instant, I was downloaded with the significance of this phenomenon taking place worldwide. A destiny unfolded before my eyes, as I was shown the book and documentary film I would bring forth cataloging the extraordinary human-dolphin connections and their import for this time. Looking back, I am amazed how much was downloaded to me, because I knew relatively nothing about this subject.

In the days that followed, I felt connected with the dolphins for the first time in my life. As I went about my work, I could feel their presence in the ocean miles away. Somehow I was on their same wavelength. Hour after hour, I could feel them drawing me. These experiences peaked my curiosity. Finally, I drove an hour across the island to a remote area on the western shore of Oahu to find the dolphins. When I arrived at the site, I was told the dolphins had already been there and gone. No dolphins were in sight. Little did I know I was about to have one of the most mind-blowing experiences of my life.

I was drawn to the edge of the shore and sat down, immediately entering a deep meditation. Three dolphins appeared before me and began speaking to me telepathically, while bathing me in a brilliant white light that spiraled up my body. They told me they were able to remove blocks. Dark matter was being released from me and I felt lighter and lighter. I found that interesting because of the similar deep transformational healing work I do with TheQuest.

These 'Oracles of the Sea' were bringing healing to the deepest parts of my being, something I had only experienced before with Angels and TheQuest work. After a while, they said they were removing a financial block. I became aware of huge cement-like block in front of me on my right side about two feet in height. A laser ray was dissolving it from top to bottom. I could hardly believe what was happening. After all, these were big fishes, not Divine Beings.

When the healing was complete, I got up and stumbled across the beach, completely stunned at what had taken place. A man from France was standing there. I told him I had just had an experience with the dolphins where they were speaking to me telepathically. He said, "Oh yes," with a big smile and twinkling eyes, "they are speaking to people telepathically." Then I told him I had been radiated with light. He said, "Oh yes, many people have been radiated with light."

I said, "They dissolved a block in me!"

He replied, "Oh yes, they are healing people." I couldn't believe what I was hearing. This was really happening to people. I had never heard about these things before. He told me how his back had been healed from swimming with the dolphins and how changed his life was. My mind was completely blown. I drove home in shock, feeling a great sense of awe. If the dolphins wanted to make an impact, they had. I was impressed, but the magic did not end there.

Later that week I was in my psychology course in California. It was late in the evening and I found myself drifting out of the classroom. Then I was in a music studio looking down at a familiar face. It was my music producer/composer friend, Paul Gilman, from Palm Springs. As I watched from above, he began playing an extraordinary piece of music. It would be another year before I would actually step physically into his studio.

Days later, I was attending IBI (Income Builders International), a powerful business conference I traveled to every six weeks to move the Earth Vision Project forward. (http://www.LemuriaRising.com). I had begun building a world team of experts, had just filed the papers on the company, and had created an executive summary to present to others. It was there I had met Paul.

That Friday he came running up to me saying, "Aurora, the other night you came into my studio when I was recording and an incredible piece of music flowed forth." I acknowledged I had been there. He proceeded to tell me in an excited voice, about an incredible encounter with dolphins he had just had on a trip to Hawaii, which had inspired a whole new stream of music. Having had my own amazing experience, I could understand.

All week at the event, I felt an incredible electric current passing through me as I traversed the halls connecting with people. It was uplifting and I felt inspired, connected, and empowered. On Saturday, I held my first investor meeting on the Earth Vision Project. Within a half hour I had raised $50,000 with another $30,000 in pledges. I could hardly believe it. I had never raised capital before and this was my first attempt.

That day, after many years of gestation, my project was born. Now it had seed money and I could proceed ahead in an accelerated way to bring it into a physical reality. I could only marvel at how the dolphins had played their unique role in orchestrating what had been a remarkable demonstration of their powers, and was profoundly touched that they even cared about my project. At that point, I realized I should at least have physical contact with the dolphins. Within days I saw them out in Malibu as I sat on the beach. Returning home to Hawaii, I began traveling to swim with the dolphins regularly.

My levels of happiness, joy, and creativity dramatically increased and I became very changed. I began living my destiny more fully, consciously creating the life of my dreams. My love for humanity also increased, as did my desire to make a difference. I had carried Sacred Visions in my heart about Earth's Transformation forever. Now my sight was opened and I was witnessing my visions coming true.

While my life continued on in the same intensity as before, it was incredible to witness how calm I was feeling all the time while I was accomplishing so much all at once. This was amazing to everyone around me. It was one of the most prolific times I have ever experienced in my life. Somehow, I could do more than ever before with an ease and grace I never dreamed possible, summoning Super Human powers I didn't know I had. I had so much creative energy flowing through me all the time and was accomplishing amazing feats, handling an incredible amount of responsibilities, and moving this vast humanitarian endeavor forward at light speed, while feeling like I was living a relaxed peaceful life.

It felt as if I had undergone some kind of time warp, where things that would have normally taken weeks or even months were accomplished in days. My sense of time shifted completely. I began to have more time than the normal human, which has continued to this day. A day for me is like a week, a month like a season. You can imagine how long a year feels. Consequently, I can get a whole lot done in a short amount of time.

Through many adventures, the dolphins continued to blow my mind. As exciting as these encounters were, and as intriguing as the project was, I really didn't have the energy to take on one more endeavor, especially of this magnitude. Strangely enough, I didn't have to. The project just started rolling by itself. I began meeting people in the most unlikely places and situations, who out of the blue would tell me their extraordinary dolphin stories and how these encounters changed their lives, when they had no idea I had any interest in the topic. After a year of this, I finally realized this project was going to happen no matter what I did. I bought a recorder and began carrying it with me everywhere.

As a dedicated research psychologist and someone who loves the Quest for Truth, I found similar mystical experiences happening to people all over the planet, from every walk of life and religious background. These were not just fun nature adventures like going on a whale watch. They were profound experiences changing people's lives.

By the next year, I had collected hundreds of stories from around the world and had begun to get a clear vision of the documentary film on the human/dolphin connection. I began meeting interesting film photographers and other key people who could lend their expertise to this project. Once again, in an effortless way, a creative alliance came together to support my efforts.

It was during that time, I attended IBI again to find yet another piece to the dolphin puzzle unveiled. I was to be shown how far reaching the dolphin influence could be. It was Friday night and I was relaxing in a chair in the back, when Paul Gilman's latest project was announced and began appearing on the big screen in front of the room. It was a short film production of dolphins swimming to showcase a song on his latest album. The music touched me deeply and tears began pouring from my eyes. I thought, "This is the perfect song for the lead-in to my documentary film."

I went up to him and asked, "Paul, what was the song that came through you the night I appeared in your studio" He replied, "This one." In that moment, an electric wave of joy and understanding passed through me. The dolphins had connected us as they released this inspired song to the world. It was destined for his album and my film.

As my magical adventure with the dolphins continued, I had to marvel at how a book and film project could come together without any effort on my part. This was a totally new experience for me. For years I had been versed in accomplishing my goals. With four children and many responsibilities and projects happening simultaneously, I had moved through my B.A., M.A. fast and Ph.D. in psychology in record time. At the same time, I was witnessing a project happening in and through me and I was not doing it. This was a powerful shift from my normal reality, but then, that is what the dolphins have shown me. There is a way to manifest a higher vision, a way to partake of life that is glorious and spectacular with little human effort. It is a very different approach than the western world inspires.

I had been told, "You have to work hard for a living. It takes effort to accomplish success in life." Now I was involved in a project I didn't have to work hard on or put any effort into. It was all coming together beautifully on its own in and through me. I was a participant in a Grand Play, which was a new experience and very exciting.

About the second year into this amazing phenomenon, I received a message that there was a running thread through the stories that I would find, that was a part of a bigger happening. One year later, I could see it. Dolphins were helping facilitate an Awakening in people worldwide, and this was just one of many phenomena that were impacting the psyche of humanity at this time. A Great Awakening was taking place on Earth, one I had received visions about in my teens and now it was clearly happening. Dolphin, angel, and other encounters were a part of it, representing a Divine Hand in our planetary destiny. There was a divine energy working to effect a positive change in the souls of humanity. Finally I was seeing the whole picture.

Through divine synchronicities of the most extraordinary kind, people everywhere were undergoing great shifts in consciousness. This divine orchestration was a part of a Grand Plan, to awaken humanity at a critical time on the planet.

It was years later I realized it was the Violet Race who were the first to receive the impact of this powerful transforming energy. They were the ones who had an expansive consciousness, who could relate to the dolphin world, and who were open to Higher Realms. They were ripe for the Awakening, Way Showers leading the rest of humanity. I was shown that it was important to create a series with a first book that represented all facets of this Awakening. With barely any effort, the first book, *Earth 2012-33: The Ultimate Quest, How To Find Peace in a World of Chaos,* was born.

Many times over the years, I asked myself, "Why did the dolphins choose me for their project out of all the people on the planet?" I was so incredibly busy. My life was so full, I could barely keep it all together. I had not been out swimming with dolphins or a part of the dolphin community, an incredible group of people drawn together through the dolphin connection from all over the world. It was much later, once I had recognized the underlying theme of the book, that I could understand the perfection of "their choice." They had chosen someone outside the dolphin world that had no idea it even existed. A serious person, dedicated to 'truth,' and to bringing important information to others.

I will never forget the incredible gift the dolphins have given me and all that they've taught me. I continue to practice the effortless way of manifestation the dolphins inspired, allowing life to manifest its glorious intention through me. I really love this way so much better than endless visualizations and affirmations to get what I want. Life just seems to know so much better what is good for me.

I realized early on, it was through a connection with my Authentic Self that I was able to 'hear' the dolphins and receive their healing. They helped link me up with this powerful part of myself, which I am ever reverent before. This gave me the ability to live in the 'altered time' they seem to live in, and to witness miraculous manifestations in my life that are being orchestrated in and through me, which is so different than the old way I used to accomplish things wearing myself out.

The dolphins inspired the Earth 2012-33 series. They are the ones who brought my attention more fully to the Awakening, expanding my vision to the positive future potential that lies before us. Their message is that we are being loved and tenderly cared for by beings of higher realms and states of consciousness, that our projects matter and we are not alone. We are being guided gently to fulfill a Greater Destiny. There is a Divine Hand in all that is taking place on Earth and we are all a part of it. We matter and the role we came to play is important.

TheQuest is a breakthrough psychological Healing System developed by Dr. Aurora Ariel after years of research and work directly in the psyche. To find out how it can help you heal your life and change your destiny, download TheQuest book FREE at: http://www.AuroraJulianaAriel.com.

CHAPTER THREE

Dreams Reawakened

by Teresa Hill

Ever since I watched "Flipper" as a child, I dreamed of swimming with wild dolphins. I would spend hours swimming underwater in our pool during the summer months pretending I was "flying underwater." After growing up and becoming a Registered Nurse, Wife and Mother, I soon forgot my dream. Then right before my first trip to Maui in 1995, I met a man who gave me a manuscript he had just written titled, "Song of the Dolphin."

His story pulled me into it. I found myself thinking about my dream as a young girl. Interestingly enough, when I got to Maui I found myself identifying with one of the characters in the story, as my "vacation script" started unfolding in an uncanny magical parallel to the story. Looking back years later, I can see the beauty of the message in this dolphin story as it became a reality in my own life.

My first encounter on Maui was with a Bottlenose dolphin and her baby who came up close to me while I was snorkeling. It looked like the mother had a bandage around her pectoral fin. Then I realized it was a plastic shopping bag. I watched in awe as she used her rostrum (mouth) to tie the straps together in a slip knot around her pectoral fin and then release it to float back in the water, only to catch it with her pectoral fin, tie it, and release it again as a way to entertain her baby. I was impressed at her intelligence to do this. I was touched by the love she shared with her baby. As this mother looked deeper into my eyes than most humans have, I felt as if she knew I was a mother also and that I understood. We shared the Universal language of love that does not require words.

Later, I took a picture of the cliffs in the background of this beautiful area. Amazingly, a spirit dolphin is clearly defined and seen by everyone that looks at the photograph. When you look at this picture, there is a distinct dolphin eye that facilitates the same energetic as when dolphins look at you. It is looking into the depths of your soul and reflecting back unconditional love.

It was after this first encounter that I began receiving messages and insights from the dolphins. This was a new experience, as I had never experienced telepathy before. Somehow I did not question this because during my vacation, I wasn't being my serious analytical adult self. Instead, I surrendered to believing in the possibilities of magic and wonder (what dreams are made of) happening in my life.

It was in this magical mindset some nights later that I silently sent a message to the dolphins, asking them if they could meet me at a secluded bay at 6:00 a.m. I felt such a longing in my heart to swim with them again and communicated my desire sending them visual images.

When I arrived at the secluded bay at the appointed hour, it was quiet and serene. The fresh ocean air awakened my senses. With great anticipation, I put on fins, mask and snorkel and entered the water with a sense of purpose, submerging my body and soul in the clear Hawaiian water. Spontaneously, I uttered a high-pitched sound underwater and continued to make these "sounds" while snorkeling.

Keenly aware of my entire surroundings, the ocean water seemed to amplify my hearing. I had only been swimming about five minutes when I heard the distinctive whistling sounds of the dolphins. Could they have heard me and were now calling back to me? My heart immediately leapt with anticipation and amazement. Then it started pounding with excitement as their whistling and clicking sounds touched a chord deep in my heart and memory, releasing emotions of sweetness and love. I was so moved, I cried softly into my mask and snorkel.

Minutes later, a pod of dolphins appeared and enthusiastically greeted me. I shrieked with joy, totally ecstatic as I was carried away in the magic of swimming with these dolphins. It was as if I were dreaming. Could this really be happening to me? My "friends" showed me how magical it is to BE IN THE MOMENT. Time seemed suspended and I felt as if I was in another world. They magically brought me back to my original self, and the innocent, trusting, child-like faith that believed in my dreams and also in me, unencumbered by the restrictions of mindsets or rules.

While in this child-like state, I felt so happy, blissful, and free, completely at home in the ocean playground of my friends. Buoyed up in their expansive magnetic energy field, my body felt light and sensual as I glided playfully along with them. I was completely immersed in the ocean of their love as they twirled around, above, below and to either side of me, all of us dancing the same kind of movements together.

As I looked into their intelligent eyes, I felt accepted and loved for who I am. Totally at one with them and myself, pure love and gratitude welled up inside of me. They felt it too, because they appeared to want the rest of their pod to come share this same experience. Somehow they were able to communicate specifically what they were going to do so that I understood it as if they had spoken to me in words.

They suddenly disappeared out into the ocean just like they "told" me they would. They said they would bring back the rest of their pod. About 5 minutes later, they reappeared and now there were twice as many of them dancing around me, perhaps as many as forty. As I blissfully basked in the center of their love, brilliant white rays of sunlight streamed downward through the core of my being, penetrating the crystal blue waters down to a depth of forty feet. As my dolphin friends danced in a circle all around me, it felt like an angelic water communion.

This gift was priceless to me because it helped heal my heart so that I could start feeling more joy and "ease" in my body instead of "dis-ease " Receiving major healing from their frequencies through their sonar, unconditional love, and joy, I underwent a major transformation in my life. I soon realized the dolphins were destined to be a steady and intimate part of my life as magical encounters with the dolphins continued over the next years. I began creating personalized Mind, Body and Soul Fitness Adventure Programs and discovered that dolphins were one of the best teachers and catalysts for transforming my clients' lives. Immense waves of bliss would flood my being as we swam with them, carrying me on waves of delight, and this would happen for them as well. As I felt more joy and purpose wholeness in my mind body and spirit, I experienced a real breakthrough in my health with levels of vitality and well-being I had never known before. I was able to dance again, even more wildly than ever, leaping, landing and jumping without any back pain. One year later, I qualified to compete in the World Championship Downhill Mountain Bike Race in Australia, and that was just the beginning.

The dolphins also helped me let go of fears of swimming in deep water and diving into the deep waters of my unconscious. They taught me to see the beautiful lights in the ocean that connected me with my own light within, and how to dive and spiral into these portals that access higher frequencies. I now can free dive 78 feet on one breath and not only look, but feel like a mermaid.

Like master teachers and guides, the dolphins taught me the health benefits of conscious breathing and how to meditate, spin and play in these liquid lights to activate our light bodies. One or two dolphins would actually spin around me in the water and then have me spin around them like a dance. Under their tutelage, I became more intuitive, felt a greater connection with nature, and became telepathic with dolphins and other animals. I was guided to spend a week with the dolphins at this beautiful bay in Hawaii where few people go. They told me where and what time to meet as they were going to work on my DNA. Right on time, the largest super pod I'd ever swam with showed up in the exact location they said they would. The water was the most beautiful aqua blue color, crystal clear so you could see the white sand bottom. There were about 300 dolphins that day all playful and interactive. It was like one great party or reunion with all your favorite friends and family showing up.

During my swim, I got a message about working with my DNA and activating dormant strands. This was fascinating to me. The sunlight had been dancing its usual pattern through the water onto the white sandy bottom. Shortly after getting this message, the pattern changed to two very distinct double helix strands spiraling in multiple pairs onto the white sand floor. It was such an incredible light show; I could hardly believe my eyes, and an experience I'll never forget. All the colors were vibrant and the dolphins very vocal. Their sonar and sound frequencies were vibrating through my whole body as I moved into a higher state of higher awareness, bliss and energy.

The dolphins were very affectionate with each other and many were caressing each other and making love belly to belly, opening me to the idea of sacred sexuality. They showed me there is no separation between sexuality, the heart, and soul. It is the disconnection that causes many problems to arise. Most people miss out on experiencing the highest sexual and spiritual fulfillment because there is no true presence and wholeness in one's being. The dolphins stayed with me all day, opening my heart and teaching me. These teachings continued in other swims several times more that week.

When I got back to the mainland, I didn't think any more about what the dolphins had taught me about the DNA. However, soon there was physical evidence of changes happening in my body, like the hazel green eyes I was born with turning a luminescent aqua blue. I had always dreamed of having blue eyes. Now, people often comment about what a beautiful blue my eyes are. My straight hair even became curly to where now I am told I look like a mermaid. Scientists have since discovered that dolphins' DNA to be amazingly similar to humans.

Another time, the dolphins called me back to Hawaii for me to learn about Lemuria and to activate the Divine Feminine energy within me. This was so foreign. I questioned myself if I had heard correctly. When I got in the waters at a secluded bay, the dolphins were leaping high into the air. There was a double rainbow above and the clouds were parting to reveal sunlight streaming downward from heaven. The download I received about Lemuria had me enraptured. A little later, I saw a boat out in the bay that had a beautiful mural painted on the side. As I swam closer, the dolphins leaping wildly before me, I saw it was depicting a crystalline city surrounded by ocean. Reaching the boat, I exuberantly asked the boat captain, "is that a painting of Lemuria?" She answered yes!

Everything was so beautiful and magical that day. I felt I was in another dimension of time. Profound insights were revealed to me. A feeling of oneness with all opened up my heart more than it ever had before. I later experienced the Divine Feminine (life force) energy arising within me, giving birth to a profound Kundalini Spiritual awakening. My entire body, especially my heart exploded in orgasmic rapture, flooding my entire being with light and unconditional love. I felt the most immense waves of joy carrying me to the heart of God, where my physical form dissolved into oneness with God and the Universe. I realized this was like one of the near death experiences that some people have described.

Later, I realized I was given this gift so I can serve as a "Human Angel" and assist people with their healing. It is not that I have some power to heal. I am simply a vessel for God's pure love and healing light. I am thankful I was guided since a small child to keep my body and mind pure as a temple of God. I have been a Christian all my life and my experiences with dolphins have brought me even closer to Jesus. Often, people are afraid or discredit things they can't explain or understand.

A few months after my big spiritual awakening, I was able to assist my Mother in healing her heavy heart and spirit at a critical time in her life. Over the next three months, I felt an incredible amount of unconditional love for my mother as I took care of her. God's Healing Light poured through so she could make her transition into the Light in a beautiful and sacred way. She told me before passing, she had experienced "more spiritual experiences and love in that short time, than most people experience in a lifetime."

Many times, at a major crossroad, a special friend or angel appears and makes a huge difference in our lives. For me, it began with this man who gifted me his magical manuscript, and then the dolphins who answered my "calls," became my teachers, and brought healing, love, and joy into my life. Now I am sharing this gift with others. At that magical place in time, the dolphins danced my forgotten dreams back into my heart. Now years later I can see how my reawakened dreams have unfolded into my reality in even a more beautiful and unimaginable way than I could have dreamt before. My life has been touched forever by this sacred dance and my special dolphin friends, who will forever remain in my heart.

Teresa Hill, owner of Aloha Wellness, is a Medical Intuitive, Doctor of Natural Health, and a Behavioral Wellness R.N. who consults internationally with clients and corporations. Her passion is to help people break through limitations to become healthier, happier and fit. Called Super T, Teresa is a Silver Medalist in the 2002 World Championships Masters Downhill Mountain Bicycling, a former Top Pro Mountain Bicyclist and Pro Off-Road Tri-athlete (Xterra). Dr. Hill has spent 5 years in her ground-breaking research in Anti-aging, including the Science of Youthful Metabolism. She now incorporates this in her Program, "A New You in Paradise," the Ultimate Mind Body Spirit Makeover Health Retreat Program custom designed for you.

Passionate about helping people have life changing adventures, Teresa's profound intimate connection with nature and spiritual awareness, helps brings others into balance and wholeness. You can contact her at: SuperTfitness@gmail.com or call (760) 703-1747

CHAPTER FOUR

Global Transformation

by Joe Noonan

Swimming with dolphins has taught me much about life. They are great coaches in the Art of Living simply and with joy. In many encounters with them, I come away with something wonderful that sinks deep in my bones, often to my very DNA.

Dolphins are known for their powerful sonar. Researchers say it's at least three times more powerful than our medical ultrasound. Others credit it with the ability to change cellular structure. I've been leading wild dolphin retreats for 15 years and it was during one of my trips to Bimini, in the Bahamas, that I discovered for myself just how powerful their sonar can be.

I had a group of about eight people and it was midweek of the trip. We were swimming with a pod of spotted dolphins and they were in a very playful mood. After swimming all around, under and between us, two of them swam up to me, stopped cold, and hung there ten feet away. I've never seen a dolphin motionless in the wild before. Their behavior took me by surprise. They're always on the move, even when they're sleeping. Here I was, face to face with two of them, time was passing, and they were perfectly still. My antennas went right up!

Then, slowly and ever so gracefully they turned, their tails sinking and heads rising, until their noses were pointing straight toward the surface. They did this without moving a fin. It was as if some unseen hand was gently turning them. What is going on, I wondered. My curiosity was on full alert. Without moving a flipper, they sank in unison, toward the bottom. It was eerie watching them sink slowly without any movement on their part. It takes me a lot of work to get down there.

We were in 30 feet of crystal clear water and they stopped halfway to the bottom. Knowing something extraordinary was happening, I placed myself directly above them. I floated there on the surface with great expectation, watching them hang suspended in time and space. Moments passed. All was quiet. I knew something magical was happening and yet, everything was perfectly calm, perfectly still. "What's happening?" I asked. I heard a whisper then to close my eyes and look inside. I did and it was like turning the corner into the middle of New York City on New Year's Eve.

There was a pandemonium of activity with a tremendous flow of energy coming from the dolphins. They were cranking their sonar at an intensity I'd never experienced in all my years swimming with them, sending wave upon wave of light, sound and color. The volume and variety of their transmission spanned frequencies and spectrums beyond my human ability to comprehend. I felt myself being stretched beyond time and space, my aura expanding exponentially to fully receive the vastness of their blessing.

Colors I'd never seen before were trumpeting forth from these two dolphins, purples, magentas, violets and oranges. Every color I looked at immediately exploded into a thousand variations of itself. Sounds and vibrations were blaring forth, frequencies I'd never known or even imagined. I would dive into a stream of light or vibration to escape the overwhelming flow of energy, and everywhere I dove instantly exploded into more. While the human part of me was overwhelmed, another part of me was ravenously drinking it all in, this part of me inhaling the vastness like a vacuum from space.

"I" became a black hole, drinking in every drop of what they were dishing out. Whatever they released, I inhaled. We were each a finger of two hands, coming together across time and space to connect and then, it went collective. The transmission was from species to species, the whole dolphin lineage tuning up the entire human lineage through me.

They were the outpouring and we were the receivers, and what they sent went into us and then, into all of humanity. We were portals between not just species, but worlds. My awareness expanded to the oneness we all come from. I was adrift in creation watching galaxies being born. Again and again my attention would focus on a single aspect of the overwhelming outpouring. Every single place I put my attention blossomed into its own exquisite flow of color and light.

Behind the illusion of a solo body was the vast presence of our collective Humanity, and this presence was absorbing and instantly integrating the energies being delivered. The match of frequencies and receptors was perfect, a divinely orchestrated delivery and fulfillment.

The transmission completed and the dolphins swam back to the surface and resumed playing. Dumbstruck, I could not move. I wanted to savor the huge charge of energy that had passed through me, but their message was to relax and let it go. The job was done. Now it was time to play, and play we did.

One of them swam over with a piece of seaweed draped across his front flipper. The other chased him and a game of tag began. They started passing it back and forth between them as they zoomed all around me. Glued to the action, I was watching with all the attention of a kid in front of cartoons. All of a sudden, they swam up and dropped the seaweed in front of me. I was shocked. They were inviting me to play. Needing no second invitation, I grabbed the seaweed with my teeth (taking in only a small mouthful of water), and started swimming.

I looked over my shoulder and sure enough, they were right behind me. I swam as hard and as fast as I could, arms and legs thrashing the water. What I lacked in grace I made up in splash. I imagine I looked like a toddler to them, barely making headway but with a lot of heart. When I was out of breath, which was pretty quick at that speed, I dove down and released the seaweed.

Wham! The second I released the seaweed they dove down, grabbed it and were off. They chased each other, passing it from mouth to flipper to tail, zooming in and out of sight. I was all grins, huffing and puffing as I caught my breath. Then they brought it over and dropped it in front of me again, the kid who's invited by the big guys to get off the bleachers and join the game. I kicked off my imaginary crutches (the dolphins don't want to play with me), grabbed the seaweed and swam my best. After another minute of splashing and thrashing, I dove down, released it, and bobbed back to the surface, winded and content to watch them continue.

The game went on as the seaweed passed back and forth between us several more times. Each time they dropped it in front of me, I felt a physical shock, for it challenged an age-old belief from my childhood, a belief that I was doomed to be left out of the game. These dolphins knew exactly what they were doing. By including me in their game, they brought me face to face with that old belief, their behavior proving it wrong again and again. I felt like I was receiving Darshan from a saint. A profound sense of peace and gratitude swept over me. This simple play was a holy interaction. I felt deeply honored they would do this for me and for being included in their game.

Off they swam and our group climbed back onto the boat breathless. I was glowing. The dolphins had played tag with me. As I was basking in the joy of the experience, I suddenly remembered the sonar blasting. On the boat ride back, I was in deep appreciation and reflection. I came to understand the incredible gift that had been given, a most powerful transmission of energy and information beyond what I, in my humanness, could understand.

I knew we received an attunement for our collective archetype, a balancing of energies for humanity on many different dimensions. We are awakening and Nature in her many forms is assisting us in the most subtle and profound ways. Whenever I reflect on this experience, I'm reminded to simply relax and return to joy. It's a wonderful message, one I take to heart. I am so grateful to these incredibly generous beings. They are a beautiful demonstration of living in joy.

Joe Noonan founded Planetary Partners to bring together kindred souls to align with the magnificence and beauty of Nature for personal and planetary transformation. His creed: "This world is already a Heaven on Earth. The tools to find joy in the moment are around and within us. Harmony is inevitable. Innately we all just love each other and sometimes we forget." Joe is here to help us remember.

Leading the metamorphosis of the masculine into a cooperative, synergistic, gentle and kind way of being, Joe helps ignite the playful child in us so we can see God in all things, ourselves and each other, bringing the lessons nature teaches back into relationships at work and at home. He teaches, "Life is a dance, harmonic and flowing. We are all 'fingers of the same hand.'"

Author, transformational speaker and community/corporate facilitator who assists individuals and organizations to fulfill their greatest vision, Joe works globally and has been a guest on FOX, National Geographic TV and Oprah. Joe provides custom Wild Dolphin Trips, Self Awakening Seminars, help Creating Conscious Corporations, Joe's blog 'Everyday Ecstasy.' Website: http://planetarypartners.com. Phone: 800.220.6925.

CHAPTER FIVE

Breathless Moments

by Ilona Selke

The ocean water of the gentle bay was surrounding me like a blanket. Crystal clear turquoise water expanded into great quiet depths beneath me. The sun was flowing in streams of light rays past my body, creating an almost surreal feeling within the still underwater world. Only the steady breath through my snorkel gave my human ears something familiar to hold onto.

Don, my Beloved, and I were swimming with a dear woman friend in a bay known for calm water and the possibility of encountering dolphins. Suddenly, out of the blue, I saw their shadowy outline underneath me in the water. In groups of two, three or more, an entire pod of dolphins came swimming my way.

I had been experimenting by sending images to the dolphins, seeing myself swim with one dolphin on each side of me as though I was being taken on a tour. I was hoping today they would hear my prayers and be with me, and here they were!

I took a deep breath and dove into the greater depth of the ocean, then veered off to the side letting the dolphins know I knew some under water social etiquette. To my great surprise, one dolphin swam up to my side catching eye contact with me. Trying to keep my excitement contained, I kept pace with the dolphin as we spiraled under water, our eyes locked onto one another. Three other dolphins ascended from the depth next to us, coming up to breathe and together with them I swooped up to the surface, catching my breath too.

As quickly as I could, I dove under water again. The three Dolphins had swooped back down and were now swimming a little underneath me. It was then something strange started happening to me. To my amazement, I was gliding under water and didn't need any air. Then I realized, I was in tow and there was a ball of energy enveloping me. The immense silence of the ocean engulfed me, as suspended in another kind of reality, I glided within the envelope of oneness with the group of three dolphins. For a moment in time there was no separation between being human and being dolphin. I felt our oneness, that we belonged together.

My human weakness was altered, my need to breath suspended for what seemed like an unbelievable and out of normal range of time. The joy of this moment was all I cared about. Gone were thoughts of yesterday or tomorrow as a wave of gratefulness filled my entire heart and mind. After what seemed like an eternity, I eventually came up for air. What had happened? Had I really been under the water all that time without breathing or had the dolphins altered my perception so I thought I was? My experience was that I had stayed under way longer than a human could without breathing but, how could I know for sure?

A little while later Don came into view just as he dove down under water in perfect timing with several dolphins. Turning upside down, one dolphin showed his white belly to Don, much like they do when they swim with each other. Don looked sleek underwater in his wet suit, gliding in synchronous movements with this small grouping. I kept watching in amazement at the sheer grace of the dolphins and their apparent willingness to take us humans into their bonds.

As I kept staring at Don I became a little nervous. Wasn't it time for him to come up for air? He was down there probably 30 feet and still had to allow enough air to come up to the surface. I got more and more anxious as the time passed. I could not believe what I was witnessing! Don continued to stay under as I watched with an increasing sense of alarm. Later I was to hear from our companion that she too was watching Don at the same time and it had scared her too. She felt like she was suffocating watching him stay underwater so long without breathing. Meanwhile, Don just stayed in sync and swam along with the pod, seemingly unaware that it was way over time for him to come up for air.

An incredibly long time after we, the alarmed ones watching, had run out of air, Don came up to breathe, swimming with the three dolphins he had come into synchrony with. Exhilarated, he shared how he had been aware of not needing to breathe. Finally, the dolphins 'told' him to go get air and escorted him up to the surface as though they knew his outer limits.

It was incredible to witness Don staying under the water for so long, when I had just had a similar experience. I then knew it was true. I had stayed down with the dolphins long after I would normally have had to come up for breath. It was a miraculous experience and I was in awe that it had happened to both my Beloved and I during this dolphin encounter. Significantly, it was three dolphins who had facilitated each of our experiences. Were they the same ones?

In great excitement Don told us of another experience, where two dolphins had come up to him on either side and flanking him in this manner, had accompanied him closer to shore where they showed him what looked like an underwater garden. For twenty minutes they had 'toured' him around, staying close and seemingly attempting to show him something of value. The feeling was indescribable and Don's glowing eyes and exuberant energy hinted at the ecstatic joy he had felt in the presence of the dolphins.

I couldn't believe that Don had been given the exact experience I had envisioned for myself and which, telepathically, I had asked for with the dolphins. I could only wonder why it had happened to him instead of me. I had become accustomed to the fact that 'as you imagine, so it will be.' I had learned by experience that dolphins seem to read our minds and respond to the images we hold inside. Today, Don had the very experience I had imagined. That was amazing.

Trying not to be envious of his experience, I wondered about this as I later floated alone like a cork on the surface of the ocean. I was relaxing and catching my breath before we would start our long swim back to shore. I wondered if the dolphins had mixed Don and me up. Had they gotten the right image and acted on it, but missed the target? Suddenly I heard a question in my mind, "Aren't you understanding yourself and Don to be One?" 'Of course we are!' I realized.

Dolphins may not see the boundary between individuals as distinctly as humans do. Don and I are intrinsically paired and what one of us experienced was almost as real to the other one. Dolphins feel each others feelings much more strongly. Their compassion is therefore much more developed. In this light, I opened my heart to receive the full joy it brought to Don, and me vicariously, thrilled for him to have had this experience. This was yet another lesson I learned from the dolphins.

To get to this point had been an adventurous and exciting journey, which got better with each encounter with the dolphins. I had been learning that the images we hold and live by influence our personal life. After many years, when I had sufficiently learned the lesson in my personal life, the dolphins asked me to help them in their plight of survival. In helping them as best as I could, I discovered the miracle of how interwoven our imagination and our universe really is, but what a road it has been.

I felt very changed from my experience that day. My perceptions have been altered as I've learned there is more to this reality than one would think. That Don and I, both good swimmers with a lot of experience, would be taken on a dolphin journey that defied the physical reality we were used to, was incredible. It opened both our hearts and minds to possibilities beyond the norm, taking us into realms we had never dreamed of. The Dolphins continue to lead us on an ever awakening journey.

Ilona Selke is an international author, seminar leader, lecturer, and musician. She has inspired thousands of people to co-create reality, discover the power of a spiritual mind in a practical way, and live and manifest their dreams. Ilona has appeared on TV and Radio, teaches seminars biannually in Germany and Switzerland, annually in Florida, Bali, and Hawaii, and has taught seminars in America, Australia, India, England, France, Canada, Mexico, and Singapore, Hong Kong, and Japan.

Ilona and her husband, Don Paris, are cofounders of Living From Vision, an institute for personal growth, multi-dimensional development of awareness, and spiritual relationship. Their Living from Vision® course, translated into four languages, is taught worldwide.

Since 1991 Ilona Selke and Don Paris have studied the lives of dolphins in their natural habitats throughout the world. Through their natural skills, dolphins exchanged telepathic messages with her that form the basis for her dolphin books. Her first book, Wisdom of the Dolphins, is about dolphins, the holographic universe and the power of our dreamtime mind. Her second book, Alin Learns to Use His Imagination, is a children's book well loved among parents and therapists for it's therapeutic value. Her third book about soulmates, Free Will, destiny, dolphins and shifting the Time Space Matrix is called, Dolphins, Love and Destiny, Yoga of the Soul. Find out more at: http://www.IlonaSelke.com.

CHAPTER SIX

Dolphin Activation

by Rytwin Lee

Before swimming with the dolphins, I had a lot of growing up type of issues, hanging on to the past, not wanting to grow up, having a lot of fears. Each time I swam with them, they were pulling layers off of me, beaming me with their energy, sounds, and love. Layer by layer I was being transformed.

One phenomenal experience was with hundreds of dolphins. Looking down, I counted a hundred and fifty beneath me. Then I looked up and saw there were way more dolphins around me, probably around three hundred and fifty.

It didn't seem like they were that playful that day, because none were jumping or leaping out of the water as they usually do. It was like they were gathered for a big convention. A gathering of the dolphins? I was thrilled. Energy shot through my body and I felt like I was floating on air, like floating in the clouds, but I was floating on water.

The dolphins began swimming away from the shallow water, which was only about twenty feet deep with white sand on the bottom. It was early morning and the light was shining through the water. Seven of the dolphins stayed and began playing with me. They would swim circles around me, in front, beside, and all around me. They were hitting me with all these different sounds, each one coming to about three feet in front of me and looking me directly in the eye as they swam by under the water.

I looked each one of them in the eye and we made a soul connection that was amazing. I felt like I was in some kind of watery heaven, with the amazing light and the dolphins playing with me as they took me totally into bliss, transforming energies coursing through me.

After this, I knew the dolphins had a special connection with me. Their message was, "You are a dolphin too. We want you to remember you have dolphin aspects to yourself so you can bring them out and share them with people. These are aspects of playing, having fun, and connecting by looking into each others eyes to connect on a soul level."

They told me, 'The eyes are the windows to the soul.' I understood instantly. By looking into the eyes of the dolphin, I could see myself in him, with many dolphin aspects. I knew it was time to bring out these dolphin aspects of joy, fun, happiness, and bliss.

Humans deserve to have these aspects drawn out in them, that the dolphins so easily embody, so they can experience greater harmony and peace. I could hear the dolphins laughing then, delighted I got it. It was a life changing experience.

Even all these years later, people who knew me before know how very changed I am. I have continued to be happy, joyful, peaceful, and blissful from the dolphin's activation that day.

Rytwin Lee is a Group Business Leader with Sunrider International, with over 400 employees. He currently resides on the island of Oahu, Hawaii. To contact him about Sunrider Products, please email him at: rytwin@yahoo.com

CHAPTER SEVEN

Trusting the Divine Presence

by Marla Maples

The dolphins awakened my trust in the Divine Presence. We all know so much, but the signs that we get through the Creator, our children, and our friends bring us reassurance. We are in our human form and these experiences help us to trust there is a Divine Consciousness that is always there. It is up to us to tap into that energy.

One way I connect with this Universal Energy is through my Kabalistic Prayers. They help me break through the veils blocking me from the light of the Creator, placing me in my higher consciousness. This brings me out of fears, doubts and insecurity to the realm where all things are connected with purpose, where I feel the unity with all life.

Ana B'Koach is a very powerful prayer I have used many times when I have sat at the beach. At those times, I love to get into a meditative state. What I came to notice is that after I would sit in the sand, gaze across the ocean, and give this prayer, I would look up and see dolphins dancing through the water and leaping into the air. Without even consciously calling them forth, I found the energy of this prayer, which is about being in unity with all creatures of God without judgment or limitation, called them forth naturally. I always feel my prayers are powerful when I am saying them by the sea. Without expectation, I open my eyes and the dolphins are there. They come forth in their magnificence from that place that I reach in consciousness. An acknowledgement of the divine in all things, the connection we as humans have to the dolphins is like a triangle of God, humans and dolphins.

Saying the prayer raises my vibration. Immediately the dolphins arrive, because they are on the same level. I rise into the Divine

Consciousness and we meet each other there. I've wondered, "Are the dolphins always in that God Consciousness? Do they live in that state, unlike humans that get so caught up in things, controlled by our own desires and fears, and the chaos that brings? Are they really at the same spiritual level as we are, or are they beyond us?"

It is incredible that the dolphins will continually respond to my prayers, and to me when I am in that Divine State. I found this was not a random experience but a divinely orchestrated one. It has finally gotten to the point where every time I go out to the beach, I want to make this connection with these magical creatures. These experiences help me understand the Divine is alive in many forms. Even dolphins respond when we respond to our higher level. It is when I am in my higher self I feel a unity with all.

Marla Maples' heart is set on one day seeing unity in the world and she works diligently to spread this message of hope. She has been honored by the Wall Street Journal, Make a Wish Foundation, American Family Housing, Feed the Children, Shelter for the Homeless, and The City of Hope. She has served as honorary chairperson and host for numerous charities and foundations and was named Honorary Citizen of Atlanta

Actress, radio and television host, songwriter and performer, Marla Maples continues to make a difference. As an actor, Marla has appeared in over 15 films and has guest starred in numerous television series over the last twenty years. She has been on the cover of over 25 magazines and has enjoyed sharing her ideas on health, fitness and spirituality in publications ranging from Vogue to Fitness Magazine.

Marla was seen in the ABC/Disney prime time show, "The Ex-Wives Club", which was praised by People Magazine as "Charlie's Angels meets Touched By An Angel." As one of the hosts she become a trusted and compassionate voice to help empower both men and women going through the pain and stress of divorce. As a songwriter and performer Marla released the Benefit album, "One World of Love" with the intention to provoke action for peace, healing, love and unity through music. In addition, Marla had the opportunity to perform her single "One World of Love" on the stage of Carnegie Hall in New York City for the Turn Up the Peace World Premier. Her album "Visions of Eternity," takes you on a mystical music journey and features spiritual teachers like Deepak Chopra, the Dali Lama, Tara Sutphen, Michael Beckwith and others. More info at http://www.marlamaples.com

Part Two

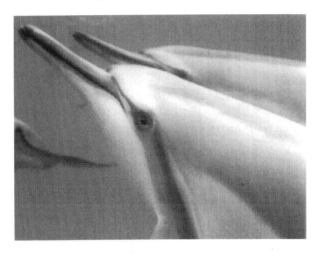

Miracles & Blessings

Miracles

Come join us in the Miraculous Dance of Life
The Journey of Sacred Selves
Living in Harmony with the Spheres
Knowing the Perfection of a Divine Plan
That Wills only good for the Earth

Bring the treasures of your Sacred Experiences
And let us bring light to that which once seemed dark
We know the answers of the Miracles of Life
That are so lovingly bestowed from Heaven Kingdoms

Bring your hearts open to be filled with Life
Ready to be Initiated into Love
Prepare yourselves to soar on the Wings of Dolphin Angels
Who will carry you up to realms you have shared

In Ancient times we called you into your Divinity
And a Golden Age was born
Once again we call those of humanity
That have heard the whispers of the coming time and who
In preparing themselves have seen the Awakening Ones arise

Yes, it is time to embrace the Miracles of Life
That are everywhere around you
That sing in your souls and bring you
To the Joyful Presence of your most Sacred Self

Live fully, Beloved
Dance in the Miracles of your Life
Bring the Miraculous Presence alive within you and
Transfer that to a world in the Dawn of the Awakening

- The Dolphins

CHAPTER EIGHT

The Dolphins' Gift

by Pamela Polland

I'll never forget the first time I swam with dolphins in the wild. I'd been coming to the Hawaiian islands as a visitor for many years. I was particularly focused on the magnificence of the Humpback Whales, (also beings of enormous consciousness), but once I actually dug in roots here as a resident, I began hearing exciting stories about contact with the Spinner Dolphins that grace these waters.

After living on the island of Maui for a year or so, we'd heard that the dolphins tended to show up in one place fairly consistently - not that they were there often, but when they did show up, it was usually in this one particular bay. So my husband and I packed up our snorkel gear and started going there once a week. This particular bay does not have a beach, so the entry is rocky and not easy on the feet. It can tend to get windy, so the water can get choppy. Nevertheless, we were determined to see these infamous dolphins and kept coming back despite many failed attempts.

We live an hour's drive from this spot, so we'd hear from friends, "Oh, we just swam with the dolphins today," and we'd go the next day and they wouldn't be there. This went on for months until we began to feel like we were 'The People Who Will Never Swim With Dolphins.' Being a large bay, we were never quite sure if they were there and if we were just on the wrong side, or too deep, or too shallow. Still, the determination continued.

One morning we got out there and swam the entire length of the bay, which took us about forty five minutes in one direction. We were on our way back, quite tired by this time, when some other swimmers started pointing into the water. We had made our cross-bay trek in deeper water, and these swimmers were closer to shore by a few hundred feet, so we started swimming in, my husband ahead of me.

I was a decent swimmer, but the length of the bay had pretty much "tuckered me out." I wasn't moving very fast at this point, pacing myself to make it safely back to our entry point. Suddenly, my husband pops his head out of the water and yells "They're here!!!" pointing his finger toward the water directly below him. I can't deny the adrenalin that shot through me at that point. I started swimming faster in his direction when suddenly out of the blue, there they were!!! A small pod of about a dozen dolphins swimming right towards me.

My heart leapt with excitement. After all this build up of months of trying, questioning if we would ever get to have this divine experience we'd heard so much about, suddenly, there they were in my face... dolphins! Not dolphins on the Discovery Channel, not dolphins confined in a pool at Sea World or some hotel. Not dolphins trained to jump through hoops for a fish. Dolphins in the wild - in *their* territory. Free, natural, at home and they're swimming towards me. Wow!

My mind was racing with the "Oh my God, oh my God, oh my God" chant, while they kept coming. As we met "face to face," literally close enough to touch, they simply rounded up to the surface for some air and glided along just under the surface of the water so we could check each other out. Then, very gracefully (because that's all they ever are is graceful), they dove down below me to cruise closer to the ocean floor, about 40-50 feet below.

This experience began what then became years of swimming with them on a regular basis. We learned they come to this bay to rest after a night of feeding in deeper water and that "cruising" near the floor is, in fact, their resting mode. We've also come to see how active they get when they're getting ready to leave the bay and go back out into deeper water.

They slowly build up to faster and faster cruising paces, speeds at which no human could keep up, and they add the jumping action the Spinners are named for where they torpedo their entire bodies out of the water, spinning around in the air. While in this bay, they also tend to swim in large circles, so if a person can't keep pace with them, there are still plenty of opportunities to meet them again when they come back around, which can be anywhere from 2 to 10 minutes later.

It was just another piece of Grace that fateful first encounter, that the dolphins were in their resting mode, because we were able to keep up, and we were able to have a tremendous amount of very close contact with them as they'd come to the surface to breath.

They'd just hang out with us for what seemed liked hours, but was probably minutes at most, gliding under the surface of the water. It was in this very first encounter I learned it was pointless to try and touch them. In that one morning alone, I had been close enough to touch them dozens of times, but each time I'd reach my hand toward one, it would move far enough away so as not to make physical contact, an inch beyond my arm's reach.

I've also heard since that arms outstretched can be taken as an aggressive action by the dolphins, so I've gotten in the habit of keeping my arms close in to my body when I'm near them, motoring with my legs.

Like most of us who are privileged to have this experience, I tend to send messages of peace and love when I'm with the dolphins so that they know I come with joy and gratitude and nothing else. Of course, I have imaginary conversations with them in my head, but my "real" experience is that these beings are far more intelligent than I can even imagine, let alone comprehend, and far be it from me to bother projecting my somewhat limited human way of thinking and perceiving onto their extraordinary beingness.

I have a slightly different take on the whole telepathic deal. The reason I call them pretend conversations is because I don't like to assume anything and I have no proof that anything I think I might be hearing is actually coming from any place else than my own head.

I definitely feel that the dolphins and I have communicated in that they've made it clear many times if they feel like playing, or are happy to see me, if they don't want to play or be touched, or they don't mind me staring into their beautiful eyes, even though the naturalists say that could be construed as aggressive behavior on my part.

It's always their game and any contact I have with them is by their allowing, by their gift. There are some who would say that any conversation we think we're having with another species is nothing more than wishful projection on our part, and I have no grounds on which to argue that point, so I don't go so far as to presume that I'm having a true telepathic experience. Just in case they can read ME, I am quite deliberate about the messages I send out, so I "talk" to them, telling them how much I love them and how beautiful they look to me, and I ask them to come to me when I can no longer keep up with them.

Although I've come to a point where I don't get the adrenalin rush anymore when I see them, I now realize there's a whole other energy source available to me when I'm in their presence. It's something I like to call DNA shifting. When I am with them, there's an energy available to me that is clearly no longer the effects of adrenalin, but something much subtiler, perhaps a result of their sonar. Whatever it is, it lasts usually for several days, sometimes it has lasted a week.

The DNA shift I've experienced from swimming with the dolphins is hard to describe, but let's make an analogy. Let's say we're fortunate enough to sit at the feet of an enlightened monk and what transpires is a kind of transmission, where even if there's nothing spoken, or if what is spoken is in a language we don't understand. We still leave the meditation hall feeling different. We may even leave feeling wiser, but at the very least, we would feel more peaceful and centered, as if some of this guru's energy rubbed off on us.

This feeling might last an hour or a day, but if the transmission went deep, literally affecting us at the cellular level, then we might feel the benefit for days or a week or even the rest of our lives. It feels like an internal improvement, literally at the DNA level. I'm not a person who was blind and now can see, who had a life threatening illness and now is healed. I'm a simple, happy resident of a beautiful island, which is part of the most isolated land mass on this planet, where dolphins also live, frolic, and grace people of all ages, from all over the world with the gift of allowing us to be in their presence and for a time, to enter their world.

At the very least, swimming with the dolphins has brought a level of joy into my life that was a significant increase from anything previous, and I lead a very blessed and joyful life. The dolphins themselves are so joyful, They live a life of play and rest. They have very few predators to worry about. Mostly man, actually. They just cruise around in the stunning underwater world, eating, resting, having sex, making and raising babies, frolicking, jumping, clicking, and cooing.

They live harmoniously in community with one another. Imagine how joyful it would be to meet a group of humans who lived with so much ease and joy. Wouldn't we feel inspired just by being in their presence? With the dolphins, there's this added energy field created by their sonar. It's their joy filtered through their sonar that I believe reaches into the cellular level of my body and literally re-arranges how I look at the world.

When we are in pain, emotional or physical, it's hard to see the beauty and perfection in this world, but when we are filled with joy, everything looks, tastes and feels better.

When swimming with the dolphins, I feel infected with their joy and their boundless energy. I also feel so grateful each time I have the experience, like I'm being blessed. To walk through life feeling blessed and grateful is a glorious gift and yes, it touches my relationships with others and the world at large.

I can honestly say, from that very first encounter, they've changed me forever for the better. Like the adage goes, "Let Peace begin with me." If I am better, I bring that upgrade to my community, to the world at large. In this way, the dolphin's gift is exponential, so perhaps they really are, as some bolder than I might say, here to heal this world.

An award-winning singer/songwriter, with three albums on Columbia and Epic as well as two more independently released albums to her credit, Pamela Polland's ever increasing list of musical credentials reads like a veritable Who's Who of artists … from all points on the musical compass. Over the course of her forty years in the business, this seasoned professional has both performed and recorded with such luminaries as Bonnie Raitt, Kenny Loggins, Jackson Browne, Van Morrison, John Denver, Taj Mahal, Manhattan Transfer and a host of others.

Fulfilling a life-long call to live in the Hawaiian Islands, and after the release of Heart Of The World, Pamela and her noted-designer-husband Bill Ernst, resettled on the island of Maui. Pamela immersed herself in studying the culture and native language, joining a hula halau (performing hula school); eventually adding the ukulele to her gig bag. In recent years, Pamela has performed both as a hula dancer and as a musician, accompanying other hula dancers.

Pamela is currently the band leader of a four-person 'ukulele band, Keaolani. Please visit the Keaolani website http://www.keaolani.com/ to learn more about the band, their history, and their current events and http:www.pamelapolland.com to find out more about Pamela, her products, vocal lessons and other services.

CHAPTER NINE

Baptized By Dolphins

by Nancy Smyth Myers

My best friend once told me, "Whenever you cross an ocean you never return the same person." In 1994, it happened to me. My husband, Brad, and I left for the island of Oahu in Hawaii on August 31st to stay at our timeshare. This particular location is of a mystical nature in the Makaha Valley on the west side of the island. We have owned there for five years, yet never knew that dolphins come in to feed less than ten minutes from our door.

When we left Los Angeles, we were both stressed and emotionally and physically in need of rest. We had not been away since I had breast cancer two years before and we needed to "ESCAPE" for a couple of weeks to be together in a totally different environment.

The first week was an unwinding time. The island trade winds, balmy nights and soothing water took much longer to infuse us than the usual couple of days. By the second week we were snorkeling with hundreds of tropical fish amongst their caverns in the sea. Life soon began to have a different meaning than you receive running to the mail box everyday to see what checks have come in to contribute to the monthly battle to survive.

Each of us has passed the fifty mark and have always enjoyed working. Only recently has the pace to survive removed the real fun from our job. There is not much we need materially but the need is there for a financial comfort zone to breathe easier. My husband was short in the "FAITH" department, always saying that "God does not pay our bills." I always reply, "Yes, He does." Immediately you get the inside picture of our different spiritual paths.

We were at a restaurant getting directions and were told the place we were seeking was just around the cove from where the dolphins come in. I said, "What dolphins?" I then heard an earful. I was told about a dolphin camp where a woman takes tourists to swim with the dolphins early every morning.

The very next morning we were up and out by 6:15 am to find this location. We found the area with little difficulty and within minutes, the dolphins arrived in their splendor. Some were jumping in and out of the water while the rest played in their normal swim pattern with fins rising up from the ocean, then curving their backs dove nose down into the water again. It was great fun to watch them.

After they left, we returned to the restaurant for breakfast and shared what we had seen. They asked us if we got in the water to swim out to them, as the lady at the camp takes people out everyday. We had not seen any lady, only a lot of tents with no one around and the dolphins were not close to shore. They were at least three hundred yards into the ocean, but this was all Brad needed to hear. He has snorkeled and dove all over the Pacific and could not wait to go back to attempt to swim out to the wonderful mammals.

I personally was overwhelmed by the idea. However, I knew I would follow my husband on this adventure no matter what, though I would be concerned about our safety. At a Sunday night service, I privately closed my eyes and asked God to watch over us. I knew that in the morning we would be off to the dolphins. I had heard that dolphins are referred to as God's Messengers who possess an intellect superior to ours. I was anxious to be with them.

When the morning came, I was exhausted from a frustrating night of little sleep and much concern. Many worries had overcome me about the distance from the shore, if Brad's knee would give out, if I would get scared being out in the middle of the ocean. I was worn out from all these worries, only to find after waiting an hour, the dolphins did not come.

I walked along the beach and saw a young man standing near some tents. As he saw me, we started to move toward each other as if he knew what I was there for. He was not at all surprised when I said we were there to swim with dolphins. He immediately began telling me he was in charge of the camp while the lady went into town to pick up some Japanese tourists who wanted to experience them as well. I thought this lady took people out in boats and dropped them over the side next to the dolphins. I had no idea that everyone swam out to be with them.

Soon the lady arrived with the tourists. I found out Teri was an author of a dolphin book and a well known lecturer in Japan on the subject. Everyone was heartbroken when the dolphins did not come. They said it was the first day this summer they did not show. Immediately, this was an omen to me we were not meant to do this until Teri and the young man educated us on how easy it is to swim to them. The key, they said, was to meet them with an open heart.

Brad and I spent an hour or so swimming in the ocean, getting familiar with the ocean floor and water conditions. I was reassured that I had no need to worry or fear anything. I quickly labeled this day as a "dress rehearsal" because of all the support we found at this camp. It prepared me for the following day. However, that night I literally got down on my knees and prayed by our bed that God would watch over us and protect us if He wanted us to have this wonderful experience. I also told God I knew whatever the day would bring would be His will. So off I went to sleep with far less concerns than the previous evening.

The following morning we awoke at 5:45 am. When we arrived we could not believe our eyes. A magnificent rainbow was perfectly formed from the sand beneath our feet over the waters where the dolphins come. It was so intense, every color vibrant. I knew this was going to be an unbelievable day. We sat on the shore sipping our coffee with a beach towel over our head for the rain. I was reading my bible and was right on the page where Jesus was demanding of his apostles 'Ask and ye shall receive.' The very next second Brad said, "Here they come!"

I felt spiritually connected and yelled to everyone asleep in their tents, "The dolphins are here!" One girl, Julia, who spends her life working and swimming with dolphins, came out of her tent and gave me a sign to get going. I put on my mask, fins and snorkel and began to swim to them. Brad, of course, was already way ahead of me afraid they would leave before he could get out there. He would turn back and beg me to hurry, but I finally told him to go and I would catch up.

A few minutes later, I looked up and saw him surrounded by dolphins. I had another hundred yards to go. I looked down and proceeded toward the dolphins when I saw a giant stingray with a tail that appeared to be at least seven feet long. I did not panic, but I hesitated to continue and thought it would be best to go back and get a boogie board. Miraculously, just as I was turning back, the young guy came out with a board and gave it to me. I hooked the strap on my wrist and continued to swim. Soon I saw the dolphins' fins within six feet of me and felt proud of myself for making it out that far. Immediately, I put my head in the water and saw my first three dolphins. They were magnificent and appeared to be about six to nine feet in length. They were perfectly clear against the turquoise water and were swimming around Brad. I will never forget the sight of those first three gracefully cruising by me.

Then I looked straight down under me and saw at least ten to fifteen more and one with a baby by its side. I thought at this moment that I was the luckiest person in the world. Prior to seeing the dolphins, I heard them. You could not miss them beeping their little high pitched sounds. Some were like one note repeating itself over and over while other beeps sounded like a tiny sigh, as though the note would drop a couple of notes while being connected. I knew they were definitely communicating.

At this point I was ecstatic to be among the privileged few in this world to swim with dolphins under these circumstances, out in the wild where they could get away from you if they chose to do so, amazed when they stayed with us so long. They began to swim parallel to the coastline and made us chase after them. This was great fun but soon we began to tire.

Julia said they tend to know when you need a rest and will take off so you can get your wind. Pretty soon they went out into the ocean and we went into shore. My husband and I took one look at each other and realized we had experienced an excitement and delight neither of us had ever known. Everyone hugged and sat on the beach sharing what had happened. Brad kept saying he could not believe I went out that far. He would have taken any bets I would not do this. He was proud of me.

Almost one half hour later the dolphins returned and Brad leaped from the sand with Julia to join them again. A Hawaiian named Mano, who lived in a tent near the camp, had been there all summer. He grabbed the binoculars and watched my husband and Julia being fully entertained by this dolphin pod. I looked through the binoculars and saw them flapping their fins against the back of my husband's head while others were jumping all around him. Mano said the dolphins never stay this long so up I shot up and went out by myself to attempt to be with them one more time.

I got to where the ocean floor drops off and this time the stingray started coming up from the bottom toward me. I looked around and saw one other girl wearing a flotation jacket and I called to her to come over to me. I explained the stingray underneath and she said there is also an eagle manta ray down there. We looked and they both came up to investigate us. We held each other's hand and slowly moved away, hoping they would ignore us. When we felt secure we went our separate ways toward the dolphins as they seemed to be split into two groups.

I soon looked back and realized the chair I used was much further than the first time so I made a decision to go back. I cannot explain the feeling of failure I experienced by this decision to retreat, but I did feel God had answered my prayers and I had no reason to push the situation. I turned around and was snorkeling my way back to shore when all of a sudden I was surrounded by dolphins. I could not believe they came to me. My heart was filled with emotion as they looked up at me and made their beautiful sounds. I had heard they understand every language so I made an attempt to communicate my joy to them by saying through my snorkel, "Thank you, thank you for coming to swim with me. I was afraid to go any further to you."

Quickly, one of them came right up to my mask, five inches from my face and started talking to me. I was positive it was smiling and sending me a love and comfort I have never shared with anything or anyone. Within a minute of this communication they all lined up, four across, and headed into shore with me following them. They stopped in waters where I felt safe to play and stayed with me for at least fifteen minutes all by myself. I could not believe the experience I was having.

They danced beneath me in pairs and swam around me while they were all talking to me in the most loving sounds. They would gently pass within inches of my arms and legs. Each time they came close, I would spread my arms to dive next to them and amongst them, but they would only let me get about five inches from them. When I tried to touch them in a very non-aggressive way, with a gentle hand motion toward their bodies, they would gracefully move in a teasing manner just far enough so my hand could not touch them. They never darted or showed fear of any kind.

There were many occasions when they looked up from beneath me and seemed to look right into my eyes, but again, only one came within three to five inches of my face. That dolphin's face I will see the rest of my life. There was a smile filled with warmth and kindness, a purity not seen in the human race. It is as if they have never known anger or confrontation. They present an aura of total peace and trust.

When you are in the midst of these exquisite creatures, you are totally lost in time. You never want the moment to end. It's a time of play beyond anything you ever knew as a child, much like a fairy tale where you feel like you have gone through the looking glass. They were never on guard with their emotions and they gave everything unconditionally and did everything they could to pleasure me. As they circled my body, my heart released all the pain I had held onto forever, my mind was transformed by all their beauty.

After this one-on -one experience, they started swimming parallel once again and I took after them until they wore me out. I returned to the beach stunned by all that had just happened to me. Julia, who does so much work with the dolphins, told me they "zapped" Brad and me for a long time. I personally felt I had seen one dot of the purity God intended for all of us from the beginning of creation. I also was sure I now knew what awaits us in Heaven. It says in the Bible that 'Eyes have not seen nor ear heard the beauty that awaits us in Heaven.' This particular level of consciousness I experienced, assured me of what joy and peace you can have if God controls your life. It is an easier path by far than when you are behind the wheel.

At this point, we all sat and again shared what we experienced and we were agreeing we were having the most DIVINE DAY when Mano said, "Here they come again!" No one could believe they had returned. I turned to Julia after watching them leap from the water and said, "They are beckoning me." She said, "If you feel their pull then go to them." Off I went again. I soon realized that Julia was right next to me, which was comforting. She would swim with them all the time without a snorkel or fins. As soon as we got to where they were, they took off and went too far for me to think of going. Julia said they do this sometime. She also said they were lined up right in front of me and wanted her to heal an injury I had. She asked if I would mind if she worked on my back in the ocean. I said that would be fine.

Now, remember, we were one hundred and fifty yards in the sea and I had this complete stranger touching my spine while I was floating as though I was a feather. She got to my lower back and said she found the spot. She was right. Nine months before, I had gotten caught in an exercise machine where the leg press would not release. It had caused a major sprain in my lower back and I was in therapy for two months. Getting out of bed, swimming any length of time, or stooping of any kind was very painful.

The dolphins continued to stay straight in front of me and when she finished with me, which was at least one half hour later, I had no pain and felt like I could float out there forever. I had no feeling of mental or physical weight and had never felt that light. It was as though I was being blown around by the wind in a place that had no gravity. This feeling of lightness has stayed with me since our return and it took days to get back into a place of reality. If anyone tries to put a heavy problem on me, I just won't allow it. Any confrontation seems so silly and absurd. Negative thinking puts a black dot on a white wall. I just want my world to stay as beautiful up here as it was down there.

On a day the dolphins did not come, I had a great desire to call the pastor of a nearby church we attended, to ask him if he would baptize me. This was not just a whim. This was something that had deep meaning for me. I had deliberately avoided being baptized after I had become a Born Again Christian years ago. I thought it meant I had to live a life without enjoyment and worldly entertainment of any kind as my strict, religious parents had done.

This vacation was another time for my spiritual thirst to be watered. The time Brad and I spent in this little church was so healing to my spirit. I knew only God could provide the road for us to take to change the grave problems we had been facing back at home.

In my heart I knew I really wanted to be baptized by this special pastor, whose inspiring sermons had touched us profoundly from the time we had arrived. I was disappointed when he told me that unless I lived there and belonged to his church, he could not baptize me. It was not until I was back home that I realized God had baptized me on my beautiful "Dolphin Day." I knew the healing of my heart, back and all the mental hurt departing from my mind was my baptism by dolphins.

The sense of not having any physical or mental weight was also a freedom I have never felt until I was immersed in those waters. As I reflect on each and every moment with the dolphins, I can feel the love they were sending me and I relate it to the love God has for all of us. That is why He gave us His son, Jesus, as a mirror of Himself for all of us to see who He is. If we could only open our eyes and hearts we would truly see Him everywhere. I had seen him that day in the dolphins.

There was a card waiting for me when I arrived home, from a special friend who knew nothing about my dolphin experience. She only knew I was going to Hawaii and hoped the card would arrive before I left. I opened it and stared in disbelief. It was one of those fold around cards. On the right side was a picture of a coastline that looked exactly like the view from our balcony in Hawaii. Beaming down on the coastline was a gorgeous UFO in pastel colors with a lot of purple hue. On the left side of the card were two dolphins in the sea and the words, "Miracles Dance in Timelessness," were written on top of the dolphins against the sunset. In the waters on the right side were written "All worlds are one village." The inside just simply said, "We are all part of the same Love."

I stared at it in awe for a long time, Being with the dolphins was one of the most powerful things that has ever happened to me. That I had been baptized by dolphins was beyond belief. No wonder this powerful experience took three weeks to stop talking about! It had also been hard to get back into any kind of 'normal human' reality.

I could see dolphins everywhere and I remained in their loving, caring world, extra sensitive to everything and everyone around me. I saw people differently, all needing love and understanding. I no longer seemed to fear the pressures that had been so engulfing before we left. I knew I had been completely transformed, the baptism by God bringing me full circle to Christ.

CHAPTER TEN

Around the World With the Dolphins

by Jason Cressey

My eyes were tired, my neck sore. The persistent tap-tap-tapping of the computer keyboard had lulled me into an irritable exhaustion, and sleep offered only temporary respite. The prospect of another day, another week, another month of this monotony seemed intolerable. I had become socially isolated through self-imposed exile from my friends and family as the need to complete a doctoral thesis, four years in the planning. Yet, on that cold Spring evening in Oxford, the dolphins swam back into my dreams.

The dreams continued and by the year's end, I had successfully gained my doctorate, moved to another country, and after scrimping and saving every penny, begun my journey in search of dolphins. There was actually nothing new about my fixation with our flippered friends. At six years of age I had witnessed the sickening spectacle of dolphins performing tricks at a local dolphinarium. I vividly recall refusing the invitation of the circus ringleader to sit in a little rubber boat that would be towed around the pool by one of the innocent captives. Something was wrong with the picture. This was not the real home of the dolphins, this was not where they were supposed to be, this was not the way we should have been treating them.

It was to be nearly twenty years before I had the opportunity to visit Australia and go directly to Dolphin Headquarters, more commonly known as Monkey Mia, Western Australia. On a balmy January morning in the early 1990's, I first met Holey Fin, the grandmother of the pod of wild Bottlenose Dolphins who had been choosing to visit the beach in this remote spot for over thirty years. In the few seconds, or was it minutes of looking into her brown, accepting eyes, meters away from the camera-hungry crowds, my love affair with the spirit of the dolphin had begun. Two years later, the dolphins called me back.

Japan may seem like a strange place to begin a tour of dolphin hot-spots. It remains one of the few countries to defiantly ignore a global moratorium on whale hunting, and until recently was the nation responsible for blood-red seas as thousands of dolphins were mercilessly slaughtered each year by fishermen greedy for ever-dwindling fish supplies.

Yet Japan is a country of paradoxes, for there live some of the most dedicated and single-minded supporters of whale and dolphin conservation, and it was the first country in the world to establish a Dolphin Healing Centre, where people can go and experience a meditative atmosphere (it is, after all, a Buddhist temple) surrounded by the sounds, images and energy of whales and dolphins.

Japan is also one of the few countries in the world where top executives of multi-national companies can enjoy stress-reduction courses run by professional psychologists, which are oriented around swimming and interacting with wild dolphins. There are, in fact, two or three places in the waters of Japan where people can, and increasingly do, pay thousands of yen to enjoy the privilege of swimming with friendly wild dolphins.

Being there in the icy cold month of February denied me the chance to meet the Japanese dolphins personally, but the video footage I was shown left me no doubt that this would be an experience worth returning for. The gracious, forgiving nature of the dolphins is a lesson for us all. Even in this most hostile of environments, at least in terms of the human threat past and present, cetaceans seem willing to hold out the hand, or should that be flipper, of friendship, and to embark upon a path of mutual trust, respect and learning with us.

Groups like ICERC Japan (the International Cetacean Education and Research Centre) are at the forefront of efforts by an increasing number of Japanese people (particularly the younger generation) to raise awareness, both nationally and internationally, concerning the conservational plight and spiritual connection with the world's dolphins and whales. Having met the individuals involved with ICERC in Tokyo, and the Dolphin Healing Centre in beautiful Kyoto, I could see clearly that the Japanese dolphins and whales have the most loyal and committed of human allies.

Traveling from the northern hemisphere to the southern hemisphere meant flying from winter to summer overnight. An obstinate wall of antipodean heat to greet me off the plane at Sydney Airport was confirmation that someone had turned up the thermostat by thirty degrees centigrade in the space of nine hours. It was to be some nine days before my body had fully accustomed, and during this time I was able to catch up with old friends and enjoy the spectacle of Sydney's incomparable Mardi Gras celebration in the vibrant company of one million other mesmerized carnival spectators. When Australia throws a party, the rest of the world packs its bags and jumps on a plane to Sydney.

Working my way up the coast of New South Wales, I soon realized that the dolphins were playing a game with me. Wherever I turned up, Nambucca Heads, Ballina, Coff's Harbour, Byron Bay, the dolphins had, apparently, been spotted in copious numbers only the day before. I soon tired of the well intentioned words from almost every local I talked to ("Hundreds of 'em as far as the eye could see. Nevah seen as mayni in mi life!") and concluded I was about twenty-four hours behind the largest pod of dolphins ever to have graced the waves. Resignation set in, and for a week I saw not a single flipper, dorsal fin or tail fluke. At least I was fortunate to meet some of the well-known and quite wonderful dolphin people who live in Australia, and a common message from these veteran cetacean lovers was that the dolphins would appear when the time was right.

One week later, in a quiet river estuary in southern Queensland, light years from the thronging tourist beaches of the Gold or Sunshine Coasts, the time was indeed finally right. Far from the maddening crowd, there I was, swimming with a mother Indo-Pacific dolphin, her year-old baby, and a huge dog. Apparently, the dog's owner had initially been concerned when his rather fierce looking Rottweiler started showing an interest in the friendly dolphins, and so decided it would be prudent to keep the dog locked indoors. For the three days that the dog could not go down to the water, the dolphins failed to appear. On the day that the owner decided to let his dog go down to the water again, the dolphins returned, and the trio of friends have been inseparable ever since.

This was the scene that dreams were made of. The baby dolphin giving two local children rides with its dorsal fin, the dog playing chase games with the mother dolphin, the handful of adults screaming and laughing like children. I had touched the magic of the dolphins, and the wait had been worth every second.

Over three thousand kilometers later on the remote western coast of Australia, my anticipation mounted as I neared the place where it had all began two years previously - Monkey Mia. Victim to a sting-ray attack, Holey Fin had sadly died during the time I had been away, though many of the dolphin folk I had met in Australia were firmly of the belief she had done her work in this incarnation, and would be remembered with great love and affection for choosing to bring her family so dramatically into the world of humans.

The first fin I spotted as I hurried onto the small beach was, fittingly, that of Nicky, Holey Fin's charismatic daughter. Nicky had become top dog, or rather top dolphin since her mother had died, and regularly escorted a select group of six or seven others to meet the adoring crowds each day. Being there in April, I hit the quiet season, with a regularly daily crowd of only around a hundred people. Christmas and Easter can bring in daily crowds of around a thousand, I was told, with visitors coming from all around the world to a location more than nine hundred kilometers from the nearest international airport or major urban center.

Every day of the week I spent in Monkey Mia was associated with the water, be it standing on the shoreline chatting (mainly telepathically) with Nicky and family, or sailing around the beautiful turquoise waters of Shark Bay, spotting dugongs (the mysterious, gentle marine mammals that resemble mermaids), multi-colored fish, sharks and yes, hundreds of dolphins against the dramatic backdrop of red sand dunes and lush green sea grass.

Sometimes the dolphins were making love, sometimes even fighting, though I saw conflicts resolved decisively and soon forgotten. I realized that the image of dolphins as cuddly oceanic teddy-bears, does neither them nor us any good. They are living, breathing mammals and yes, they have conflicts too, maybe even bad days, but their evident desire and ability to overcome problems and strive for group harmony contains a lesson for us all.

I noticed that every bus load of tourists who came to Monkey Mia arrived with a set of expectations about performing dolphins, and left with a very different perspective. I witnessed people spontaneously laughing, crying, shrieking and sighing at their first sight of the famous residents, and it was clear they had touched the magic of the dolphin spirit too.

About one thousand kilometers further down the western coast of Australia lies Bunbury, a small industrial town just two hours drive south of Perth (the pretty, if somewhat inanimate state capital). Bunbury boasts the Dolphin Discovery Center, an impressive museum dedicated to the pod of local dolphins who cavort in the waters just off its doorstep. Although the owners of the center have tried to cultivate a Monkey Mia-type image of dolphins freely swimming to the beach and interacting with visitors, the reality is that these dolphins prefer to keep clear of knee-deep waters.

The best way to see the Bunbury dolphins, I discovered, was by a two-hour cruise around the crystal clear waters of the bay and the dolphins loved it. They leapt around the small boat, swam beneath and in front of us, peered up inquisitively and I swear, enjoyed the experience as much as the eight humans on board.

In the following weeks I saw dolphins at close quarters in Strahan (Tasmania), Sorrento (Victoria), Port Stephens (New South Wales), and Moreton Island (Queensland). I firmly believe that Australia, a magical land of harsh beauty and forty thousand years of Aboriginal spirituality, is truly blessed when it comes to meeting cetaceans. It is as if the dolphins and whales have nominated Australia as the global hub of their efforts to raise the consciousness of humans, to make us aware of the beauty and bounty of the oceans before it is too late to reconsider our role on this planet, and our immutable connection with the myriad of life forms to which Gaia plays host.

A brief stop in New Zealand en route to the Islands of the Pacific gave me the opportunity to see (albeit for just ten seconds at a two hundred meter distance) the mighty sperm whales of Kaikoura, an increasingly popular but terribly commercialized whale-watching spot on the east coast of the South Island.

One day later I was in the beautiful little town of Akaroa, New Zealand's only French settlement, to see the world's smallest dolphins unique to this area, the Hector's dolphin. The contrast could not have been sharper. For half the price I had paid to see the whales in Kaikoura, I was taken out by a friendly and knowledgeable skipper with just three other people to see the Hector's dolphins, allowed to get close and personal, and to spend almost double the time out on the water compared with the Kaikoura experience.

I declined the invitation to jump in the water and swim with them (I had made the teeth-chattering mistake of swimming in New Zealand waters three years earlier) and in fact, it seemed the best place to be was above the water rather than in it, as it became clear that what the Hector's dolphins lacked in size they made up for in speed and athletic agility. Like silver bullets in the water, they gleefully jumped around the boat, at times only millimeters from each other, but never bumping into one another by accident.

Watching these little dolphins made me marvel at the wonder of evolution, for just a few million years ago these creatures were trotting around on all fours through the swamps and undergrowth of primordial forests. I snapped back into the here-and-now when the skipper announced to the small crew that it was time to return to the harbor, and at that moment two of the enchanting dolphins jumped two meters out of the water with the kind of synchronized timing that Olympic gymnasts yearn for. Seconds later they were all gone, having quite clearly and telepathically, understood that this human-cetacean meeting of minds and hearts was over for the day. For me, the South Seas now beckoned.

Few people have ever heard of the Republic of Kiribati (pronounced Kir-ee-bas) in the Central Pacific. This tiny atoll republic (albeit a huge country if ocean area is taken into account) is like the Pacific of fifty years ago. On thirty-one of its thirty-three atolls there exists no electricity, running water or sewerage system. The country has no television or daily newspaper, the main transportation is by sailing canoe (as it has been for centuries) and outsiders are still regarded with a mixture of wonder, respect and fear, particularly on the outer islands.

Snippets of stories I had heard over the years led me to the northern island of Butaritari, close to where the equator and the dateline meet. This was where Robert Louis Stevenson, in his wanderings around the Pacific, spent two tranquil years in the 1890's, and where he gained the inspiration to write Treasure Island. Butaritari is still a treasure of sorts, with its lush vegetation on the narrow strip of sandy atoll land, which encases a dazzling tropical blue lagoon. Yet this paradise harbors a dark tradition in the village of Kuma at its northern tip.

For centuries, two families practiced their magical art of calling dolphins (and small whales) to the beach. This was achieved by the head of the family entering a state of trance sometimes for as long as three days, during which his or her astral body would travel to Mona (the underworld beneath the ocean) and greet an assembled group of dolphin spirits all in human form. The dolphin caller would then invite the dolphin-people to a party in his or her village, and a number of the dolphin-people accepted. As soon as the astral body of the dolphin caller had witnessed all the guests commence their journey to Kuma's beach, he or she would wake from the trance and announce to the village that the dolphins were on their way.

The exact time of arrival later that day, or the next, was predicted with great accuracy, and the villagers prepared themselves for the arrival of their guests. Exotic garlands of flowers were worn, as well as fine perfumes and the most beautiful traditional costumes. When the dolphins appeared (invariably right on cue), the villagers would each choose an individual dolphin and spend the next few hours stroking, playing and even flirting with this guest. On a given signal by the dolphin caller, the villagers would then lead their guests to the beach and once all the dolphins were out of the water, they would be ceremoniously slaughtered and eaten.

I was fortunate to speak to one of the women who still has the ability to call the dolphins. My mind and heart were torn. In front of me was an old and locally revered woman who possessed the gift of directly communicating with dolphins, of entering their world and conversing with them in much the same way as humans converse with each other. Yet here was a woman who was leading the dolphins to their death, at least in the three-dimensional view of things. Through my dear friend and interpreter Winnie, to whom fate had steered me when I had arrived on the island, I spoke at length to the dolphin caller.

Her basic philosophy was that the dolphins who came to the beach (and there could be as many as five hundred in one calling, enough to feed all the islanders for weeks) did so voluntarily, in the knowledge that their physical bodies, for which they had no further use, would be put to good use in the nutrition of land-based humans.

I neither reject nor agree with this viewpoint. It is not my place to judge a whole culture after the briefest of visits, but I did gain some satisfaction in telling the villagers how much dolphins and whales were honored in the West in their functioning physical bodies, and how their presence was seen as very important for people to care for the oceans and ultimately each other.

This was greeted very warmly, and the villagers assured me that the tradition, which had all but disappeared over recent years anyway, would probably pass into history with the knowledge and understanding that dolphins and whales had important work to do in helping the I-Matang, or white people, treat the Earth and each other with more respect.

Just before leaving Butaritari, and after attending a mesmerizing display of Micronesian singing and dancing staged in my honor, I fell quite suddenly and violently ill. Winnie, my host, teacher, interpreter and surrogate grandmother on the island, decided it was time to use some of her tried and tested magical techniques to nurse me back to health. At about two o'clock in the morning, after I had been vomiting and running a high fever for several hours, she started massaging my stomach and chanting indistinguishable words beneath her breath, immediately making me feel much better.

Something then happened which I can neither explain nor dismiss, and which was to change my connection with dolphins forever. As I lay on the straw matting of the hut floor, I saw three beautiful gold-tinted dolphins floating above me. Unhesitating, I told Winnie that three friends had arrived in dolphin form, and without showing the least surprise, she started asking me questions, to which the visitors immediately provided answers.

I cannot describe how the communication occurred, though I can say for certain that the dolphins' jaws were not moving in any way that might imitate human speech, nor could I be certain what language any of the communications were in. Perhaps the nearest I can get to describing it would be to say that I saw and felt images. I was communicating by instinct, by a kind of telepathy or stream of thoughts and emotions. Information started coming into my head and my heart of which I had absolutely no previous knowledge. I clearly remember telling Winnie about a local village woman, who had a name resembling that of a flower, responsible (through evil magic) for the recent deaths of several children, and who had a shark-tooth necklace hidden in her house. Within two days this story had been confirmed, the woman confronted, and the deaths stopped.

The dolphins have appeared several times since then, often at the most unexpected moments, and represent something akin to an inner voice, a voice which has access to information my conscious mind is unaware of (or chooses to ignore), and which manifests itself physically via a form with which I feel an immediate affinity - the dolphin.

It is my belief that this gift (or awakening) was given to me with the help of Winnie, an elderly lady living in a tiny village in the middle of an ocean on the other side of the planet from my birthplace. I had felt before I set foot in Kiribati that it would become clear to me what the real purpose of my visit was (the initial motivation to visit had been a strange attraction of the country's beautiful flag printed on a world map!). The reason had ultimately unfolded in a spectacular and unpredictable fashion.

Following a relaxing week in Raratonga, recovering from a strand of cholera, which had been a rather unpleasant souvenir from my latter days in Kiribati, I ventured to Maui, in the Hawaiian chain, at the north end of the Polynesian triangle. After spending two powerful weeks in the foothills of Haleakala, the sleeping volcano in which the goddess Pélé resides, I traveled on to the Big Island, spending three days kayaking with the dolphins in the dramatic setting of a beautiful bay. These were Spinner Dolphins, and as they leapt out of the water like giant, playful corkscrews it was obvious to us why they had been given their name.

Not for the first time on my dolphin journey, I was left with more questions than answers after this first encounter with the pod of Spinner Dolphins. Why do they spin? Why do they sometimes choose to come close and at other times swim away? Why does this pod swim so close to shore and interact with people, when almost every other pod of Spinner Dolphins prefers the open ocean? One thing was becoming very clear. My empirical, left-brain approach to life, which had steered me through eight years of academic study in psychology, had little to offer in understanding the oceanic world of dolphins and whales.

The final cetacean encounter of my journey was in the waters of British Columbia, Canada, close to my (then) new home of Vancouver. Having seen the world's smallest dolphins in New Zealand, I was now treated to the mesmerizing grace of the world's largest dolphins, the Orca. The tall, black dorsal fins silently cutting the water's surface and the huge pppwwwfffff, as the blowhole ejected salty condensed air at three hundred kilometers per hour was quite spell-binding, and had the small group of us on board the cozy sailboat entranced for the serene three hours we spent in their company.

To me, the Orca embodies the magical essence of British Columbia with its native Indian heritage and tiny coastal islands smothered in evergreens and early summer morning fogs. The Orcas also welcomed me home, back to the land where the lessons and experiences from my Cetacean journey would touch every part of my life, both personally and professionally, as they become integrated into my very core. That into which years of academic psychology had failed to provide any insight; the dolphins had managed to penetrate, quite literally, in the blink of an eye... a big, brown, understanding eye. Everywhere I had visited, the dolphins held up a mirror and showed me myself, and gave me the gift to accept what I saw without reservation and only with love.

CHAPTER ELEVEN

Adventures With Dolphins and Whales

by Catherine Espinoza

Growing up with dolphins in Florida was incredible. They were in our backyard every day. We used to whistle to them and they would come. We knew a lot of them by their colors and markings. Being around dolphins was an invitation to be playful in the water. I lived in the water all the time and this really affected my character. There was so much I picked up from them like the way I seem to just undulate through life. It is a feeling of being really flexible and fluid. Since then, I have done much work on myself with breath, Tantra, and working on my inhibitions, including shame programming from my Catholic upbringing.

Being in the water with dolphins would bring me to that place I had begun to know through my healing work. It was a place of deep meditation, which seemed to substantiate the work I was doing on myself. I would meet them in that vibration and resonate with their energy. It seemed to be a confirmation I was on the right track.

Now I have done a lot of work with people undulating in the water and in my workshops. It is a way of moving the whole spine in a fluid kind of motion. I have found a metaphor that people relate to very easily. I tell them to move like a dolphin, moving their whole spine in a fluid kind of way as they breathe. This has been an incredibly healing experience for many. It is a very freeing thing, very primal, and very essential to our nature. The combination of the breath with movement of the spine is what yoga is all about and I think the dolphins just live in that conscious dance all the time.

I play the Irish harp, penny whistles and flutes, sing, and tell stories. Some years ago, I was called to produce a recording of my music along with whale and dolphin songs. This inspiration came from hearing the recordings of their songs made by scientists in the field like Roger Paine, a person who has recorded the white whales as well as the song of the humpback. It intrigues me they sing and that their singing is so haunting. I realized the cascading sound of the flute and the harp, which is an instrument of the mood and intuitive side of water, would sound incredible in a combination with the haunting sounds of the whale songs. These can be absolutely beautiful and poetic without using words.

I was in Baja California, Mexico, whale watching the California Gray Whales down on the lagoon at San Ignacio, which is a very beautiful place. I was on a very small fishing boat, which probably held around ten people at the most. I had a little tiny Kinder Harp with me, which is a harp for children tuned to pentatonic scale and I also had a very small Guatemalan flute.

As we flew over the water, I would go back and forth playing the harp and the flute singing wordless songs. We began seeing these huge whale tails all around us and were all hoping to have a friendly experience with a whale, envisioning one coming up to the boat so that we could touch it.

I was playing my little heart out, playing and playing when suddenly this whale came up. It was a mama and with it was a baby. The baby was so excited and friendly. It wanted to come over to the boat, but the mother was protective, placing herself between boat and baby. The baby began climbing up over the mother's back, trying to get at the boat. It was incredible to watch. Finally the mother realized it was OK and got out of the way. To our amazement, not only baby, but the mother too, came up to the boat and allowed us to touch their heads. I was trying to take pictures of what was happening, but then realized this might not last long and I had better go be with the whales before they left. Somebody pulled me toward the whale and I touched its head. Then I looked into its eyes and I couldn't speak. All I could do was cry. It was a massive creature that with one whip of its tail could send the boat and all of us flying and yet, this mama was totally gentle, relaxed in being with us, and adoring the way we were touching it. It looked into our eyes with the greatest peace I had ever seen, a true gentle giant, completely accepting our human interaction.

Since that time I have gone back two or three other times to that same lagoon and incredibly, I've had a lot more experiences like this. It is just amazing the way the whales will play with you, but if they know you are afraid, they won't approach the boat. They usually want to get a look at you before they will approach the boat. Because of their anatomy, the only way they can really do that is if they bring their heads straight up out of the water high enough so their eye is exposed so they can take a really good look at you and see what you're all about. It's an incredible experience to see these huge heads above the water, while their bodies remain stationery like they are on a pedestal.

For such huge beings they are really gentle creatures. When your energy is in sync with them, they approach the boat and will do all kinds of things. They will swim under the boat so everyone will go to one side of the boat and then the boat will seem to almost tip over and it will feel like everyone is going to fall in the water. The people will lean out to touch the whale and then the whale will swim under to the other side, going from side to side under the boat playing this game with the humans. Sometimes they will push the boat around with their heads and they will also get underneath the boat and start to lift it up, they are so playful!

You think of dolphins being playful, riding the bow, looking up into your eyes and jumping around, but the whales, when they are playful, is awe inspiring. The dolphins look so tiny and their energy is totally different. It is lighthearted and joyful. The whales are deep, still creatures that carry the whole record of civilization in them.

The mating encounter is also an incredible experience to witness. There was a Mexican TV crew that had been there filming and they had yet to film the mating, which was what they were waiting for. Forty days they had waited. The fortieth day, we arrived and went out in the boat. It was late afternoon and a little bit cold, but we were excited. We had been driving all day and were happy to finally be out on the water. All of a sudden we saw this massive churning on the top of the water. The water was frothing and foaming white and we could see these tails and bodies going in circles as if they were dancing in the water. We all wondered what was going on and then realized the whales were mating, which is very rare to see.

We moved the boat out as close as we possibly could and watched their beautiful dance. There were two males and one female. One male is the helper while the other one is getting ready to go. We watched them on the top of the water going round and round in their lovemaking ritual, while the television crew was filming, everyone shrieking with excitement. What is incredible is that the whales are the only creatures besides humans that mate face to face. The helper whale assists by moving the female around so that she can receive the other male. Sometimes when the one male is done, the other male will take over, just to make sure the female is impregnated. It was an awesome experience for us all, one we will never forget.

I've also spent a lot of time kayaking in Maui with dolphins and whales. The thing I find about them is they put out a real emotional energy. If you are in your heart, they seem to be much more interested in you than when you are being mental, thinking about how to find them.

The whales and dolphins are all in the same family and dolphins are actually considered small toothed whales, and together with the whales they form the cetacean family. Whales are highly intelligent the same as dolphins. The blue whale is the largest living mammal alive. They are three times as big as any dinosaur that ever lived and are like the colossal bull elephant, which is the largest land mammal. The blue whale is so big that the elephant would fit on the whale's hump. The blue whales use sound vibration. Their echo location will travel the entire circumference of the Earth. All the blue whales are in direct communication with each other all over the planet at all times. Their song echoes through our world, shifting the vibration of the Earth.

Once there were millions of whales on the planet before the whaling started. They were all communicating with each other through the water, which is the main part of our planet and a powerful transmitter of frequencies. There is so much more water than there is earth, Earth being three quarters water. Imagine all the time there was this ohming zero point energy going on around the planet as whales communicated with each other and what that must have been like. Today, we have definitely gone through a vibratory shift from their absence.

Through my experience with dolphins and whales, my life changed dramatically. I entered a rebirth into something greater and deeper than I have ever experienced before in both my philosophy about life and way of being. This led me into my music career and expanded the horizons of my special gifts and ability to contribute to the world.

CHAPTER TWELVE

Dolphins Make a Wish Come True

by Bennie Kante

I worked as a boat captain on a Scuba dive boat on the Kona Coast of Hawaii. One morning I had a very special charter. The Make a Wish Foundation brought a small child who was diagnosed with a terminal disease. His wish was to swim with dolphins. I prayed the dolphins would feel my sincere desire to assist in his dream coming true.

The boat was appropriately named the Blue Dolphin. Once on board, the child, his family, and myself left the pier in search of dolphins. I headed for a bay an hour away, a well known place spinner dolphins inhabit. We had only been cruising five minutes when a pod of Spinner Dolphins began jumping and spinning around us.

We coasted to a halt, and the small boy enthusiastically slipped into the water. The dolphins immediately surrounded him and my entire body felt electrified. As his mother entered the water, the dolphins dove down seemingly disappearing. Once everyone was back on board the dolphins resurfaced. We started back on our journey to the dolphin bay and were escorted by our cetacean friends for quite a ways being entertained by their joyful energy. The boy was delighted.

As we came close to our destination, we were surprised to encounter a small pod of Bottlenose Dolphins. They rode the bow wave of the boat and looked right into our eyes, escorted us right into the dolphin bay and then vanished. Once in the bay, Spinner Dolphins, known to play in that area, quickly greeted us. I stopped the boat and the small boy entered the water alone. Immediately he was surrounded by dolphins, as once again, waves of electricity moved through my body. Then, his mother got in the water and the dolphins disappeared deep underwater. The moment she got out, the dolphins returned to the boy.

Once back on board the Blue Dolphin, we headed back towards Kailua-Kona and were met at the entrance of the dolphin bay by the Bottlenose Dolphins, who once again escorted us, this time back to where they had 'picked us up' earlier that morning.

Everyone was amazed! The boy, his mother, and others were hanging over the front of the boat, connecting with our escorts. As we came to the area where the first dolphins of the morning had left us, we found them waiting to give us a spectacular show of acrobatics. We stopped and cheered them on for a long time and then continued towards Kailua. As we neared the pier at the end of our trip, a lone dolphin leapt way into the air giving us a spectacular farewell salute.

The energy and love generated in the boat was amazing. Tears of joy filled everyone's eyes. I thanked the Universe for blessing us with this beautiful experience, and the gift that allowed the boy to have such a deeply personal interaction alone with the dolphins. The dolphins had singled him out, orchestrating the whole series of events to make his dream come true... an experience he (and we) will never forget!

CHAPTER THIRTEEN

Red Sea Dolphins Keep Peace in Middle East

by Doug Hackett

Having had a strong connection with dolphins over many years, I was thrilled when my friend, Joan Ocean, asked me to join her to do dolphin swims in the Red Sea. Different from Hawaii where dolphins are embraced with respect and love, I soon learned dolphins in this region of the Middle East were normally shot at, making them shy away from boats and people. Having been there the year before, Joan had quite a task, given that people flying halfway around the world were easily disappointed when no dolphins showed up to swim with them.

My experience at the Red Sea was an initiation in itself. On the first day out, we were on this rickety boat. So different from U.S. standards, it was one of the better boats in Egypt. The captain of the boat was taking us to where he believed the dolphins hung out. About ten minutes out of port, I happened to spot two large Bottlenose Dolphins behind us on the left. A wave passed over me as we circled them, like an ancient energy and wisdom and I knew, these dolphins were the greeting committee coming to acknowledge we were there.

We stayed with them for twenty minutes and then all of a sudden they disappeared. Though we circled around several times trying to find them, they were gone! We finally came to the place where the captain thought dolphins would be, but there were none there. He was puzzled, because that was the place he had always seen them. Joan said, "Just keep going."

After a little while, we gathered in a circle as we often times do to connect with the dolphins and their energy. We have found this helps draw them to us. We were deep in it, when jolted by a flurry of noise and activity, we looked up to see six crew members running around, talking excitedly in Egyptian. Dolphins had appeared and were playing on the bow wave of the boat, something they had never seen before. In that area, the Dolphins stay away from boats because people usually shoot at them.

The crew members were all excited as we followed the dolphins, but even though we got into the water to be with them, the dolphins just kept going until we couldn't see them anymore. This was so unlike the dolphins we had met in Hawaii, who were always eager to interact with us.

The second day, the owner of the boat came with us. We headed out, looking for dolphins and after forty five minutes or so we hadn't seen any. Our Egyptian guide, Dr. Morad, came to Joan and said, "Joan, don't you want to do a circle." He had been with her the year before where he had incredible experiences with the dolphins. This year he had requested to be Joan's guide for the trip. Joan said, "No, let's just keep on going. "

After about fifteen minutes, he returned and asked again if she was sure she didn't want to do a circle. He explained that the reason the owner of the boat was with us was that he really wanted to see the dolphins. The crew had told him about the dolphins showing up on the bow and since he had never seen that, he had insisted on coming along.

Joan still felt we should keep going. Finally we got to a place where it felt like time to do a circle. Immediately three dolphins showed up. Like the day before, we followed along after them, but never swam with them.

On the third day out, we had barely gotten going when two dolphins showed up. Expectant and excited, we believed they would lead us into a bay, stop, and swim with us, similar to what our dolphin friends back home do. After about 45 minutes of following them with no sign of this, I decided to do a meditation to see what was going on. What was *their plan?*

Once in meditation, I felt a connection with the dolphins and asked them, "Do you want to swim with us?" I got this enthusiastic 'Yes!' Then I realized I hadn't asked a very clear question and I would have to improve on it as wanting to swim with them is a lot different then dolphins stopping and letting us in the water.

I reframed my question saying, "Are you going to stop and let us get into the water with you?" The answer I got just blew me away. It was, "Yes, but we are busy right now holding together peace in the Middle East." It was so clearly stated, I had no doubt in what I heard. I told them, "That is also what our work is about, to create peace in the world."

I never knew there were dolphins in the Red Sea, nor would I have ever imagined the great work they are doing there. Now it was all becoming clear... Dolphins - Middle East - Peace. Dolphins holding peace in our world was an incredible realization.

Since then, whenever we go out and don't find dolphins, or they are quiet or doing something unusual, I remember this experience and wonder what kind of mission they are on.

After the second year at the Red Sea, Joan Ocean decided it was better to set up swims in Hawaii. I believe our time there had been important. A higher purpose had been fulfilled, with us showing dolphins a different side to humans and that not all people were out to harm them.

Doug Hackett cofounded Dolphin\Spirit of Hawaii with his wife, Trish Regan, in 1994 in response to a powerful calling by the dolphins (and Spirit) to take a leap of faith, leave their professional lives behind, and move to Hawaii to work with the wild dolphins. Since that time, they have co-facilitated life changing dolphin-swimming retreats in Hawaii and whale swim retreats in the Kingdom of Tonga.

Doug was in a meditation group in San Francisco for thirteen years before moving to Hawaii and since 1994 has been a respected spiritual teacher bringing higher consciousness retreats and workshops worldwide.

Along with his spiritual work, Doug is founder of Financial Mastery Now! LLC, whose goal is to help people move from lack to abundance consciousness, and become debt free.

For information on Doug and Trish's products, services, and offerings please see: http://www.dolphinspiritofhawaii.com and, http://www.financialmasterynow.com

CHAPTER FOURTEEN

The Leaf Game

by Cecily Miller

It's been nearly twenty years now since I first felt "The Call." It happened when I was taking a break from my schoolwork. Sitting on my bed, sorting through papers in my boyfriend-shared studio apartment in NYC with 20/20 on my television, I looked up and saw dolphins. 20/20 did a piece on a little boy who had healed remarkably as a result of his time spent in the water with the dolphins. Something indescribable happened to me as I watched. An overwhelming feeling came over me and I knew I had to swim with dolphins. The problem was, I was terrified of deep water. I had never swam in the ocean because I was too scared. And yet, the call was too strong to alter my course. I knew I had to go and see the dolphins.

My goal set, I began to prepare for my dolphin adventure. I bought snorkeling gear and took swimming lessons at the New York University pool for a couple of months. I started swimming laps while holding onto the ledge of the pool until eventually I could let go.

The next winter was my first time swimming in the ocean with a normal heart rate, comfortable breathing, and no irrational fear, though I had been out with the dolphins before. My first day in the water was magical. That morning I woke up breathing plumeria scented Hawaiian air, waited impatiently for the sun to show itself and put on my suit. As I walked down to the bay, I acknowledged my nerves and walked through my fear.

I was so excited to see my special friends. My sense memory of the kind of joy dolphins evoke was already lifting my heart. Journeying to be with the dolphins felt like coming home. It was a sense of joy and relief. The water was like a lake. I was thrilled there were no big waves. Entering the water would be effortless and completely safe. In the distance I could see dorsal fins. Yay!!! I swam towards the handful of snorkelers, hearing the dolphins echo locating. "Oh my God, you're here! Hi!" I laughed and cried through my snorkel.

In eye to eye contact we swam together. My heart expanded as I realized I was seen with my flaws, fears, shame, imperfections, sadness, loneliness, joy, love, happiness, hope, and longing and yet, accepted wholly. This was unconditional acceptance.

"Oh Hi! Wow you are swimming so close to me, so close, so intimate, so safe, so free. Thank you for coming to be with me. My heart is so happy." I looked to my right and saw the pod around me were playing the leaf game. Big, thick leaves fall into the water and dolphins "toss" the leaves to each other. It's more like half tag, half water ballet, a combination of mischief and grace.

The year before, I had watched dolphins invite people to play this leaf game with them, but I was not invited. I figured it might be because I am so slow and shy in the water. "What? Me? You're tossing the leaf to me? You're tossing the leaf to me! Wow! But I can't dive that low. Oh no, when you see that I can't get it, you're not going to want to play with me anymore."

My dolphin bud swam back over to the leaf and brought it up closer to the surface. I undulated over to it as fast as I could. "I got it! Woo Hoo!" I felt included and welcomed. I swam in my turtle-like style and released the leaf for another dolphin to be "IT." I watched to see what would happen. Sure enough, a pod member came and got the leaf right on its rostrum (nose).

"Thank you for including me right away, even with all 'my stuff.' Thank you for seeing me for who I really am. It helps me to remember myself and to reconnect with why I am here." Every child deserves to grow up remembering who they are. Every person deserves to know what it is like to greet the day with open arms, confidence, and to embrace life with joy and trust. Instead, we are so fear driven. Pouring my gratitude out to the dolphins, I telepathically said, "I love you so much. Thank you for helping me to feel love and be loved. Love certainly helps put things in perspective. You remind me of what we, as people, have the potential to do for one another. The potential to love and accept one another is so great. I wish everyone could feel this."

I had thought I was on a journey to overcome my fear of deep waters, but I let go of so much more, the dolphins guiding me each step of the way.

Part Three

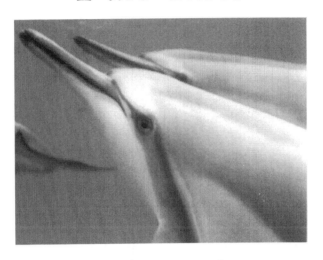

Miraculous Healings

Healings

You have called for Healing
And we have come
From the Regions of Starfilled Beings
And Ocean Realms

We bring Healing to humanity
That souls might find solace in our Presence
And seek to know the Joy that we live in
To bring that Joy back to families and friends

We are Healing the Souls of Humanity
Those who come for the Initiation of Love
To our shores, entering our waters
Playing, moving, knowing the Grace we live in

Come to us, Beloved
We are friends, long and true
For eons you have forgotten us
The family you once knew

We dwell in oceans that are like universes
Spaces between time
We know the Grand History of this planet
And the secrets of your race

Come, take our Medicine of Light
We share it lovingly
Enter the Joy of our Presence
And become a friend to this Earth

- The Dolphins

CHAPTER FIFTEEN

Cetacean Healers

by Lily Townsend

Dolphins, and later, whales, have been deeply affecting my life since I began swimming with captive Bottlenose Dolphins twenty years ago in the Florida Keys. After a three-month immersion into their world, my life took a turn. As human-dolphin connection pioneer, Dr. John Lilly, would say, I joined the Cetacean Nation.

Within a two-week span, my adored mother, Elsita and my beloved teacher, Hale Makua passed on; changed worlds, died. During the heartbreaking events surrounding their deaths, powerful experiences I'd just received from close contact with Atlantic Humpback whales in the Dominican Republic sustained me.

John Lilly often made the size comparison between a dog's brain, a human's, a dolphin's, and a whale's. What he hadn't spoken about was the whale's heart and that is what I had found in the Dominican waters.

I gazed in thrall at a courting pair of humpbacks. I drifted like seaweed towards the whiteness of their pectoral fins, which appeared underwater as a vivid turquoise. Their blue-black shapes moved tranquilly around one another, lazily circling. Then a longish period of communication occurred between them as they hung suspended at right angles to each other. One gently ascended directly to us, swiveling her huge eye to make contact with each of my companions.

My heart flew open at the beauty, grace and sheer closeness of them. I couldn't help but coo and laugh through my snorkel and tone out "Aloha!" Like a bubble bursting, revealing another bubble beneath it, my heart expanded forever. I was "Vasted!"

This vastness sustained me when I returned to Maui and experienced my Mother's stroke and Makua's surprise exit in a car crash. I could, in an entirely new way, embrace the profound grief and shock, functioning clearly, yet feel everything from a deeper perspective. I was able to experience my own heart as Vast Love. So vast, the doors of perception opened to me in new ways.

As I watched my Mother take her last breath in a room full of flowers, candles, and beautiful music, I saw an amazing sight. I saw her Spirit leave her body. A purplish wisp spiraled out of the top of her head. It continued for over two minutes. I exclaimed to the nurse beside me, "Can you see it? Can you see it?" She couldn't. I realized a great gift had been given to me.

The next morning, I joined dear friends on the small, famous boat of Captain Samone who had powerful connections to our local pods. She took us to a particular spot near Molokini where two Bottlenose Dolphins came to greet us. One swam between the hulls where he proudly showed us a large remora clinging to his back. We putt-putted along as they guided us to a pod of nine Bottlenose Dolphins with three lovely new babies. They, in turn, led us to a huge pod of Spinner Dolphins, (we guessed 98, in honor of my Mother's age.)

I slipped into the water, alive with piercing dolphin calls, chirps, whistles, croaks and trills. Two Spinner Dolphins swam towards me, sonaring my body with a low crackling call, then a third joined them to give me the once over. Only then, did they lead me into the main pod, which surrounded me with a moving circle.

Different characters interacted with me as I dove among them for a timeless enchantment. I felt their high frequencies penetrate me to the core. I was aware of my heartbeat and the shape of my skeleton, a fluid body undulating through the sparkling cobalt of deep water. I sensed Light pulsating in my bone marrow like vibrant opals. Exhilaration and joy filled me.

I took a big breath and dived deep. A huge single whale bellow penetrated my whole being, exploding my heart open. I felt it to be a message from Makua, who knew himself to be part of the Whale Amakua. I bellowed back and was still wailing when I broke to the surface. Pain erupted as I thrashed about, shaking and vibrating, releasing the past and tendrils of my fractured self, while being held gently by the ocean. In that openness, I received the wonder of the dolphin orchestra, their healing sounds filling me with profound peace and gratitude. I emerged a prayer in my heart: *May Blessings of the Cetacean Nation continue to open the hearts of humanity, so Peace can return to Earth.*

CHAPTER SIXTEEN

Dolphin Initiation

by Judith Greenwood

I am a healer and Intuitive, as we now call ourselves. A client had become aware of my interest and special connection with the dolphins. As we shared tidbits about dolphins, she mentioned her daughter is the Medical Director at the Dolphin Research Center (DRC) located on the west coast of the Florida Keys. One of the dolphins there named Aphrodite was critically ill and at the same time was pregnant with a calf. The daughter contacted me and asked if I could be of assistance.

In an intuitive 'reading' on Aphrodite, specific procedures were recommended which included having me send healing energies to her. The medical treatments and the healing energies were effective and I was invited to go to DRC to explore further ways of being of assistance to Aphrodite. I immediately made arrangements to go. This promised to be an excellent opportunity to be with dolphins again and in particular, for me to bond with Aphrodite and the other dolphins there.

When I arrived at DRC early in the morning and stood on the sea wall bordering the dolphin enclosure, a dolphin named Santini swam up to me. Santini swam about playfully chattering and showing off. Suddenly she disappeared into the lagoon, surfaced and tossed a hunk of seaweed at my face. As I caught the seaweed and tossed it back to her she "laughed" and caught it with her nostrum. Thus our game of seaweed tosses began. I was in seventh heaven as other dolphins approached and joined in the fun. It was a delightful welcome.

During my days at DRC, I participated in the caring and training program of all the dolphins under the supervision of staff members, feeding, giving back rubs, and lovingly being present to the dolphins. Many hours were devoted to Aphrodite and her need for healing. I also observed the child-dolphin swim program in which severely handicapped children benefited from the playful loving relationships available to them through the dolphins and staff members. This was a precious opportunity to observe the dedicated and loving care made available to these dolphins and my heart filled with the shared love and joy of those involved.

As the time approached for me to leave DRC, I was struggling with feelings of sadness that came as I thought of leaving this delightful group of friends. The evening before my departure I sat on the dock watching the dolphins in their quiet and rhythmic swimming patterns. With tears flowing down my cheeks I watched the sun drop below the horizon. Silently without my being aware of her, Santini swam up to my feet and looked up at me, then dove down and picked up a rock from the bottom and offered it to me in her mouth. I thanked her, then stroked her nostrum and back, whereupon she dove down again.

This time she came up with a hunk of seaweed and tossed it at my face soaking me in the process as she 'laughed' with delight. She stayed with me for some time, maintaining eye contact and swimming close by. I knew I would return and a deep connection had been made. I saw the dolphins could read my thoughts and feelings and wanted them to know how much I appreciated being a part of their lives and for the wonderful experiences we had shared. In that moment, there was a sense of knowing the message had been received and I would return one day to continue this relationship.

On awakening the next morning, every cell in my body seemed to undergo a significant shift. Moving about slowly as I prepared to return to the cold and dreary weather of Chicago, I felt a pervasive dizziness. Another major cleanse was beginning and this fuzziness would stay with me for some time.

For over a month I underwent a deep cleanse as all the old cellular memories were released, my energy field realigned and my vibratory rate increased daily. Driving an auto became a challenge and unsafe for days at a time. Messages and gifts from the dolphins poured into me day and night in meditations and dreams.

I had no conscious choice but to allow the transformation of my being as lifetimes of old patterns were being released. I also became a vehicle through which past generations and lifetimes were released and healed. I felt like I was dying and I surrendered to it. I cried and mourned, released and surrendered until I was empty. It was the death of who I had been. Slowly the new me emerged. I felt like a new born child in many ways and at peace with the whole process, more clear, much more calm, with a deeper connection to God.

The following year I returned, bringing a group of twelve people to DRC to participate in a week long dolphin program. The very first morning I quickly walked to the sea wall where Santini and I had parted the year before. From the depths of the water came a hunk of seaweed aimed directly for my face. She 'laughed' with delight as though to say, "Just like old times. Welcome back!" Tears filled my eyes and my heart sang out, I radiated love to the dolphins and felt it reflected back. It was wonderful, a feeling of deep connection to them and to all.

While there, I was delighted to find Aphrodite had regained her health and joyful presence. The week went so quickly and every one of the twelve people gained immeasurably from the wealth of loving and joyful experiences interacting with the dolphins. For everyone it was a life changing experience and my whole life has changed.

I am experiencing more love, seeing through the eyes of love and healing lifetimes of pain and sorrow. My relationships with others are more joyful and exciting. I look at life in a much lighter way. I play more and become more of my Authentic Self, one with Source each day. Each time I see one of my dolphin friends, I feel my heart open more and more. Love is constant in my life now and my desire is to help everyone experience love, inner peace and joy.

CHAPTER SEVENTEEN

Dolphin Ride

by John Kahele

Growing up a Native Hawaiian, we have many traditions that bring us into a close communion and respect for Mother Nature, our Ancestors, the Aina (land), and the animal and ocean kingdom. All families have an Aumakua (protector) from a certain species that speaks to the essence of that family lineage and where it draws its wisdom and power from.

From an early age, my Grandfather taught me about the Naya (dolphins). He took me out in the ocean as a small child and I felt an immediate connection to them. They became my best friends. I had names for each one and together we would have amazing adventures.

I've never shared my stories before, though many people over time became aware of my special connection with the dolphins. Somehow, it never felt right to share about it, so even though many offered to do interviews and even pay me for them, I always turned them down. I was not ready to speak about my experiences with the dolphins. They were deeply personal and also quite incredible. Now I feel it is time to tell my story.

When I was young, I had a really hard time speaking and would stutter most of the time. I grew up in a family who were all very well spoken and at times, felt out of place, so I turned to nature and swam with Naya a lot. All the way through high school I barely said a word. I could never do an oral report and felt very nervous whenever I had to give one. So, on those days, I just wouldn't show up at school. I was lucky I graduated.

I had passed through many years with this condition and the pain and discomfort it brought. It seemed to be a life-long handicap that I would just have to live with. Unfortunately, it caused me to be a loner and as the years went on, the ocean and dolphins were my only solace.

Looking into their eyes, I felt total and complete acceptance. They knew me for who I really was.

The morning of my nineteenth birthday, I felt drawn to swim with the dolphins. My family wanted to celebrate, and I told them to come down to the beach. The water was crystal clear, a beautiful turquoise you only see in the tropics. As soon as I got out in deeper water, a dolphin began zooming towards me really fast, then another swam over. For a moment I felt scared.

Then the two dolphins moved into a strange position in front of me, pointing their nostrums directly at my neck. I had never seen dolphins this intent. Immediately, I felt this strong electrical current running up and down my throat. Next, it started to expand outward in some kind of rippling effect. My whole throat had this tingling feeling. They then broke "formation" as one of them playfully splashed me in the face. For a long time afterwards, we played in the water. I would lift my arm up, and they would lift their pectoral fins in response. I would roll over in the water and they would follow, mimicking my every move. We were having so much fun that I forgot about my earlier experience.

Finally, I swam back to shore. People on the beach who had been watching us were amazed by my interaction with the dolphins, and someone even asked if I was a dolphin trainer. Still flushed with excitement, I ran over to greet my family. "Did you see them playing with me," I yelled to them as I approached. They stopped and stared back at me with their mouths wide open. I continued talking excitedly about my encounter, when I saw my mother had tears running down her face. Then I realized I was talking without a stutter. It was a miracle!

Mama said, "What happened out there?" I told them how the dolphins had sent electrical energies to my throat. They had healed me! I had received the most incredible birthday gift from the dolphins, and have been able to speak without a stutter ever since. I remembered that my grandfather had once told me to swim with Naya and they would help me. When he heard about my miracle, he nodded his head and said, "I knew Naya would help you, when you were ready."

In time I realized he was right, that I had been swimming with the dolphins for years, but if they had healed me earlier, I might not have formed this incredible bond with them and nature, one that keeps me going today.

After that experience, I went back to the bay looking for those two dolphins, but I have never seen them again. This is unusual. Dolphins swim in the same area, or at least return to the same spots after a while. I now wonder if special dolphins were "brought" in like outside surgeons to perform an operation.

I will never forget their gift on my birthday. It changed my life and gave me confidence, as did their friendship. I'm grateful to them, and to all of the dolphins and marine life that have played such an important role in my life over the years.

Many years later, I moved to Oahu and found that dolphins frequented an area near where I lived. Soon I was swimming with them every day. I had just gotten out into the clear blue expanse of water one morning, when unexpectedly Loki, one of my Oahu dolphin friends, swooped in and nudged me to hold onto his fin. The moment I grasped his fin, he took off through the water, the other dolphins trailing behind and beside us. Some were leaping joyfully out of the water beside me. We were all having great fun. It was a mile ride down to Hercules Rock and back, exhilarating and amazing. On the way back, we stopped in a mating area and I let go.

I was so caught up in the experience, I forgot where I was for a moment. Then, I called Loki. Immediately he zoomed through the water beneath me and came out of the water ready to have more fun. He started circling me, looking at me and yakking away. I felt he was trying to tell me something. Then I got it. His message was: It is time to tell your story about the dolphins.

When Loki looked at me like that and started circling me, I looked right into his eyes. He was only eight inches away and he just looked at me saying, "It is time to tell the people." Since then, that idea was strong in my mind. So that is why I am sharing my story today.

My whole life I have had a reverence for the Divine in Nature. Much of my life has been spent in underwater adventures with dolphins and other sea life. I've learned and grown so much from my personal interactions with the dolphins and the many gifts they've given me.

I feel like this information about the dolphins is meant to be let out now. It's time for people to understand and appreciate what is out there. The dolphins have a lot of messages they are sending to people and a lot of people like us are hearing them. There is so much we can learn from all marine life, everything in this ocean, and the dolphins are an important part of that.

CHAPTER EIGHTEEN

Columbine Story

by Paul Doty

Oddly enough, this dolphin story starts on an airplane. My first wife, Deborah, was returning from the Bay Area when she met a family from Littleton, Colorado. They had a daughter and her friend who had been in Columbine the day of the shootings and who had actually had bullets shoot over their heads in the gym. Their friends had died and they were in a state of "post traumatic shock." Deb told the family about all the fun aspects of our business at the time, Adventures In Paradise, on Maui, especially the Dolphin Kayak trips.

After a few days I received a call from them wanting to do a kayak trip and hopefully to see dolphins. I said, "Great!" We planned to meet in a few days. As luck would have it, the day of our trip was windy and the optimal dolphin bay was out of the question. I reluctantly headed us to a different area. This is a place the dolphins never frequent. You might see them there one day out of one hundred.

Well, call it fate, or karma, or just plain good luck, but after paddling out for about ten minutes, I saw a huge pod of over one hundred Spinner Dolphins, swimming toward us. The girls were together in a double kayak and soon they were surrounded by dolphins. They were all around their kayak, and were actually letting the girls reach out and touch them. Now, I had never experienced this behavior in over two hundred trips with the dolphins. This was special!

The girls were giggling and splashing and getting splashed. A few dolphins even jumped over their bow. It was as if the dolphins were on a mission to cheer these two sad girls up, and they did! I could see their life force come back into their bodies and the sadness leave.

I don't know how the dolphins got the message to find these girls. One could say it was coincidence. I feel it was a little miracle. A bit of magic that doesn't happen often, but when it does you just know it is special. It lasted for about thirty minutes, then it was over. The dolphins swam off, but their impact remained for the rest of the morning, and I'm sure longer. I, too, was blissed out from the experience and realized I had witnessed a gift. Mahalo to our finned friends once again.

Paul lives in Byron Bay, Australia with his beautiful wife, Juliet. He continues to enjoy kayaking with dolphins and whales. He can be reached at: padoty26@yahoo.com.au.

CHAPTER NINETEEN

A Healing Song

by Matisha

I sit here amidst spiraling feelings and emotions after the most amazing dolphin encounter to date. I feel very blessed to have had so many experiences, each one surpassing the previous encounter. In truth, every moment with these playful, gracious, graceful beings is a touch of the sweetness life offers.

Rose, a friend from Germany, and I headed out into the sparkling Hawaiian waters late morning in the kayak. The skies were beginning to cloud over, the water was a rich aqua, a color that always has my attention as I breath in its beauty. We reveled at the clarity of the coral on the ocean floor, commenting on how good the visibility was going to be for us.

Shortly after paddling out, we saw dolphins coming up for air over on the other side of the bay. They seemed to be staying to themselves, not really giving much attention to the people in the water. We decided to watch for a few minutes as they swam from one end of the bay to the other underwater. On one of their passes by us, we gently entered the water and they did just that, passed by us.

My back was hurting from a tight muscle, so I was not feeling able to fully enjoy the experience. With a little disappointment, I swam back to our kayak, pulled myself up onto it, lay back, and rested for a while. Rose swam by the kayak and I heard her say, "They're definitely not in an interactive mode."

I said, "That could change in a moment," half to myself, hoping for something more. By this time, I was feeling a little grumpy about not being able to enjoy the experience, so as I lay there I called to the dolphins in my heart and asked them to come and assist me if it worked into their schedule of play, enjoyment, and rest that day in the bay. I imagined them coming over to the kayak, me getting in, them swimming up to me, singing and circling me, beaming me with that powerful group song I had experienced as very healing ten years previous, while swimming with dolphins for my second time.

A very few minutes went by and I felt the impulse to sit up. I actually questioned this as I pulled myself into sitting position. I thought, "Why am I sitting up now when it is really comfortable lying here?" No sooner had I formulated the question, I looked to my right and saw a rather large pod swimming toward the kayak. "Well, maybe they'll come close and want to spend a little time," I thought to myself. I heard my inner voice say, "They're coming over to be with you, as you requested."

I put on my fins, mask, and snorkel, gently slid into the water and dove down, instantly feeling like a dolphin, as I swam in a slow, dolphin-style fashion. All the excitement of that moment comes back to me as I write this. The pod numbered about sixty dolphins weaving intricate, gentle patterns all around me. A group of about six or seven came very close and surrounded me, while a couple swam along side of me, looking in my eyes, singing. After a few seconds, they distanced themselves from me, and I heard this continuous note of the song being repeated, while other dolphins sent their songs through the shimmering aquamarine water. I immediately recognized this repeated note as the note I heard sung ten years previous that had healed me in Florida.

The next thing I knew, a young male dolphin swam in front of me and turned to face me. He let me know clearly he wanted to play and take me through a few maneuvers, so I dove down to be with him. He got noticeably excited and started a slight shaking of his head. I twirled and spun in the water below him. He dove down and I came up. I dove down and he came up to meet me and swam circles around me. We then floated on the surface of the water looking into each other's eyes.

I was overcome with a feeling of deep love for his sweetness and playful behavior. While I was with him on the last couple of twists and gentle turns he took me through, I realized he was preparing me for what was to come next. I noticed the adult dolphins he was swimming with had given us a lot of room to do our dance. As soon as I noticed their seemingly intentional offering, allowing our time together, these adult dolphins turned and began encircling me, singing out. *Oh, how that song resounded!* I became overjoyed with the thoughts and pictures filling my mind, the power of emotion from our dance, and the intense feelings of communion I was having. The older dolphins encircling me swam closer and closer, each coming in for a look, or a chance to beam me, or whatever they were doing. Every direction I looked, there were dolphins. Then I felt something over me. By the time I turned to look, a dolphin had swept his fluke downward with considerable force right over the area of my back that had been hurting.

I felt a powerful current of energy run down my back. As I looked at him, he swam a distance away, making room for the next dolphin who was now swimming beside me. This dolphin paused in the water, as if waiting for me. As our eyes met, he gave me a signal that he wanted to dive down. We dove down belly to belly. He twirled around, hung upside down in the water letting me know it was my move. I made my move for the surface, twirling and undulating like a dolphin. He got quite excited at this, darted downwards and came up circling a few feet from me.

Closer and closer he came. I started matching his behavior, swimming the same pattern as best I could. He got even more interested and swam his circles closer, tighter, and faster, until I had to swim in place, in a circle on my right side. This was quite a challenge with how my back was feeling just minutes before, though I trusted he knew what he was doing. The circles he was swimming got so tight and close that I had to point my feet to the bottom of the ocean and do this spinning-swim. I held eye contact with him until he swam such fast circles, I had to pause and resume our gaze on his next orbit. Never before had a dolphin swam with such speed while circling me like that. After a few minutes, I had to take a breather and saw Rose and our friend watching the whole thing. "What a workout that was!" I exclaimed almost out of breath. I laughed and barely could believe the intensity of play I was experiencing.

This continued for well over four hours of close, ecstatic dancing and simply being with the dolphins. Their spirals became more evident as the day progressed. Something I experienced more powerfully than ever that day, was the feeling of being so much a part of the pod. The dolphins responded to my every thought instantly. I would look at a group about twenty-five feet away and send a thought/image that I wanted to be close to them. Within two to five seconds, they would all turn and swim right at me until they were a few feet away. Then they would turn to position themselves and swim along side of me, each one taking turns to have eye contact with me. When they swam off, another little pod within the pod would be there to share the experience with me. If not, I would look around, decide which dolphins I wanted to be with that moment and call them to be close with me.

I was continually amazed at their willingness and desire to be with us. It didn't matter whether it was one, two, or a group of dolphins, whether they were five feet or fifty feet away. When I called them they came, turning 180 degrees at times to come and join us. For hours, we each were off with our dolphin or group of dolphins, having the time of our lives.

That morning in Florida, I had suffered from a stiff neck and a knee that had been bothering me. After swimming with those dolphins and being in their song, I didn't remember my neck or my knee had been bothering me until about ten days later, when I realized something extraordinary had happened. The pain and stiffness had disappeared that morning with the dolphins. On looking back at this experience, the elusive nature of the dolphin comes to me, almost dream-like. Are they elusive or are we just a bit slow? I have heard for a long time that dolphins are aware of how we feel. Something they told me while they were circling me was, they can feel our consciousness shift, our moods change, and when our minds expand. They find great joy in waking up sleeping parts of us by swimming patterns, and when we catch on, having us swim those same patterns. They are aware of the subtle energy levels every moment as they live in that place.

What they shared with me that day has continued to come to me, getting clearer and clearer. I find myself saying things I never thought of, things that barely feel like mine. I now know they are feeling with me, the accelerated frequencies running through my body, all that is opening, my altered states, as they take me through the gates of expanded consciousness. They are here for us all. It is a great joy for them to be a part of our return home.

What I experienced that day becomes clearer and clearer as my own awakening unfolds. As they were circling me, I could feel subtle shifts in my awareness or consciousness that have become more pronounced with time. Their swimming patterns, the sounds of their songs, every movement and every maneuver seemed geared to wake up or activate sleeping parts of myself. This experience changed me, and gave me a greater appreciation for these "Shamans of the Sea."

CHAPTER TWENTY

Dolphins Help Cure Cancer

by Shivani Goodman, PhD

In September 1992, after I had a mastectomy on my left breast and my first treatment of chemotherapy, I decided to come to Hawaii to the Big Island to take a workshop on connecting and swimming with dolphins. My friend suggested I swim with dolphins as a healing experience with my cancer. She said they are very playful and they spin up in the air and make you laugh. I decided to give it a try. I was feeling quite sick from the chemo and traveling such a distance from New Jersey was very difficult. At one point I almost fainted.

When I entered the water to swim with the dolphins, I was worried that I wouldn't be able to swim because of my surgery. My arm was still painful. I was told that you can communicate with the dolphins telepathically. I sent them a message telling them not to come too close to me, as they are so big I would be scared, but to please not stay too far away, because I wanted to see them.

As soon as I sent them that message, I saw them coming towards me. It was a whole group (called a pod) about six to eight spinner dolphins. They were circling around me and yet keeping their distance. Then they started circling underneath me. I asked them if they could help me heal my cancer. I saw one dolphin send rays of light in my direction. I knew that the response was "Yes, we are helping." I thanked the dolphins and they started swimming away. I decided to follow them. I sent them a message to please not swim so fast as it was difficult for me to keep up. I saw them return and then slow down so that I was able to keep swimming at their pace.

That same evening reflecting on this experience, I felt hopeful I could heal from my cancer, but doubts kept on creeping in. Voices were in my head of my husband, family, friends and colleagues saying, "That is a lot of nonsense. Dolphins can't help."

I had undergone a modified radical mastectomy. A two and a half centimeter aggressive cancerous tumor had been found, and two out of the nineteen lymph nodes removed were affected. The doctor said I needed one year of chemotherapy. The prognosis was 50% chance of recovery with chemotherapy.

After the first chemotherapy treatment I felt like I entered a concentration camp. The torture was unbearable. It felt like I was being bombarded with machine guns inside my body, like a total destruction was taking place. My brain was badly affected. For a few days I could barely function and I became very paranoid and started speaking strangely. It frightened my husband and sister who were with me and it frightened me as well. Nonetheless, I decided to embark on this new adventure with the dolphins. I am so happy I had the courage to do this.

The same evening after my first encounter with the dolphins, I sat outside looking at the sky and suddenly I took a vow saying, "If I make it through this, I will devote my life to help erase sickness and suffering from the planet." At that split second the clouds rearranged themselves in the sky around the moon and the moon became like a pupil in the center of an eye. The eye was so perfect looking directly at me that I started shaking inside. It looked like God's eye looking at me, witnessing this vow, an eye witness. I knew right then I was going to make it. However, the thought of having to face another treatment of chemotherapy brought me back into feeling nausea and terror. Some of the students at the workshop told me I didn't have to do chemotherapy if I didn't want to. I remember crying and telling them I had no choice. The doctor said I must have one year or I would not survive.

I was wondering whether I could take such a risk. I wished I had the courage to do it. If I knew then what I know now, I would have definitely not continued the chemo. At the time, though, I was too frightened to stop. The barrage of attacks by my physicians, family, friends, and colleagues that I must follow the medical route was too powerful. I was too vulnerable and open and it was very difficult to trust my own inner voice. I was longing to believe those people who encouraged me to stop chemo. I kept on asking God for guidance. However, as soon as I got back home the memory of my vow, the eye, and the dolphins became so vague and dim, it felt like it was just a dream. My inner voice and God disappeared under the barrage of fearful faces of the well meaning people in my life. To them, cancer meant death and soon my weakened mind started feeling the same way, that I am doomed to die.

From time to time a glimmer of hope remembering the dolphins would come back and rekindle my spirit. However, as soon as I had undergone the next chemotherapy treatment, I felt hopeless and desperate, like I was dying and nothing could help.

I had six more treatments after swimming with the dolphins, at which time the chemotherapy nearly debilitated me completely. I felt like a zombie and could barely function. After the eighth treatment I decided to stop chemotherapy. This was in December 1992, three months after I had swam with the dolphins. To my shock and horror, in July 1993, only 7 months later, cancer reappeared in my other breast. I was totally devastated, because I had researched and tried numerous alternative therapies and I thought I was getting better. I had a lumpectomy, refusing the recommended mastectomy, chemotherapy, radiation, and medication.

Then in December 1994 the biggest shock of my life took place when a four to five centimeter hard tumor on my right breast was found. I had swollen lymph nodes and pain in my bones. My physician warned me that cancer would soon end my life and that I must go to the hospital right away. It looked like the cancer had spread throughout my body. At the last moment before entering the hospital, I decided to drop everything in my life and come to Hawaii to swim with the dolphins once more. I decided I would rather die in a fairly healthy body than to be poisoned by the chemotherapy again and have pieces of my body cut out. I knew if I went into the hospital I would die within a very short period of time. I felt the physicians would start taking out pieces of my body until there would be nothing of me left.

I practiced all the self healing techniques I had been teaching for years that I had gathered from amazing healers and teachers all over the world. I did not tell anyone what I was doing. I flew to Hawaii and began visiting many of the islands. Within a few days of being alone and practicing my self healing regime, I started feeling so good I knew I was on the right track and wasn't going to die. I kept thinking, "There is no way I am dying if I am feeling this good." I celebrated by having a cup of coffee, ice cream and other things that I had denied myself for a long time because I had been on a very strict healing regime.

I knew I couldn't tell one person where I was going or what I was doing, because I would be barraged by well meaning friends with their concerns. They had already told me, "You are risking your life, you are committing suicide," each time I would move away from conventional medicine and try something new. Because I was so weak from the illness and all the fears that came with it, I knew they would be able to influence me, and I would buckle under and end up going to the hospital, which I knew would be my death.

In Hawaii it was so wonderful to be alone. I felt a great relief and my energy returned to me. Over the next few weeks I began feeling good about myself and my life. I was optimistic about my future and that my cancer could be healed. I traveled to different islands in search of the dolphins and had many experiences with them. Even seeing the dolphins and whales from far away helped me feel hopeful and gave me a reconnection with the possibility of my total healing. Just being near the ocean was so nurturing and healing.

After about five weeks, I could no longer afford to stay in Hawaii. I returned home and began losing hope again. The healing energy I had felt began diminishing and I felt like my cancer was returning. The very strange symptoms I had encountered before began reappearing as I became caught up again with the stresses of life. However, I kept on practicing my self healing techniques three times a day and from time to time I would have inner experiences with dolphins. This gave me hope and courage.

In November 1995, my doctor confirmed that I was in radiant health. His words were, "A miracle happened, your cancer is gone!"

"No, it was not a miracle, doctor," I responded, "I practiced self healing three times a day. If I can do it so can anyone else."

"You must write about this," my doctor said.

"That would be too stressful! I want to enjoy my life," I replied.

In December 1999, I was magically led once more to Maui to celebrate the new year as we entered the new millennium. The thought suddenly occurred to me, "You can live here for the rest of your life if you want to." My energy grew in Maui surrounded by the dolphin's consciousness. I regained my strength and was able to focus on writing my book and fulfilling my vow.

My experiences with the dolphins continued. On September 11, 2001, I woke up in the middle of the night, feeling a huge explosion inside my body. A dolphin emerged from within me as though changing the energy of terror of the explosion into an energy of love and playfulness. That morning I went to swim with the dolphins on Captain Simone's boat with some students who came to study with me from Los Angeles. Captain Simone told us about the bombing of the Twin Towers.

"So that was the explosion I felt," I uttered in shock. Six dolphins appeared and we followed them throughout the day. "This is very rare that they come to play with us for so long," said Captain Simone. I knew they had come to help heal our sorrows.

Miracles were happening in Maui regularly the more I flowed with feeling joyful and my healing work assumed a new dimension. I finished writing my book, *Nine Steps For Reversing or Preventing Cancer*, while the dolphins and whales often visited me as I watched from my beach front condominium.

During that time a physician called me saying he was diagnosed with colon cancer. "Practice this exercise for 5 to 10 minutes 3 times per day," I suggested. I taught him the exercise, which took about 5 minutes to teach over the phone.

"But I don't believe in this," he commented.

"That's all right, you don't have to believe in it. It still works as long as you do it."

"But I am going for surgery next week," he continued.

"Well, imagine that when your surgeons open you up the tumor is gone." I was thinking that way he wouldn't need chemotherapy or radiation.

"That's impossible!" he laughed and then said, "It would be wonderful. I guess I have nothing to lose doing it. I will do it!" he exclaimed. A week later he called saying that when the surgeons opened him up the tumor was gone.

"Did you practice the exercise?" I asked him.

"Yes, I did," he responded, "they were all surprised. I was surprised too," he added.

"Did you tell them about this exercise?" I asked.

"No, they termed it Entersusseption, which means the tumor disappeared within itself."

The ancient self healing exercise I had given him was intended to erase sickness and suffering from the planet. It has helped me and many people heal all kinds of ailments, pain and sickness, as well as mental, emotional, and spiritual suffering. The benefits of this exercise are on many levels. When I became aware of the power of this exercise, I realized that erasing sickness and suffering from the planet is within the realm of possibility. It used to take me several years to explain this exercise to people, and to be quiet enough to be able to practice it myself. It then took me several months, then several weeks, then several hours. Five minutes is something new that just happened after I swam with the dolphins.

I often wondered if I had taken on a crazy vow, thinking I was kidding myself, that it's impossible to erase sickness and suffering from humanity. Then the idea began to appear in my mind that we have the potential to shift humanity's consciousness within 33 days. 2 to the power 33 is equal to 8.8 billion. We are currently around seven billion people on the planet. If we pass on a powerful healing message to two people we love and care about, say within one day, and they pass it on to two people they love and care about within one day, within 33 days, every human being on the planet can learn to heal themselves. Even if they pass on this exercise within one week, then in 33 weeks humanity can be in a healing process.

I am now hopeful that it is doable. I did it and now I believe that everyone else can. I thank the dolphins for being such wonderful messengers of joy, love, and playfulness. Through my whole ordeal they were always present with me and gave me the strength and courage to keep on through my darkest hours. If I was far away from Hawaii, then they would come to me through inner experiences. They were ever present with me. I love them and am so humbled by their wisdom and great caring. I feel so blessed to have them in my life.

Not only was I healed, but I now had a gift to give humanity. This gift was fulfilling the vow I made to God on that night when the eye appeared in the sky, to help erase all illness and suffering from humanity. Now I am doing that through my book, *9 Steps for Reversing or Preventing Cancer*.

Dr. Shivani Goodman is the author of 'Babaji Meeting With Truth', and '9 Steps for Reversing or Preventing Cancer.'

CHAPTER TWENTY ONE

Rite of Passage

by Kiki Corbin

For a long time I had been Divinely guided to go live on the Big Island of Hawaii, but I had waited many years before I felt I was totally invited. The dolphins had been a big part of this inspiration. I had connected with them about four or five times before. After that, I was in constant touch with them and they would stay in touch with me no matter where I was.

Many times when I would meditate, they would come to me and say "Remember, you are supposed to be getting ready to come to Hawaii." Yet, at these times I would be in the midst of life changes that had a way of taking away my attention. I would think, "How am I ever going to be able to leave here? How is this ever going to work financially?" My mother needed my help as she was getting old, my children were needing me, and my clients were too. Finally, after many years, I was ready to make the journey to my new life in Hawaii, but while in the process of the move, I was a passenger in a car accident and hurt quite badly. I was still intent on going. I wasn't going to let anything stop me this time, but the move became so difficult, I wondered if I really wasn't supposed to move after all. I didn't know if I had the strength to make it through the move and yet, everything in me just knew somehow that it was all meant to be.

I was wondering why this accident happened and began to go to all these readings to find out what was going on. Through astrological readings, I saw how my move to the Big Island was part of a big change I was in and that part of that new cycle was for me to come out of hiding. A woman in Colorado, who didn't know me at all, blew my mind when she said out of the blue, "Are you familiar with the dolphins in Hawaii?" I said, "Yes!" She continued, "Well, they're with you constantly and they're here now. They're telling me to remind you that you have a lot of work to do with them." I could hardly believe it. It really helped me overcome every obstacle and soon I arrived on the island. The first thing I planned to do was to visit Pele, but now I had to wait two months before I could go on that journey, as it was still difficult for me to drive and the volcano was two and a half hours away on the other side of the island.

Finally I was able to take the trek. I took four days to go on a Vision Quest to the volcano. I brought my offering to Pele and then meditated beside the lava flow. Going to see Pele was a massive surrender for me. I looked over the edge saying, "Ok, I put my life at your feet. What did you bring me to Hawaii for?" While meditating overlooking her caldera, Pele told me my life was now indeed going to change. She reminded me how I had spent most of my life dealing with hardships, chronic fatigue, and all kinds of physical challenges throughout the years. She told me part of what these life situations had taught me was to be responsible with the power I came into this life with and which I have always hidden from people.

I've always felt like I made some mistakes in other lifetimes and so in this life I have been very cautious about using my power. It has almost been as if I have been hiding this powerful part of me from myself so that I would not misuse it. I wondered if these challenges had also been a way to repay the karma from another time. Pele said it was time for me to stand up tall now, and what I got was she meant for me to be all that I can be. In that moment I felt a strength and power come back into me I didn't know I had. It ran through my whole body and became a physical sensation. I knew she was taking my hand and helping me take a step forward into claiming my Authentic Power.

The next day all I could do was spend a day in meditation, the impact of my experience with Pele had been so huge. I was in the midst of dealing with all the shifts going on inside me, which were very strong. The following day, my girlfriend, who is a meditator too, went with me to swim with the dolphins at a beautiful bay. When we arrived, the dolphins were already there. They were jumping up as if to say, "Come on and play!" That day they were swimming and frolicking on the surface of the water, something I hadn't seen before. They were so joyous and kept swimming circles around and under us.

There were about six of us in the water all quite separated from one another. I was by myself in one area when two dolphins came up.

One moved right in back of me, while the other came right in front of me, stood still, and looked deeply into my eyes. This was such an incredible experience since dolphins are always in motion. I knew I was receiving Darshan (blessing) from these dolphins. It was a total acknowledgment of being here on the island at last, welcomed, and supported in my big life change.

A little while later, the whole pod of dolphins came out to me and began swimming under me. I had the sense I was going to be helped with all the challenges I had been having health wise. They began beaming me all at once, together as a group. I stretched out my arms and floated on the water looking down at them. Then I closed my eyes and felt an energy move through me. It was like every cell of my body was being shifted and put into the right order. I had never had that happen before in all the times I swam with the dolphins. There are no words to describe it.

In the days that followed, the healing continued from the accident until I was completely healed and able to move my body normally again. Between Pele and the Dolphins, I went home changed, honored they had accepted me into the clan. Though I had been with them over the years numerous times and had wonderful experiences, I had always felt like a bit of an outsider. Now I don't feel like that anymore. After that experience, a therapist was working with me and asked if I had swam with dolphins, as she could see them all around my head. I was also aware of them and have felt them with me ever since. I was going through a massive spiritual change. My astrology confirmed this as a time of major transformation for me. These changes helped me know these experiences are real, that its not just in my imagination. A lot of doors opened and my destiny was laid out in front of me, putting me on a very straight and narrow path.

Years ago, it used to be a very windy road with lots of lessons. It's not that way anymore. The way is straight and my guidance is super clear. Anymore it feels like what is shifting is not what is outside me, like receiving guidance from my angels and guides. It is starting to be a knowing, like the Self knows. One big thing is, I'm not afraid of it anymore. I feel ready for the first time in my life. I've been given lots of work in this life. I was a minister of a New Thought Church, giving all kinds of lectures, though I never felt ready. Even though I followed what I was supposed to do, I always felt like I was a babe out there feeling like, "Who am I to be talking about these things, when I barely have a sense of myself and not much confidence." I was still in my 20's and pretty naive. I felt like Pele woke up the strength in me and the dolphins supported it. Whatever was left of my lack of self confidence, security, and inner knowing was burned up. Pele had simply burned it up in me. This has been very much a Rite of Passage for me both Pele and the dolphins contributed to. What I get from this experience is that the New Millennium energy has been birthed in these last years and Hawaii is the place of the birthing of new dimensions now possible for us all.

There are many of us living in the 5th dimension already, with some living in the 6th and 7th dimensions. It has become very easily attainable by many who have come to be here at this time for The Shift to happen. The dolphins are part of that shift. We are really all one people and all one soul. This planet is in very serious trouble. It may be one of the darkest times we've ever seen. We go through many epochs where there are dark times and this is one of them. Since there is an equal amount of light and dark, this is also the time of greatest Light.

I've been shown that millions of souls are coming here and we've all chosen to have bodies to hold light and support each other to have clarity. It doesn't matter what our professions are. There is an amazing influx of love vibration, which the dolphins share freely. The dolphins are here to help us joyously celebrate Life and yet, like the Awakening Ones, the dolphins have a very tough job because so many of them are sacrificing their lives and suffering a lot. Even still, they're very hopeful and help us remember what we're here for. Our mission is to keep communing with each other, be a constant reminder to stay centered in who we are, help one another awaken to who we are, and hold on tight no matter what happens on the planet. Since this experience with the dolphins, I have been so happy, my heart is bursting open with joy. I can see the whole picture now and all we're accomplishing together.

Kiki Corbin, author of The Gift of Light, Stories of Hope and Inspiration From Near Death Experiences and owner of Hualani Productions publishing co., is a spiritual teacher, Certified Traditional Naturopath, New Thought Minister, Certified Integral Yoga Teacher, and Pastoral Counselor who holds Gift of Light workshops and lectures, and is available for 5th Dimensional Counseling and consultations. See: http://www.thegiftoflight.net.

Part Four

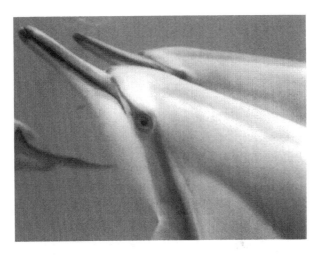

Activations & Inner Visions

Inner Visions

We bring
New Visions to humanity
Opening up treasures of the Ocean Kingdoms
Come humanity
Play with us in our Glorious Realm
Away from strife
Learn to live in harmony with all Life
Seek to know the reason you are living on Earth
Seek to find the Truth of why you are here
Then in knowing
Join your energies for Peace
Find the Center that allows you to live it for yourself
Journey with us into Regions Fair
Dwell with us in the Sacred Sanctuary of Life,
Be the fullness of your True Creative Expression
In a world that is calling for Healing
To a humanity calling for Truth
In a planet that has long waited for Harmony
To Hearts that are longing for Love
Come humanity, it is not so hard to live in Peace
It is not so hard to share loving
It is the Breath of
who you are

- The Dolphins

CHAPTER TWENTY TWO

Dolphins Activate My Next Book

I was in Aspen, Colorado, immersed in the glorious nature wonderland that has inspired my creative expression year after year. Being drawn back to this Rocky Mountain paradise once again, I wrapped up a book precious to my heart, Letters From the Inner Self: The Indwelling Spirit, and prepared for its formal release on 11.11.11.

Having been through a major metamorphosis as I edited it from March to November, I was in a heightened state of illumined awareness. With joy radiating from my being, I spent time each day hiking in the spectacular wilderlands. Snow capped peaks, trees in full golden array, and blue skies lent to the magic of this special time.

Reveling in the sense of completion and loving every moment alone in nature I could get, I was surprised when the dolphins showed up and began appearing every day. First it was like they were flying in circles around me, similar to their circling pattern in the ocean. Next one began nudging me in the back! Surprised, I realized I was being pushed west. I began to long for Hawaii, my homeland, its warm turquoise waters, tall green mountains, and flowering jungle growth. At the same time, an inspiration welled up to begin editing this book on the human dolphin connection. With over 200 stories gathered over many years, I would choose forty nine to be in the book, keeping the Earth 2012 template of seven parts, seven chapters.

Between the dolphin visits, awe inspiring nature adventures, and dolphins ethereally weaving their magic daily, the Earth 2012-33: Oracles of the Sea, the Human Dolphin Connection book was activated. At that same timing, I was inspired to send out word to my Hawaii friends, but though I had lived twelve years on Maui, it was to the Big Island of Hawaii I directed my inquiries. I joined the dolphin pod community internet network and started connecting with people there.

A few Divine Synchronicities and ten days later, I arrived on that beautiful island, stepped out on the lanai where I was staying, and looked in awe over the wide expanse before me. All three bays where dolphins frequent to swim with humans were in sight. Around the home, flowering jungle growth, fruit trees, and rain forest humming with life kept a protective field, while the view gave a feeling of expansiveness. The home was filled with sacred art, statues, crystals, and a pure, sweet essence. Perfect I thought! My Creative Self was already being activated.

Soon thereafter, I awoke early to swim with dolphins. Arriving at a gorgeous bay, I saw the dolphins offshore, donned my gear, and quickly entered the water. The beautiful transcendent blue water was like liquid crystal light. I journeyed forth and soon came to an area where the dolphins were leaping and playing in the water. A lady dolphin came over to me and placed a beautiful golden leaf inches from my face. I was so touched by this offering, I held it in my hand in awe as I swam. Another dolphin zoomed in inches from me and leapt up out of the water. I raised my head above the water and saw him come down with a dramatic splash right in front of me.

Amazed by these greetings, I began swimming with a pod of dolphins, who opened up the middle area between them for me. As I became part of the pod, I realized there were three dolphins on either side of me with dolphin babies beside them on the outer edges. Together we traveled in unison, until I finally realized how slow they had been going. They were cruising at my speed so I could keep up with them!

Sometime later, I was swimming with another small pod right next to a gorgeous baby, with only a couple feet between us. This is rare, as dolphin clans are extremely protective of their young. I felt so gifted, honored, appreciated, wanted, and welcomed, in awe of how I was being greeted. Did these dolphins know I was working on their book?

Dolphins leapt out of the water, spinning in the air. Babies danced underwater in graceful movements, while some dolphins glided serenely beneath and beside me.

I emerged out of the water hours later in that same peace. The peace continued throughout the day, like a time capsule release that kept going. I felt grounded yet light, quiet yet joyous, blissful and serene. This continued into the night and graced my next days, infusing this book with their sacred essence.

The Dolphin Magic continued as stories made their way into the book. I was uplifted and inspired by the high transcendent state they called me into, as I was weaving through the stories. I was transfigured by the gifts of the dolphins, the beauty of the Aina (land), and the sacred Mana (energy) one feels in the islands. I was home... drinking in the magic of these ancient Lemurian lands. Steeped in Hawaiiana, with a mystical weave of Kahuna Wisdom, my soul drank in the frequencies of my favorite place on the planet. That precious energetic flowed into this book, infusing my heart, mind and soul as I edited and prepared it for its birth.

As I moved into the final edit, I was unexpectedly transported to the next place I was to stay. A new friend, Michael, whose birthday I share, graciously opened his home to me, which was even closer to the dolphin frequented bays. Not only that, he enthusiastically became my early morning dolphin swim partner.

Amidst spectacular dolphin encounters, nature adventures drinking in the beauty of magical Hawaii, the full moon total lunar eclipse in plain sight at 5 am one glorious morning, sacred music playing in the background as I edited this book day after day, and chocolate wafting on the air as Michael prepared his next magical cacao bars for market, (allowing me to dip in whenever inspired), I proceeded forward in record speed, flying on a high wave of inspired enthusiasm caught up in the magic of these dolphin stories.

With joyous expectation of how this book will impact an awakening humanity, the project came to completion. I was then able to see the depth and breadth of the sacred energies I had been a vessel of and the joy the dolphins infused as I worked.

As the days had passed, I had become more and more uplifted and joyous, riding waves of inspired insights about our present planetary equation and the ramifications of massive dolphin facilitated awakenings in astounded participants worldwide. I had melted into the sacred vibrations of Hawaii as histories cleared through my inner work, leaving me in a quiet elation.

Finally, I emerged from the experience on a whole new level, completely renewed, restored and transformed, ready for the next divinely inspired project that would call me into yet another Sacred Journey.

CHAPTER TWENTY THREE

Shamanic Journey

by Paulette Chang

I went sailing with some friends and took my six year old son and two of his friends along. It was a great windy day for sailing and we left the harbor with sails up and moving at a rapid pace.

We encountered a pod of dolphins that swam with us a few miles. They were so swift, moving under, in front of, and behind the boat. The boys were screaming with delight and I was especially pleased and felt blessed by their presence.

A week later, I joined my Shamanic drumming group to do a journey. My question to my guides was, "Is my present vocation in line with my true purpose?" I began my journey as usual at the entrance to a large dark cave. Mountain Lion greeted me and I thanked him for showing up to be my guide. I rode on his back through the cave and asked that I remain in this present body, so I could receive the answer to my question in my present situation.

We came out of the end of the tunnel into a lush tropical forest, meandering through the forest awhile admiring the great trees and flowers. Suddenly, the forest became very thick. I was no longer able to stay on his back and had to struggle through the many thin and strangling tree trunks. I asked my Spirit Guides for the meaning of this struggle on my journey. My answer was that the current path is full of obstacles I was learning to overcome. I asked again if my vocation was the cause of these obstacles. They said it doesn't matter what I am doing, the obstacles are there because it is the right time for them to be there. I was to learn how to face them and move through them in balance. *Balance!* My number one struggle at the moment was frustration. I felt out of balance in my relationships, family life, and career.

I asked that I be given an alternative to this current struggle. Immediately I was nose to nose with a dolphin. I was looking straight into his eyes as we were dancing upon the ocean's surface. I asked Dolphin how I was to find balance. He laughed. He said, "What you need to find first is fun. You need to reconnect to the childlike fun you don't allow yourself to have because you're so serious about your obligations. To maintain balance, one must maintain one's sense of humor."

Yes, humor! Another fine quality I had been struggling to bring into my life... and Joy, which also had been evading my attention lately. So we plunged deep into the ocean and I was surprised to find I could breath easily in the darkness of the depths. I swam next to him as an equal and we burst out of the confines of the water into the open, free air again. I asked him, "What is my true purpose at this time?"

His answer was, "You are a teacher and your number one priority student at this moment is your son. Your focus should be on teaching him to connect with his intuition so he can learn how to find his answers from within and not depend on the outside forces to guide him." He gave me a game to play with my son. He said, "Hide a rock in one hand and a feather in the other and encourage him to use his intuition to find one of the items which you call out."

I asked, "What is the significance of the rock and the feather?"

He replied, "Balance. The rock is his masculine, intellectual side, the feather is his feminine, creative side. Using these two items grounds his energy and guides his intuition to remain balanced in both hemispheres." I realized then that this game would help me stay grounded in my dual energy at the same time.

I've played this game quite often since, with my son, Riley, who loves it and is very good at it. However, I need a lot of practice and sometimes he reminds me when my intuition is not working very well.

CHAPTER TWENTY FOUR

Great White Dolphin

by Paul Overman, PhD

I am a transpersonal therapist who specializes in altered states of consciousness for healing emotional trauma. I do a great deal of dream work with my clients and since an early age, I have had a very active dream-life.

Some years ago I began having the most amazing series of dreams that later evolved into telepathic communications during meditation. It all began with a dream where I was with a pod of highly evolved dolphins. One of the pod was its spiritually evolved leader. In the dream I was realizing his special nature and calling him the Great White Dolphin. I kept saying, "I did not know there was a Great White Dolphin."

Later in meditation, I re-experienced this dream and began receiving telepathic communications from this Great White Dolphin and his pod members. They told me they were in communication with me because they needed the waters of the Pacific protected. They said they contacted me because we were familiar with each other. I had known them from another time and place. They were concerned about pollution levels in the Pacific Ocean and had asked my help in making this known. They invited me to come to Hawaii to assist with this work.

In another meditation they showed me the Pacific Ocean region and explained it was in an environmental crisis approaching a catastrophe. Synchronistically, that spring I was unexpectedly invited to present the research and work I am doing on transformational dream states at a new center on the Big Island of Hawaii. I saw this as a way to lay the groundwork for the work the Great White Dolphin's messages were inspiring.

I learned the Pacific Ocean is greatly polluted, is becoming too warm due to the greenhouse effect with many consequential problems like El-Nino and according to some knowledgeable of the esoteric sciences, in difficulty due to rifts in the etheric web of the Earth in this Pacific region from atomic testing. I find it amazing how the Great White Dolphin and his clan wanted to alert me to these conditions so I could be one more voice of conscience in this world.

Paul Overman is a transpersonal therapist specializing in altered states for healing emotional wounds and creating new futures. He is the author of The Dreaming Self: Dreams, Transformation and Evolution of Consciousness and Sage: A Journal on Dream. See more about his work at: http://www.thedreamlistener.com. His blog is: http://www.theshamanicdream.com.

CHAPTER TWENTY FIVE

Awakening the Light Body

by Emerald Starr

We were floating in kayaks in a bay of the Inland Passage between Vancouver and mainland Canada. It was July 1996 and a group of explorers had come to communicate and commune with the Orcas, the largest species of dolphins made famous by Willy and Sea World, better known as Killer Whales.

We were searching for connections to ourselves, nature, and each other, desiring to take the next step in our evolution spiritually and physically, while trying to make more sense of our lives. Our journey to this remote place was a sort of Vision Quest, a place to slow down and open up to the voices within, surrounded by wilderness. A place to really listen, to ourselves and each other, and to read the signs placed before us by Mother Earth.

Our "Mother Ship" was a yacht outfitted with a sound recording studio complete with instruments and underwater speakers. Friends had orchestrated this event destined to be a concert with the Orcas.

Our first night we sat quietly in a circle with instruments before us. We were waiting for the first sounds of the Orcas in the passage. At last the first whistles and clicks were audible. We listened and as the sounds grew louder, we took to our instruments and slowly began to mimic our brothers and sisters of the sea. The response was immediate with variations, enhancements and more complex passages. We rode the musical communications and the Orcas drew nearer and nearer to our position. The concert was under full steam and soon our boat was surrounded by the Orca pod, with huffs and puffs of air and sea mist above the water while our "conversation" continued beneath the surface of the sea. We filled two tapes with this orgy of sound, and then as quickly as the Orcas had come, they were gone. We were exhilarated and exhausted. This was a great and auspicious beginning.

The stars were magnificent on the second night. Our kayaks rocked gently in the silence. I was at the helm of a two person kayak. My friend, Linda, was in the aft seat. Bioluminescence trailed and swarmed around our every paddle stroke. We were surrounded by stars in heaven and the sea. It couldn't have been a more perfect night.

Then we heard the first "blow," a sign of the Orcas approach. Our friends in the "Mother Ship" were beginning to play and the "blows" were getting louder and more frequent. We knew the Orcas would soon be upon us. My heart leapt into my throat. This was my first encounter with Killer Whales in the wild, and a large pod was coming hard and fast upon us. At first I was sure we would be rammed, and then at the last moment the entire pod submerged and everything was silent, at least for a few seconds. They were checking us out, I was sure. I could feel our light kayak being hit with sonar and then the pod was back in full force playing all around us exuberantly.

Moonlight and bioluminescence fell off the rising bodies of our friends, and we could now see them close up. Their powerful bodies could have sent any of us tumbling into the freezing waters at any moment. In the chaotic frenzy, I wondered that none of the kayaks had tipped over. It was then I felt the first "blast." My body trembled and I closed my eyes. Light was igniting inside me as if my cells were suddenly illuminated from within, one by one from my toes to my head in rapid succession.

I called out to Linda and she was experiencing the same thing. The Orcas were scanning us, activating our Light Bodies, and energizing our physical bodies. During the next hour of play we were "scanned, activated, and energized" three times until we were filled with the most amazing sense of oneness and well-being.

The next morning we were gathered at the beach. Tai Situ Rinpoche and his faithful companion Gene La were expected to arrive soon. This was a special honor and sure to be a great treat. Our friend, Joan, was already with us and it was destined to be a magical reunion of kindred souls. Linda and I took off into the forest to search for elves and fairies while Joan showed Tai Situ and Gene La the camp. By evening we were gathered around a fire and soon decided on our plan for communicating again with the Orcas. Joan and Linda were to be in single kayaks. I would take Tai Situ and Gene La in the larger kayak with me in the back, Tai Situ in front, and Gene La in the middle.

We set off, floating above the freezing waters under the full moon. This night was still and starry as the night before. We all paddled gently into the bay. Gene La and Tai Situ were like children watching the bioluminescence falling off our paddles, giggling and surprised. Our three kayaks began to triangulate in the bay. Joan and Linda were equidistant from us and far enough away for the OCR pod to enter in between. Gene La and Tai Situ began to chant and chills went up my spine. I felt the deep power of their call to Spirit and our ocean dwelling family.

Soon enough the Orcas started their approach from the deeper waters of the Inland Passage, making their diversion to our location for another communion concert. As they drew nearer, the chanting grew louder, a coming together of ancient tribes from the tallest mountains of Tibet and the deepest ocean depths.

The pod swam toward us as before in full force, aiming straight for our fragile kayaks. The sounds of their blows were wild, furious and close by. Seconds before colliding into us they slipped beneath the moonlit surface, barely creating a stir in the water. Everything went silent. Our enlightened friends stopped chanting at the same moment as the Orcas submersed. The silence was tense with energy. No one could move or speak. Without warning, emerging from the exact middle of our triangle, a single and great Orca erupted from the water to a huge height above us all, dripping bioluminescence in the moonlight.

In total awe we witnessed this enormous being looking down upon us with a single eye as if to say, "I see you and know who you are." After that penetrating look, she slowly returned back into the dark and luminescent waters. As the last of her body disappeared, the entire pod emerged blowing and playing in all directions around us. We all laughed in pure ecstasy and Tai Situ and Gene La began their chanting once again. We were all scanned, activated, and energized several more times that night and stayed up for all hours around the camp fire recounting our stories of the magic that we each experienced.

The next day I woke up early and took a kayak to another uninhabited island nearby. Along the way I met several families of seals and floated under the wings of bald eagles flying in all directions. There were many logging roads on the island and I had been warned to look out for bears that might not be too friendly. I was still in a state of blissful communion as I disembarked from my vessel. The seals had seemed to speak with me, and I could almost make out the eagles talking with each other, I was in such a heightened state of awareness.

I paused for a moment before I took off for the interior to sense if there was any danger there waiting for me. Feeling safe, I took off and started to run. I needed to feel the wind on my face and exercise my body after such a huge opening in my being. With each movement of my body and pounding of my heart I felt myself expand. My ears and eyes became sharper, my sense of smell clearer, and my skin felt more sensitive and alive. There was a rumbling in the underbrush and a bear stood up in surprise at my passing. After a moment he was running in the other direction. As I ran, I heard the seals talking and then a story came to me, "The Wise Woman of the Emote." It was the first of many stories that I later received from the eagles and the bears.

My sense of self had shifted, and my ability to understand and commune with nature had expanded. Meditations took me directly to my innermost core and I began to hear the needs of others in a new way, with greater love and compassion. A new self was emerging and has continued to evolve to this day. From the cold depths of the dark ocean rose a great being carrying ancient wisdom as a gift for our souls. That gift has assisted each of us to enter into deeper states of Loving Kindness and Compassion, the cornerstones of enlightenment. From out of the darkness came the power to illuminate and energize our cellular structures and awaken our Light Bodies.

Understanding and respecting the power of the shadow can give us compassion for those lost in ignorance, who are in denial of the negative forces that dwell within all of us. We are then free to choose a path of kindness, tolerance and love. This is the gift and blessing we receive when we are open to all possibilities. It gives us strength to face the many challenges that we all confront living a conscious life.

Emerald Starr has been an advocate and educator for environmental health and sustainability for over 25 years. He became aware of the Balinese principle of Tri Hita Karana: Humans in harmony with Nature, other humans and Divine Spirit. This has inspired his environmental and human rights advocacy ever since, from his home in Bali. Emerald is currently active in organic gardening, education and raising awareness for the health of our planet and the vital need to reduce toxic pollution and environmental destruction worldwide. For more info see: http://www.tirtagangga-villas.com and http://www.turtlebayhideaway.com.

CHAPTER TWENTY SIX

Golden Light Activation

by Shanta Hartzell

A woman friend took me out to swim with the dolphins on the west coast of Oahu. She was older than I was and not in as good condition. I became frightened as I did not consider myself strong enough to swim such a great distance, but felt heartened by her seeming ability to swim out to them. We did a short meditation to connect with them and then in we went.

As we swam, she told me dolphins orchestrate what she calls a "swim program." They take people out farther and farther so you can experience magic with them. We were the only ones out in the water that day. Soon the dolphins came and began swimming around us in circles. They were Bottlenose Dolphins and at one point, they turned pink, a very bright pink! I stuck my head out of the water to see more clearly and still they were pink. They were leaping and circling under us. It was the most exhilarating playful joy I have ever experienced.

My fear completely disappeared and I felt strong and able to swim along with them. I had been swimming quite a distance and I still had a lot of energy. I was completely awestruck and delighted when I saw their babies. Afterwards I said to my friend, "Did you see the dolphins were pink?"

"Definitely," she replied. After that we tried to tell some people we had seen pink dolphins. They were skeptical and said,"Besides, Bottlenose Dolphins don't even go there." Later we found out that the dolphins can turn pink when they are excited.

For days I had a smile on my face that wouldn't wipe off. It was exhilarating. I was blissful for a whole week. I felt their presence with me as I have felt the angels presence at times. It was very powerful.

The second time I swam with the dolphins, I was with a man friend. We were dangling in the water way far out. Somehow we got parted and he ended up really far from me.

I began thinking of the oneness of all life, and preparing myself for their visit. A song started to go through my mind and soon I was singing to the Earth, and connecting with the Presence of the Mother.

All of a sudden I saw what seemed to be around 300 dolphins leaping in the water swimming towards me. It was the most awesome experience I've had. These dolphins were all illumined in golden light. They were swimming in circles around me and I had the sense they could see right into me.

Then I felt like Christ as I lay there in the water. I had my hands out and the golden stream of light began going through my body. I stayed in this amazing communion with the dolphins in what seemed like endless time and felt greatly impacted for days afterward. Illumined and transformed, the golden light continued to stay with me for a long time.

Shanta Hartzell is known for her Angel Messages Book and Card Set: Practical and Inspired Support for Day to Day Living; her Angel Readings, and Balancing and Attunement sessions. You can buy her book and card set on Amazon.com For sessions, call Shanta at: (808) 239-5433.

CHAPTER TWENTY SEVEN

Dolphin Journey of Self Discovery

by Takara

You've probably heard of the Dark Night of the Soul. I woke up one morning not feeling well and called in sick. Before I knew it, I was lying on the floor in a fetal position, crying my eyes out as I relived being raped. This was fifteen years after the experience actually happened and when I had never before shed a tear. Fifteen years of denial is a very long time. The emotions I felt were completely foreign to me.

I grew up without witnessing strong emotions. No one in my family ever expressed anger or fear. I didn't know it was normal to have those feelings. So whenever they were present within me, I just shut them down. That doesn't mean they go away however. They get stuck in the body and turn into illness.

This Dark Night brought them all to the surface. Alarmed, I had no reference for the intensity of the anger and fear I was experiencing. For the first time in my life I felt completely out of control and found that terrifying. I realized in that moment that if these feelings were a part of who I am, then I didn't really know myself AT ALL. My journey of self discovery had begun.

I went for the first time to a New Age bookstore. I picked up a brochure for someone that did Energetic Clearing. I had no idea what that meant, but it felt like the right thing to do and I made the appointment anyway. It's funny that when the ego is shattered, new doorways suddenly become available. If I weren't in such a desperate place, I never would have been open to new concepts or alternative therapies and I wouldn't have been so quick to follow my intuition.

While in the bookstore, I bought an audiotape called Ocean

Dreams by Dean Evenson. It contained beautiful music and real dolphin sounds. I played it throughout the day, over and over again. The soothing music bathed me with its melodies and the dolphin sounds whispered to my soul. It soothed my pain as I continued to shed fifteen years worth of tears.

When I went for my energy healing session that evening, I was completely amazed by what transpired. The woman had a stereo and about fifty tapes to choose from. The one she played was Ocean Dreams by Dean Evenson. All I could think about was how on Earth she chose that music.

As soon as the session was over, I asked her why she chose THAT ONE. She said it was the one she felt I needed. Wow! That's when I first realized something much bigger than myself was at work and there might really be something to this New Age stuff.

I quickly became a regular customer at all the New Age bookstores. I began reading, listening to audiotapes, and attending seminars. I was learning a great deal about myself and about emotional healing.

During that time, I was feeling very drawn to Native American spirituality and turned my second bedroom into a meditation room. In it I built a gigantic medicine wheel. Using the newly built wheel, I tried a guided visualization meditation for the first time. I discovered that I had an instant affinity for voyaging into alternate realities and could easily experience what I was visualizing with most of my senses.

The meditation I was following guided me around the medicine wheel in my mind. In each direction I was to stop and ask for guidance from the energy or animal. I was amazed at how vivid and real the experience was.

I was visualizing the South Direction, working with Coyote medicine, when suddenly the Coyote began running around in circles. It transformed itself into a dolphin swimming in circles. I began to cry tears of joy. This was my first dolphin encounter.

After that, practically every time I closed my eyes, the dolphins appeared. The encounters progressed and transformed into much more. I soon began seeing the images and having the feeling of being in the water with them, not just seeing them from a distance.

In the water I would be belly to belly with a dolphin, my arms around it, and it would spin the two of us through the water like a torpedo. Tears would stream down my face every time these encounters happened. Afterwards I would feel completely cleansed and renewed. Eventually I found myself shape shifting into a dolphin and seeing the world through its eyes.

The dolphins greatly assisted me in healing my wounds from the past. They taught me how to thrive, not simply survive. I began to understand that what I once thought had value, really did not. Fame and fortune were simply illusions of the ego. The things of lasting value were love, wonderful enduring friendships, my own happiness, sense of self worth, connection with Creator, living my truth, and being of service.

Since those first encounters years ago, the dolphins have become my greatest teachers and source of inspiration. Through my Dolphin Journey of Self Discovery, I've become much more joyful and fulfilled, and now teach others how to do the same.

So much has shifted for me since that fateful day. My psychic, intuitive, and healing abilities have been greatly enhanced. I left the corporate world to head out on my own doing what I love and to make a positive difference in the world. I met and married the man of my dreams who had also been visited by dolphins numerous times while diving in Honduras. I have a beautiful son who was born at home in a heated pool with only my husband present and dolphin sounds playing on the stereo.

Each day the journey continues as an ever unfolding revelation of who I am. I am constantly learning, growing, and releasing those things that keep me from being all I choose to be and the dolphins are ever present, offering insight, inspiration, and joy.

Debbie Takara Shelor is an award winning author and teacher as well as an engineer and mystic. Her most recent book is Peering Through the Veil: The Step by Step Guide to Meditation and Inner Peace. She is the creator of Dancing Dolphin Energy Healing Products and offers workshops online, on land, and at sea. Thousands of subscribers from over 100 countries enjoy her free email newsletter, Here's to Your Magnificence. Visit her website http: www.AbsoluteJoyNow.com and get two of her ebooks for free. She can also be contacted by email: takara@ dolphinempowerment.com, phone: 540-639-1633, or mail: P.O. Box 1363, Radford, VA 24143.

CHAPTER TWENTY EIGHT

Hidden Treasure

by Rona Smith

Each night our spirits rise out of us to
explore all the wonders of this universe
Wayfarers beyond time and space.
We fly together until the
safety of the morning light
calls us back to our sleeping body.

Where, my friend, does a story that is centuries old begin? Well, I suppose, since this is my story, I am a good a place to start as any. Born at the middle of the 20th century, I had betrayed the dear doctors prediction on two accounts. First I came early, in January, almost 6 weeks before my February 14th due date. For this I spent a little over a week in the hospital experiencing the world in a plastic incubator, only taken to my mother during feeding times. Perhaps this was a fair enough trade, but the biggest trespass was the piece that was missing from my little body when I arrived.

Before the invention of ultra-sound, the prediction of the gender of the child was based on heart rate. Mine, it seems, was on the speedy side… a boy for sure! In fact, my parents were so set on the idea, not a girl's name did they ever once consider. Hence, several days after my birth and at the insistence of my primary caregivers, the nurses, "lD" was deleted from my male name and I was to be called "Rona" instead of Ronald, the boys name that had been decided upon. Not "Donna" with an "R," but "Ron" with an "A". Despite a lifetime of misspellings and mispronunciations, I still love my name.

My father, childless until the age of 42, soon forgave me for the gender mishap. But to a mother who had experienced life in a female body as one of being "less than," I could never do enough or be enough to redeem myself for being a constant reflection of her most hated aspect, her femininity. Still, I learned to get by, leaning toward strong male role models. I played at Tarzan, the Lone Ranger, and any stories that offered a connection with animals, an opportunity to connect with the instinctual nature inside.

It was around my fortieth year the visions began, sometimes coming during meditation, but often they would be part of my dreamtime. The scene was always the same. I was a part of a group of women living in a sanctuary at the edge of the water. Something about the women was illuminated in my mind. They were not just "normal" women. They were more of the Priestess genre, and the place was no ordinary spot on the planet. It glowed in my vision.

I knew it was a place of great Mana (spiritual power) where things existed in harmony. The setting was a white, open-air palace surrounded on three sides by the sea with steps leading into the water. Dolphins were in the water surrounding this place, both guardians and guides of the women. The vision became clearer and clearer bringing with it a visceral response that resonated like the sound of a sacred tone within me. I was being called.

All of this was unusual for me, as my experience of women had not included any visions of the Great Divine Mother or Goddesses. It was not an image or lifestyle I was used to or comfortable with in any regard. Since I did not grow up Catholic, I did not even have the imprint of the Virgin.

Women in my family were the glue that held the daily life together. They were strong, resourceful, capable and enduring, worker bees, not the Queen. They were needed, but not revered in any true sense. Yet somewhere in the hallways of my unconscious, there was a coup brewing. A revolution that was to undo the weavings of centuries of women that came before me, whose genetic memories swirled in the recesses of my deepest places.

It was on a late summer afternoon in upcountry Maui I received the invitation. It came from a woman I had not known long or well. I suppose the three key words; women, dolphin and retreat, were too much for my guarded self to resist and I became a witness of an enthusiastic affirmative response that escaped from my mouth to my own surprise.

Less than six weeks and a couple of thousand dollars later, I arrived with my friend on the Island of Hawaii, which was destined to be the place of my Awakening. Ariana, the woman leading the retreat, picked us up at the airport. Her shoulder length hair was wild with auburn curls and her eyes the vibrant green of the rolling hills above my home. She was beautiful and petite with an arm full of golden bangles and a silk sarong wrapped tightly around her shapely curves.

Her age was hard to guess, but she surely exuded the sense she had been well taken care of and the giant emerald on her finger was of a cut, clarity and size fairy tales are made of. My mind rested easily on the thought that she carried the archetype of some form of the Goddess.

We had only gone about a couple of miles down the road when she turned and looked deeply into my eyes. "You have come here to heal," she stated with full authority. This was true, because in the time between signing up for the retreat and arriving, my father had passed suddenly, leaving me saddened, shocked and numb. The information she gave was very accurate. There was no doubt I was in need of healing.

Upon arrival at the private home where the retreat was to take place, I stood in awe. It was the realization of my visions… a white, open air palatial home situated on the edge of a sacred bay, directly adjacent to a heiau (Ancient Hawaiian Temple). The ocean surrounded the home on two sides and in every imaginable way it was similar to what I had been seeing in my dreams and visions.

The two women leading this journey seemed sure of their connection to the Goddess, something I was not even sure I understood, let alone could align with in any personal way. Yet, I arrived open, surrendered to the possibility of gathering glimpses of my own feminine divinity.

It was late afternoon when we finally immersed ourselves in the ocean. There were clouds blocking out the sun and it seemed like a liquid sepia tone movie instead of a snorkel adventure. Already, I was getting the feeling this retreat was not to be an ordinary experience. Everything seemed so surreal.

There were no dolphins and in fact, no fish in the water to speak of. Only the underwater remnants of a dock, with large pieces of concrete laying on their sides and a big concrete ball, which gave me the feeling of being on an underwater archeological expedition.

We followed the group leader closely and because of the darkened sky giving less light in the water, we were all somewhat relieved, when after about forty minutes, we returned to shore. Little did I know at the time, there were other women, ones from the Mainland, who were very unnerved we were in deep water at a time of day usually associated with unspeakable creatures, which come out to feed at dark, namely sharks.

When all the women had arrived, we were given time to settle in before gathering for our first meal together. The setting was pristine as thirteen of us found our seats around the large table on the lanai over-looking the bay. The sun had just gone behind a layer of clouds, which gave a glow to the now calm surface. I looked out over the water, as it gently lapped against the stark black cliffs that framed the northeast corner of the bay.

A hand on mine brought me back to the moment – the women, following the lead of Ariana, had embraced hands, connecting us all through touch. A silence fell on the circle. Suddenly, at the very moment Ariana began the blessing, an opening in the clouds sent a column of light down to illuminate a spot on the water in the middle of the bay.

"Dear Ones, we have come here to claim our birthright as women on this feminine planet. This time together will bring us an opportunity to embrace our potential as divine incarnations of the creatrix and explore those parts missing from the culture and time in which we currently live."

Ariana kissed the hand to her left and then to her right as we all followed suit. It was as though the circle between us had been formed by touch, strengthened by words and sealed by breath. We all lifted our glasses in a toast to the life affirming Goddess in each of us.

After dinner, we gathered in the open-air living area. There on the floor at the center of our circle was a magenta silk scarf. On it, jasmine flowers floated gracefully in a large blue bowl. A thick white candle glowed in one corner next to a statue of Kuan Yin, the Chinese Goddess of Compassion. In another corner, Mary, the Great Mother took up residence. The other two corners of the scarf housed a statue of Green Tara, the Tibetan Goddess of Protection, and the Greek Goddess of Love, Aphrodite, which lay in the corner nearest Ariana and her assistant, Gayle. There in the middle of our altar was a teal blue glass vessel shaped like a dolphin.

Once we had all settled in our seats, Ariana opened the circle. "I am Ariana and I am a temple of the Mother's Grace." I was struck by these words, the thought that we could be a temple, embody the grace of the divine mother, our bodies a receptacle and vessel for such a powerful essence. Still, I believed this was possible of Ariana, who created with such ease and beauty, who seemed to resonate grace from her very core.

What came next was far more difficult for me to grasp as one by one each woman took her place in the circle by reciting these same words. My heart beat faster as my turn approached. I took a deep breath hoping to dispel the panic rising in me. How could I be a temple? How could I hold the vibration of grace and proclaim this out loud?

As my turn approached, fear and anxiety took a stronghold within. At that moment, having the power to make myself invisible seemed far more feasible then being a residence of such an immensely healing vibration. My voice broke as I began. "I am… Rona… and… I am…" my vocal cords seemed frozen and my mind went blank as the woman at my right whispered the words for me to follow, "a temple of the Mother's Grace."

The shock and numbness lasted the rest of the circle for me. I only caught glimpses of what was shared in regards to the Goddess. Somehow, I did understand we were all to have a task to perform daily for the benefit of the circle. Mine was to connect with the dolphin energy by choosing a "dolphin card" from the teal glass vessel on the floor before me. I felt a relief to be assigned something that was easy and I believed, would not require me to step out of my comfort zone.

Then as an experience for us to bond together and also with the pod of dolphins, Ariana turned on some soothing music that had dolphin and whale sounds swimming through it. She instructed us to stand facing one of the other women.

Gazing into each other's eyes, we were directed not to speak or make any gestures, only gaze silently connecting with the soul of the other. We took turns connecting with every woman in this way and I was surprised to find in each one, parts of my own story - shadowed or revealed. We were then directed to go off to slumber in silence and we would awaken in the morning prepared for our communion with the dolphin pod.

For me, dreams have always been easy and prolific, revealing all of the glory and disappointments, hopes and worries…a splitting open of my everyday life. This time at the retreat was to begin to shift the quality and essence of the dreamtime.

The first night, I felt in the sweet call of slumber, a safety and peace that had been absent from my night explorations for a very long time. As I closed my eyes and began to drift off, I felt the presence of something divine swirling around me, calling me, inviting me to join in a circle out in the middle of the bay.

Soon, I found myself swimming in deep water, moving through it with the power and ease only known by creatures born and raised in that domain. I could see my body was the same, yet it appeared I had certain gifts not associated with my waking hours. I noticed I did not have to concern myself with laboring to hold my breath, as it seemed my lungs were large enough, designed in such a way I could continue breathing internally, not needing to replenish my oxygen. It is a freedom I have experienced many times since, in my dreams with the dolphins.

That night a large dolphin came and invited me to follow it. First the interaction was somewhat playful, sort of a follow the leader and also a sourcing out my aptitude to connect, follow, surrender, perhaps even to be trusted. At some point, it was clear for both of us I was able to follow the unspoken lead of this amazing creature. It was as if our minds had melded into one and her slightest thought would register in my brain simultaneously. I was then given permission to go to another level.

I was taken to the bottom of the bay where there was a soft, pink glow. The dolphin used its snout to brush away the sand and a vault door was uncovered. The dolphin hesitated for a moment, waiting to assess my reaction. When it was assured of my openness and curiosity to enter the vault, it used its sonar to release the lock and the door opened.

Now the light was much stronger and slightly more magenta colored. Without hesitation, I followed my guide inside as we traversed a series of tight passageways. Keeping up with every twist and turn, we finally came to our destination, an illuminated rose-colored chamber.

In the Inner Sanctum something opened and I found myself staring at a gigantic pink diamond, the magnitude of which had never been seen on the Earth. Somehow, I felt the emanations of this remarkable stone were penetrating my very being, righting something deep within me. The dolphin waited as I soaked up all that I could of the rays of this brilliant healing light. The change in me must have been evident, as again, as if operating from one brain, we both concurrently knew when the work was finished. I followed my guide back to the surface and then once again found myself peacefully curled up in my bed, refreshed and ready to awaken at the first sign of light.

The sanctuary swirled with energy in the morning light. Remembering the night before and eager to perform our devotional service for the whole, the rooms were buzzing with activity. Surely the dolphins would be in the bay today and we would be invited to join them.

The two retreat leaders had slept in the open air meeting room and were now on the lanai with binoculars looking for dolphins. They could feel them, they said, but their eyes had yet to pick any out on the choppy surface of the bay.

As we completed our morning routines, Elizabeth, Guardian of the Prayer Bowl and Gatherer of the Energies summoned us into circle. The candle was lit and the blessing bowl of water in the center of the circle had been replenished with fresh, fragrant plumeria flowers from the garden.

After a few moments in meditation and our ritual of proclaiming ourselves Temples of the Mother's Grace, it was time to share the various divination cards of the day. I closed my eyes and sensed inward to ask for a communication from the dolphins. As I reached into the glass vessel, one card felt warm to my touch and I retrieved it from the dish. When I opened my eyes, I was surprised to find the words written on the small round card to be so revealing of my experience in the dreamtime. I looked around at all of the beauty that had come together to form this circle of women. Softly I spoke, sharing the communication from the dolphin pod, "Hidden Treasure."

We had been told that if the dolphins were to come, they would usually do so in the early morning and by now it was mid morning. Yet, the experience of the two group leaders was that they would come, they always had. Little did we know at the time that this scenario of "no dolphins" would play out each morning for the whole week we were at the retreat. Yet, each night in my dreams, I would be summoned to enter the bay and swim with the pod. My encounters were remarkable, healing and illuminating experiences and until now, I did not once share them, in or out of circle. I had learned early in life my "visions" or dreams were not believed and certainly not valued by others. They were mine to hold close…they were my "hidden treasure."

Slowly, over the coming week, this group of thirteen were introduced to simple yet profound rituals which opened the doorway of acceptance and love for the feminine in all its incarnations. We came to live the nurturance, compassion, cooperation, sensuality, power, fierceness and rationality of the Goddess. Together we created a peaceful and harmonious existence. Slowly, we were brought, both personally and collectively, into the service of a higher calling, willingly baptized into the essence of the Goddess.

Our days were focused both outward and inward as we journeyed on our path of healing. Each day we participated in an adventure into the heart of the Goddess. We went to the City of Refuge to perform a ceremony of forgiveness for not only ourselves, but also for those who might have wronged us.

One night we were introduced to the lost art of anointing, with essential oils blended by Ariana for each specific energy center of the body. We had danced at dawn on the rock wall surrounding the property, calling out to our female ancestors to join our circle, as the waves crashed against the rocks, soaking us with the salty lifeblood of Gaia. We had entered the body of the Earth, following Pele's labyrinth until it opened onto a cliff high above the pounding surf. We had swam with wild sea turtles and kayaked the bay at sunset, when the surface of the water was slick like glass and you could almost hear the voices of the ancient villagers that once shared this sacred place on the planet. In each moment, the barriers were revealed in the unconscious script which devalued the feminine in me and in the world.

On the final morning of the retreat, the hope of swimming with the dolphins had spun a visceral web of expectation throughout the circle and yet, we arose to discover that once again, the dolphins were absent from the bay.

It was just after lunch when I asked my friend to take the double kayak out into the bay with me. "There's something I need to do," I whispered.

The waves were calm and the week had made us courageous, so this time we met at the edge of the property and pushed the vessel into the water. Waiting to go between sets, we maneuvered the craft through the surging water and out the narrow path to the bay. The sun was high in the sky and there was no cloud cover. It was bright and hot and the water that came in from the sides of the boat were cooling and welcome. When we had paddled to the middle of the bay, I stopped her. "Wait!" I said. "There is something I need to do here."

"Here?" She turned looking puzzled.

"Yes, here in the middle of the bay."

Slowly, I reached down my swimsuit and pulled a Herkimer diamond from between my breasts. It was a special stone for me. My father had given it to me years ago when I was just a child. He had found it on one of his hikes in the mountains and I had carried it to the retreat to help keep him close. I now knew it belonged here – a gesture of gratitude to the dolphins. My friend was now turned fully around in the kayak with a curious look on her face.

"The dolphins have been coming to me every night in my dreams and I want to thank them." I closed my eyes and held the stone tightly in both hands. The words came freely and the tears with them as I attempted to share my deep gratitude for my many luminous experiences with them in the dreamtime. I could feel my heart opening wider as I spoke, the feeling of knowing that it was all perfect, the fullness of such intense gratitude for my encounters here, the dreams, the dolphins, the healing water, the circle of women, this ancient power spot on the planet. All of it!

As I dropped the diamond into the water, I watched as it cut a jagged path of light reflecting the prism of water and light down, down, down, until it became a tiny speck of luminosity falling into the darkness of the deep.

"Oh, did you see them? Two dolphins, there, look!"

Before I could turn to see where she was pointing, two more had surfaced behind her. Soon there were two more and then two more and before long we were in the center of a dolphin mandala. We sat spell bound, as we found ourselves in the middle of a circle of dolphins numbering close to fifty. We could not move, hushed by the power and unexpectedness of our experience.

At last, we came to a profound desire to enter the water with them. We looked to shore and could see several of the women still sitting on the lanai finishing their lunch. We waved our oars, alerting them to the fact there were, at last, dolphins in the bay.

Our service to the others completed, we abandoned the kayak and slipped into the water. The circle of dolphins tightened and became a crisscrossing of visitors as they swam close to explore us, the ones who had come to thank them.

Suddenly, from directly beneath me, a large dolphin emerged and seemed to hover in the water only a couple of feet below. As the dolphin continued to float, maintaining the perfect space between us, our eyes locked in a knowing of mutual recognition. Just like in my dreams, my thoughts arose and seemed to be immediately seeded in the brain of the other.

"Are you the dolphin who led me through the labyrinth?" I thought. This time the dolphin surged at high speed, producing a series of clicks and whistles as it spun a tight circle around me. I took that to convey an affirmative answer.

I felt my whole being become full with a sense of wonder, joy and profound gratitude, as a concept entered my awareness and was expressed as thought. "Oh, I see, we come to you in your dreams too."

The dolphin looked as though it was smiling as it continued to deepen its gaze. By now the other women had entered the water and some of them were swimming in to the realm occupied by the dolphins. We were all taken into the inner circle of the pod that day. We were all celebrated and we all received what had called us to that time and place.

Innovative educator for the past 35 years, Rona remains dedicated to exploring creativity, imagination, intuition, story and the transformative process. She is an artist, SoulCollage® Facilitator, storyteller, teacher, Women's retreat leader, author, and Master of the Usui System of Natural Healing.

Rona grew up in Northern California and moved to Maui in 1990 where she has built a life around doing what she loves and what touches the lives of others in meaningful and creative ways. As a child, she had many visions and dreams of dolphins and in 1995 was gifted with the first of many mystical experiences swimming with a pod of wild dolphins off the coast of the Big Island of Hawaii. She regularly joins these amazing and intelligent creatures in the water and they have become guides on her spiritual journey. She currently lives, plays and creates art on the slopes of the dormant volcano Haleakala (House of the Sun). Rona can be contacted at: rona@soularthawaii.com or visit her website at: soularthawaii.com

Part Five

Intervention & Protection

Protection

You come bravely out
Into our World
We watch over you that you may be protected
Precious Souls seeking Enlightenment in our waters
Finding the Joy we choose to live in

We are your Protectors
Watching over you as you venture into dark waters
We know you are brave and true
Or you would not seek us
You, Valiant Ones
Out of all humanity
True seekers are
The Ones who find Truth

In deep waters
You have opened your hearts to us and
Others soon shall join you
For we have called them forth
That they might learn a New Way of Living
True to the Essence of the Soul
True to the ever present Joy Within
True to the Divinity that is their True Spirit

A Spiritual Quest it is
To venture into our waters
To play among us and receive our Initiations of Love
Have you not thought that this is quite wondrous
That we, your Elders, have drawn you out into our Realm
To bring you to your Truth?

- The Dolphins

CHAPTER TWENTY NINE

My Dolphin Song

by Bennie Kante

I was working on a dive boat off the coast of Hawaii when I had my most memorable encounter with dolphins. After helping all the tourists back onto the boat, the dive master surfaced and told me he had found a rare frog fish. I hopped into the water and took his mask and scuba gear and, following his directions, descended.

Instantly I recognized the sounds of Spinner Dolphins. I found the spot where the Sergassom Frog Fish was. It was beautifully patterned with red and white. I could tell the dolphins were getting closer as their calls were getting louder.

I was at a depth of thirty feet when I began to swim towards the sound. I came to the edge of the shelf I was diving on and the water dropped off into a deep blue abyss. The dolphins sounded very close and playful.

I continued to swim at the thirty-foot depth into the Big Blue. Rushes of energy started to flow through every cell of my body and I felt an immense feeling of joy. Knowing no one was around to see and hear me, I stretched out my arms and started making high pitched sounds trying to imitate the dolphins. I released all restrictions and really enjoyed myself as I sang my dolphin song and felt love.

Suddenly out of the blue, hundreds of dolphins appeared and began to circle me. Water began to leak into my mouth because my smile got so big. I had never felt such euphoria. I continued to sing and began to dance with my new friends. I just let my body move to a quick childlike beat and the dolphins swam around and around me.

I then looked down and saw a large shark below me. A quick jolt of fear swept through my body as the unexpected visitor showed up. As quick as the shark appeared my emotions switched. The dolphins moved in to totally surround me, above, below, and on all sides. The feeling of love and joy again filled my heart and I smiled. I had stopped dancing and my arms were back at my side. I just floated weightlessly in the inner space of the ocean realm and fell in love with my new friends. Then, as if they were all one being, the dolphins disappeared into the abyss as they all dove straight down.

Looking to the surface to get a directional bearing of the sun, I thanked God for my special moment. I then returned to the boat with memories of a lifetime. Now, whenever I catch myself being anything but happy, I think back to my dolphin experience and a large smile always covers my face.

CHAPTER THIRTY

Swimming For My Life

by Paul Overman, PhD

I accepted an invitation to present my work on transformational dream states at a new center on the Big Island of Hawaii. I planned to make this a scouting trip for a potential move to Hawaii, where I hoped to continue my dream work while being open to further communication and interaction with the dolphin pod I had for some time been receiving telepathic messages from. This may seem to be a very tenuous "connection" to base such a life-changing move, but my work has repeatedly shown me the validity of altered states and their import on our lives. In fact, my most important life decisions have been based on dream symbols.

On my way to Hawaii and immediately upon arrival, I ran into some difficulties. The morning after my arrival, I found myself in the ocean swimming with my lecture group. I got injured in the high breakers attempting to get out to calmer waters with this group. I had hurt my foot, was knocked out of breath twice, and had taken water into my lungs. I spent some time on the other side of the breakers attempting to calmly float, rest, and catch my breath. I had told the others to go ahead without me, but then found the prospect of returning to shore alone a little daunting. I decided to swim out to them and get assistance. I became severely nauseated and started losing physical strength. My roommate, Mike, saw me floundering and swam over to help me.

Due to the swift currents, we could not swim directly back, but had to swim parallel to the shore for the longest time before catching the right currents for the swim into shore. By this time, my body had rapidly lost energy, and Mike offered to pull me as he swam into shore. Floating on my back, I helped him by using backstrokes and kicks, but eventually I became exhausted and could offer little assistance. My body temperature had fallen, and I was having flashes of sinking deep into the waters. My consciousness and life force were leaving my body, and I began to experience what death must feel like.

I prayed to the Divine, repeated a mantra, and meditated. I believed in divine intercession, that some intermediary or medium would bring about a miracle and save us. All I could do was try to stay conscious. I repeatedly had to surrender to the ocean waters, letting my body just float on its waves, and trust this man Mike. It was difficult not to be in despair, for we were still pretty far out from the beach. I had no idea how we would survive this ordeal. Nobody on shore or swimmers in the water saw our predicament, and there were no boats nearby to rescue us. Even if we got close to shore, I could not move a muscle and didn't see how Mike could get both of us through the breakers.

I thought of telling Mike to leave me so he could save himself, but some inner awareness kept telling me to trust him when he said we were doing all right, even though I believed he was having his doubts. I thought of the dolphins and the legends down through history of how they've helped those drowning or floundering at sea. I connected with them mentally and asked where they were. I thought of asking them to come and nudge us to shore, but it sounded too fantastic or childish. I did ask them to send me energy, the energy I had felt so many times in my meditations with them. I began to feel their energy flowing into me, but it was faint, as if transmitted from a distance and did not replace the energy draining out of my body.

When it looked the bleakest with Mike steadily losing his own strength, water getting into my lungs, and my physical strength totally depleted, I discovered we were right at the breakers, only thirty yards from shore, though for all our diminished resources, we could have been two miles out. Then an unexpected energy flooded into me, pulling my consciousness back into my body, which was instantaneously filled with a white light energy as strong as steel.

It filled me like air pumped into a balloon. I used this energy to move my muscles, and then an emphatic silent voice said, "You must flip yourself over now and swim with all your will or you and this man will drown."

I immediately drew upon the energy and flipped over on my stomach. I asked Mike where on shore we were aiming. He pointed to a spot about 20 yards down the beach. The energy in my body increased more than tenfold. It felt like I had the strength of a hundred men. Not in my wildest dreams did I believe the human body could hold so much energy. At that moment I knew, without a doubt, we were going to make it. All I had to do was swim with all my might and let Mike swim on his own power. I told him to let go of my arm, shouting as the waves splashed in my face, "Let's go for it!"

We both swam with breaststrokes in perfect unison for another twenty-five yards, and then we found ourselves rising over a large breaker that took us down and under, smashing us with a powerful jolt on the ocean floor. We scrambled up to the beach to avoid being hit by the next breaker. I fell on the beach totally exhausted and continued to lose energy and body temperature. At times I fought a tendency to go unconscious from the energy loss. My body kept shaking ferociously as if in a monstrous shock. Rather than fighting, I gave into it, going deeper and deeper inside myself for another level of healing.

After a couple of hours, I finally revived myself enough to head back to the van where Mike was recuperating. Inside, Mike turned to me and asked, "Did you see the dolphins?"

I said, "What dolphins?"

He said, "Right before we reached the breakers, I tried to rouse you, shaking your shoulder and yelling above the roar. I didn't think I could get you through the breakers alive with you being unconscious. I was losing my own strength. Then these two dolphins appeared ten feet off to our side and swam with us. I felt this surge of energy come into me, and then you turned over and said, 'Let's go for it.' You went from unconscious to total awareness in the blink of an eye. It was amazing to see."

I realized then that my prayers had been answered, that the dolphins became the medium of this tremendous power transmitted into Mike and me, which literally saved our lives. In the years since that experience, I have used the New Life given me to help spread the message my dolphin friends have given to me.

Paul Overman is a transpersonal therapist specializing in altered states for healing emotional wounds and creating new futures. He is the author of The Dreaming Self: Dreams, Transformation and Evolution of Consciousness and, Sage: A Journal on Dream. See more about his work at: http://www.thedreamlistener.com. His blog is: http://www.theshamanicdream.com.

CHAPTER THIRTY ONE

From Broken Spirit to Healed Heart

By Cindy Brower

My father left our home when I was five and died two years later. My mother suffered from a variety of chronic illnesses that frequently forced her to the hospital for extended periods, often months on end. My two older brothers, Danny, twelve and Johnny, thirteen, assumed the duties of running our household and raising me. We circled our tiny wagons against the world, with Danny taking the lead. He did a remarkable job, and as you might suspect, we three developed an extraordinary bond beyond that of most siblings.

My big brothers made sure that I ate properly, went to bed on time, and got to school with my homework done. They never left me at home alone, actually requiring me to tag along in their comings and goings when mom was hospitalized. They defended me, standing as the toughest boys in the toughest of neighborhoods. I was safe wherever I wandered. They nurtured me, seeing to it that I played on the school athletic teams as well as in the school band. Bless his heart, Danny even took me to get my first training bra, perhaps the most courageous effort ever for a blushing teenage boy. The boys were my security, my guides, my refuge, and my life. We were three, but were also one, the boys and I.

I was sixteen when Danny committed suicide. One year later, Johnny followed. I had lost my anchors, the only reliable people in what had otherwise proved to be a totally unreliable world. Our church and community at large eagerly handed down judgment without compassion. I felt alone, betrayed, and angry, but most of all, I missed the boys with an unimaginable hurt and felt responsible.

Rather than healing the emotional cuts, time caused them to

fester. What began as a downward emotional spiral soon began to take a physical toll. Year after year, rightly or wrongly, my feelings of grief and guilt deepened and my health grew worse and worse. At the age of twenty-three, I was hospitalized with heart problems. At the age of thirty-two, I hit bottom.

I had been married a year when my husband and I headed out from Arizona to Virginia for an eighteen month sabbatical for my husband to complete graduate studies and me to take some personal inventory, collect myself, get back on track. You know all the buzzwords. I had been seriously struggling at home, but my health took an even more drastic plunge as we traveled across the country. Within our first hour in Charlottesville, we found a doctor through the yellow pages who measured my blood pressure at 80 over 40.

I can mark that day as the beginning of a medical ordeal that in hindsight was as inevitable as it was horrific. No doctor could diagnose my illness, neither in Virginia, nor in the years following our return to Arizona. While I occasionally had 'good days,' my decline was steady and unrelenting. My muscles, for some reason, were shutting down. I had no energy. It took me days to recover from the most minor of activities.

Medical instruments showed that rather than recovering after a brief period of exertion, my muscles actually continued to tire. The pain was unbearable, translating through my shoulders and up my neck. Migraines became a way of life. Because of the muscle pain, I could not sleep. Because I could not sleep, my muscles could not recover. Because they could not recover, the pain grew. My body was locked in an insidious, self-destructing cycle.

After a year of bouncing from specialist to specialist, getting scanned, poked, thumped, wired, and medicated, I was still undiagnosed. I had become bedridden, barely able to make it from bed to a chair. Those few steps left me exhausted for hours. My neck and shoulder muscles delivered unrelenting pain. I had gone from a trophy-winning track star to what could only be described as an invalid.

Slowly, in the depths of despair, the miracles began to unfold. Through a series of extraordinary and seemingly unrelated events, I found a healer. He was an M.D. who, as a result of quite different circumstances, suffered from similar symptoms. He began to ease my muscular problems, but he was also quick to address my spiritual sickness as well as asserting that above all else I was suffering from a broken heart. With his guidance and urging, along with the help of many others, I began a spiritual odyssey, searching for spiritual resolution while we all searched for a solution to my retreating strength. I started to dream vividly at night, wild dreams whose memories would remain accurate to the tiniest detail in the days that followed.

My intuition began to assert itself, and I slowly came to trust what I had for years discounted. More than once I awoke to two 'blue lights' hovering in my bedroom. I learned that if I looked for connections between my dreams and happenings during the day, and that if I trusted my intuition, events would unfold in the most mysterious and wonderful of ways.

Through much hard work and appropriate (finally) therapy, I had managed to stop my decline. However, I was not improving. I maintained a status quo through a regular schedule of trigger point injections, including injections into my occipital nerve at the base of my neck. My husband learned to give me shots at home in conjunction with what I saw as a worrisome, but necessary, regimen of painkillers.

Like it or not, for good or bad, I was hooked and now had the added fear my prescription might someday not be refilled. I needed the pills to get me through the day. The thought of losing my pills filled me with constant dread. It was the cruelest of ironies that the only relief to my pain was also a source of added anxiety. I was putting out the fire with gasoline, and the insidious cycle continued.

Then one night, I had one of my most spectacular and curious dreams. I was in the ocean, swimming near the shore but under the water, with a group of dolphins and a two-headed creature. My pain was gone and I was gloriously happy. Then, I looked up through the swirling current and could see a crowd of people on the beach, staring down at us intently through the water. They were hunting the two-headed creature, trying to drive away what to them was a source of fear, but what was to me a source of comfort.

I felt safe with the two-headed creature and our dolphin friends, and wanted to stay there with them under the water forever. The two-headed creature spoke to me, saying that I must return to the world above with the people on the beach, and that it must return to the deep. Neither of us were where we belonged. We could be together no more. I awoke the next morning and realized that the boys had spoken to me that night, telling me that I had to let them go.

That very day, a magazine arrived in the mail. My husband brought it to my chair in the bedroom. I opened it to an article describing Dolphin Spirit Hawaii and the work of the program directors, Doug and Trish. The article described how some people believe that dolphins' sonar heals at the cellular level. This string of events could not be ignored. Trusting my instincts, I decided that somehow I would go to Hawaii and swim with the Dolphins, though I could not walk as far as my kitchen to get food!

My husband, a 'scientific kind of guy,' bravely packed me up, took me to the airport, and waved encouragingly as I headed down the gangway. Slowly working my way to the plane, I felt like a little child heading out for her first day of school. I was full of excitement but also was haunted by self-doubt. Would I be strong enough to make the trip? Once there, could I manage in the water? What would happen if I really did encounter dolphins? I wasn't sure I had enough strength to make it to the plane, let alone swim in the ocean. Was I out of my mind???!!!! I couldn't do this! I had to fight to keep from returning to the safety of my home and support of my husband. I took a deep breath and thought, 'One foot in front of the other.'

I gained a bit of confidence once in Kona, as Doug and Trish put me patiently through my paces, learning to use the snorkel in some fabulous offshore locations. It took a mammoth struggle to keep up with the group, but they were compassionate, understanding and helpful. Then the big day came, and we loaded up on a catamaran and set out across the waves in search of our friends. I was filled with hope that we would hook up with a pod, but also filled with trepidation on how I would stand the physical test. Amazingly, on our very first day at sea, we met up with what Doug and Trish described as an unusually large pod of dolphins. I believe in my heart they found us rather than we finding them. Doug and Trish estimated the pod to number over one hundred.

The beautiful creatures seemed to call us into the water, waiting patiently and playfully as we all slowly but surely lowered ourselves into their world. Ever so slowly, I made my way from the boat until I found myself surrounded alone with a portion of the enormous pod. I was simultaneously marveling at their grace and at my own location. I was a long, long way from my bedroom in Scottsdale, Arizona.

As if on cue, the dolphins began to make their sounds. It seemed as though the entire group was bouncing their signals back and forth to us and to each other. As the sound waves bounced off my chest, I could feel my body begin to vibrate from the inside out. I became extremely, immediately ill. There I was, bobbing up and down in the ocean, sobbing, sputtering, throwing up, surrounded by singing dolphins.

I survived, but had to be helped back to the boat, then to the bus, then to my room at the hotel. I collapsed in my bed, exhausted from the intense physical and emotional experience, still feeling the after effects of my day with the dolphins. It had become typical for the wildest of my dreams to follow the most tiring of days. That night was no exception. I dreamed that while I lay in my bed, spirits of what seemed to be island natives ran over the top of me, chanting in a strange language. I awoke to find my pain level down, way, way down. For the first time in years, I went without taking my pain pills. In fact, that day I stopped taking them completely.

I left the plane in Arizona, and retraced my steps back through the gangway tunnel, only this time I ran to my waiting husband with a smile from ear to ear. The only smile in the airport that was bigger than mine was his. A week earlier, I barely had the energy to walk the same route! Now I was trotting along joyously, my heart full from the dolphin's gift.

That trip was a turning point for me. I had made this forbidding trip and endured a physical testing that reverberated deep into my soul. I had begun to release my brothers and let go of the pain and inner torment their deaths had caused. The cell shaking experience with the dolphins had restored me to such an incredible degree, I now had heart to continue my healing journey.

As the years have passed, I've made steady progress and finally know what it means to have good health. I truly believe my adventure with the dolphins was ordained. To this day, memories of my healing with the dolphins make my spirit soar!

CHAPTER THIRTY TWO

Relationship Intervention

by Mirra Rose

The first time I had a connection with dolphins was in Chicago at the zoo when I went to see the Dolphin and Whale Exhibit. I went in, sat down and watched while the dolphins and whales were playing around in the water. All of a sudden, I felt this consciousness come in and begin to speak to me. They let me know they were the dolphins and they loved me very much. I got the feeling their whole purpose in life was to play, have fun, experience joy and show human beings how to live in that consciousness.

Another significant experience was when I was in Florida visiting Key West. At the time, I was in a dysfunctional karmic relationship. I was deeply troubled and yet compelled and drawn to this person. I didn't know how to not be with him, even though I could see the relationship was holding me back. I was so consumed in the emotional instability, I couldn't work at all during that time. Finally, I was at a point where I had to make a choice between this dysfunctional relationship and doing my work, being held back or progressing spiritually.

In a particular key in Florida there was a wild dolphin named Sugar who had chosen to maroon herself. She was free to go back into the ocean, but chose to stay in this little bay and interact with humans. She had been interacting with people for quite a few years and was getting pretty old. When I went there, she was on the other side of the lagoon. I jumped in and began singing under water to her, and she came to me. I danced in the water and she got completely vertical and did the same thing, mirroring whatever I did. I felt it was a way to be with me, showing me she was aligning her energies with me. Finally I felt this overwhelming love and wanted to make some kind of connection, some kind of gesture of love and trust. I put out my hand and Sugar imme- diately opened her mouth and completely enveloped my whole arm. It was the lightest touch like an angel holding my hand. We looked at each other as she held my arm in her mouth and I trusted her. She trusted me. Finally she let go, and it was a complete blending of energies.

I felt like I had been embraced in my humanness in some kind of dolphin way that I didn't understand. It was a measure of Divine Consciousness with an aspect of Divine Love I had been seeking. An amazing transference of healing energy, it was helping me understand and reconcile my pain and loss, let go of my relationship, and go on with my life. Her choices as a dolphin were being reflected to me in a way that was profound. I felt it was a call for me to enter a life of greater service. To do that, I saw how important it was to free myself from that painful relationship.

Sugar's mission was to work with human beings, so she had given her whole life to that. It was her choice, a conscious choice and I am sure it was a big sacrifice, as dolphins are social beings who like to be in a pod. The ocean was open for her return and yet, here she was, helping me and others heal their hearts and change their lives. As my partner and I swam with her, it felt like she gave both of us a message to a part of us that wasn't fully conscious. In my case, I felt the message was, "You can trust the Universe. The Universe loves you and is going to embrace you no matter what you do, so you can leave this situation and go on to a kinder gentler world and create a story that is sweeter for yourself. Everything will be okay."

With the unexpected help of this dolphin, I was able to free myself from that painfully dysfunctional relationship and move on into a more rewarding and fulfilling life, where I was bringing out my work, progressing spiritually, and fulfilling a greater destiny. Like Sugar, my life path led me to helping many people throughout the world, which I have continued to this day.

Mirra Rose is an internationally acclaimed spiritual teacher and healer who has been sharing her gifts world-wide for over thirty years, touching thousands of people with her Loving Presence. Her primary mission is the empowerment of individuals to attain Divine Consciousness through a direct connection with the Soul. http://www.MirraRose.us.

CHAPTER THIRTY THREE

Purple Ray of Compassion

by Trish Regan

One morning, I was awakened at 7:00 AM sharp with a huge message to go see the dolphins. They were calling to me saying, "You must come now." I told my husband, Doug, the dolphins were calling and asked if he wanted to come with me and he agreed to come along, as did a woman who was staying with us. Both of them were busy preparing breakfast and I knew I could not wait. I made plans to have them meet me down at the bay near our home on the island of Hawaii.

I went to the first place where the dolphins come in and there were no dolphins. I knew I was going to see them because I could feel them calling me. I went into my heart and asked, "Where should I go?" The answer came, "Go to the next bay." So I drove to that bay, which was much smaller. When I got there, I counted 78 dolphins. I noticed there was no one else around. I went into the water and soon, I was surrounded by dolphins. There were so many swimming all around me. It was very powerful and amazing.

After I was swimming with them for about five minutes or so, I suddenly got the message they were there to help me bring through the Purple Ray of Compassion. I had just learned about this ray at the dolphin seminar we had held that had ended the day before. A Universal Angel had come to work with our group so we could bring this light through our crown chakra to our heart and then send it out into the world together. This had been a very profound experience for everyone present. Now I was being guided to do this exercise again to send this purple ray out to all the areas in the world where there was strife, conflict, and war. I understood the dolphins were going to assist this energy to flow through me.

I started consciously bringing in the diamond shaped Purple Ray of Compassion as the Angel had taught us. I brought it through my crown chakra into my heart and then I sent this ray of light out to the Middle East. Immediately I saw an Arab and a Jew hugging each other, both with deep compassion for each other. I could feel it in my whole body and experienced being each of them and what they had gone through. I felt all of the past aggression, with the thousands of years of strife and conflict, melting out of my body as my heart opened to receive the love from the other person as my love went out to him. This compassion was surrounding us and filling us. It was so real.

Then I took the Purple Ray to Ireland and I saw the Catholics and the Protestants coming together in the same way. Once again I felt I was them, experiencing both sides of their ongoing drama and what their lives had been like. The compassion once again surrounded and filled us and love prevailed.

The next place I went was to Bosnia. I experienced the two factions coming together with compassion and love. Then I went to Africa and continued this process. To my amazement, after fifteen minutes of doing this, the water turned a brilliant purple around me. I was incredulous. I shut my eyes and thought, "Oh, it must be the way the sun is shining on the water." I opened my eyes again and the dolphins were all around me and the water was bright purple.

I continued bringing the Purple Ray of Compassion all over the world and also worked with all the people in my life. Soon I became filled with a blissful ecstatic state of consciousness that was the essence of love and compassion. I would bring this compassion to each person, hug them, and feel this incredible blissful state of oneness with them.

I continued this process for a long time with the dolphins, when looking at my watch, I saw it had lasted an hour and a half. All of a sudden, I was drawn out of this incredibly expansive state when I felt this presence next to me in the water. I pulled my head out of the water and looked up and right next to me was a woman in a kayak who was screaming and yelling at me. She was enraged because she felt I was harassing the dolphins by swimming with them.

A Caucasian woman married to a Hawaiian man, I learned she lived in the area right by the ocean. She told me, screaming, cussing, and cursing, "You're harassing the dolphins, get out of here, get away, move away. What are you doing? My husband has been yelling at you for an hour and you haven't even looked up!" I looked over to the shore and saw a Hawaiian man screaming and yelling at me with all this rage and the interesting thing was that while all this rage was coming toward me, it was just going right through my body. I wasn't taking it in at all. Normally I do not like people getting angry with me. It usually scares me, but I was in this state of grace and remained untouched by the force of negative energy blasting me from these angry people.

All I could do was look at her with love and compassion. Finally I started to explain, saying to her, "I'm not harassing the dolphins. I am here on a spiritual mission." I didn't defend myself. I simply stated the facts. In this spirit of love and compassion I continued, saying, "I am sorry you are so upset about this, but the truth is, the dolphins brought me here to do this work."

Angry and locked into her position, she couldn't hear me at all. Finally she became so enraged, she just turned around and left. By then, the dolphins had gone way down to the other end of the bay, while I remained in a state of compassion. I said to myself, "I know I have done the work I was here to do. I don't want to upset these people anymore.".So, I began swimming in to shore. I could see her husband running over to meet me. Normally, I would have kept swimming even if I had to swim two miles to get away from conflict. It was a strange feeling to find myself still swimming towards him.

As I swam over to him, I was amazed by the state of love I was remaining in. Meanwhile, there were now a lot of people watching the scene, and of course I wouldn't have wanted to be humiliated and screamed at in front of them, but something within me kept moving me forward. I got out of the water and the angry screaming man was right in my face yelling at the top of his lungs, while the people around us stared at what was going on stupefied. He was calling me horrible names and saying, "Get out of here, you're harassing the dolphins! What do you think you are doing?"

I remember looking into his eyes and feeling to myself, "I bet he is really a wonderful guy inside. I bet I could really like him." I felt all this love for this man and his anger was just flowing right through me. I began to explain to him, "I am sorry I am upsetting you, but I know I am here on a spiritual mission with the dolphins. We believe the dolphins are here to teach us to live in harmony." I was speaking in a normal voice simply stating the facts and I could see he was beginning to soften a little bit.

All of a sudden I burst out crying because I realized this experience was a metaphor for war. We were two good people. He was a good person who really cared about the dolphins and I was a good person who also cared about the dolphins. We just had different belief systems about them. Here we were having a conflict over our disagreements and misunderstandings.

Tears poured down my face as I cried for people in strife everywhere and the conflict taking place all over the world. I felt a connection with all of the people of the world, one with all that they were experiencing in their individual conflicts, and it broke my heart. Somehow, when I got it, he got it. Suddenly he shifted. He came over to me closer, put his hand on my shoulder and said, "Look, I can see you are really a good person and I should never talk to anybody like that. I am so sorry. I can see that you do care. I am never going to do that again."

At that point I knew we could have a dialogue so I said to him, "Are you concerned that it is their sleep time because it is so early?"

He said, "Yes, in another hour there will be twenty people out there."

I said, "Maybe you are right, maybe I could come down a little later next time. Does it look to you like I am chasing after them?"

He said, "Yes, when you dove down it looked like you were trying to catch their tails."

I said, "Oh, no, no, I would never do that! They like us to play with them. They enjoy it when we dive down. Its fun to swim around and be with them." By then his wife came over and she had this piece of paper in her hand. She was still very angry and said, "I called the authorities."

He said, "No, no, no, she's okay, she's really okay." So the wife came over and we were able to talk and she said, "It looks like they are really angry because they keep blowing out of the top of their heads."

I said, "No, actually that is how they breathe." These people had total misconceptions of the dolphins, but at last she had come to a place of dialogue where we began to understand each other. Finally it was time for me to leave, so I asked their names. We shook hands and I said, "They are our spiritual teachers. We believe they are here to teach us how to live in harmony."

He answered, "We are spiritual too. Maybe we can help each other."

I said, "Yes, whenever we are out there swimming, if we see people who are trying to chase the dolphins, we can gently teach them the right way to be in respect." He shook his head in acknowledgment. Then I said, "We also always ask permission of the ancient Hawaiian Spirits before we enter into their sacred waters."

He said, "Okay, then we really can work together." We both noticed the dolphins were still out there. Looking at me he said, "Go ahead," somehow knowing I had to go. As I left, we hugged each other and said goodbye. Through compassion, the whole situation had completely turned around.

I believe the dolphins brought me down there to experience the Purple Ray of Compassion through the planetary healing work I did, and also through this personal experience of healing conflict with another person. I had learned the Art of True Compassion and seen for myself how the most intense situation can be turned around. From this experience, I believe in my heart that if any two people can come to that healing space we entered, no matter how challenging the division, then it is possible for the world to do the same. It takes each one of us to make that conscious choice to move into compassion rather than stay in the conflicts we are in. Through compassion, we can come to understand the other person and to find resolution, creating peace on Earth rather than perpetuating the conflicts that lead to war. I believe this is what the dolphins are here to teach us.

Trish Regan, Visionary Writer and Intuitive Soul Reader, is the author of the book series, Essential Joy: Finding It, Keeping It, Sharing It. She cofounded Dolphin\Spirit of Hawaii with her husband, Doug Hackett, in 1994 in response to a powerful calling by the dolphins and Spirit to take a leap of faith, leave their professional lives, and move to Hawaii to work with wild dolphins. Since that time they have co-facilitated life changing dolphin-swim retreats in Hawaii and whale-swim retreats in the Kingdom of Tonga. Trish travels the world facilitating uplifting spiritually expanding workshops. She also has produced many enlightening CDs and DVDs for spiritual enhancement. She offers Soul Readings and Light Activations globally. Find out more at http://www.dolphinspiritof-hawaii.com and on Trish Regan's Blog: http://www.trishregan.com.

CHAPTER THIRTY FOUR

Dolphins Protected Our Beaches from Sharks

by Robert Frey

Throughout my childhood, I used to have a lot of dreams of dolphins. I dreamed of swimming with them, of communicating with them underwater, and having physical contact with them in the water. I have dreamed of them jumping into the sunset and amazing things like that. I had an experience that very few people have had.

When I was a kid growing up in Florida I learned that the dolphins controlled our beaches and protected us from the dangerous predator sharks that frequented that area.

One time I saw a pod of dolphins kill a big shark. It was an astounding thing to see happen just offshore from one of our favorite beaches, which was always filled with people.

The dolphins circled around the shark and then trapped it in their circle. Then one of the dolphins broke out of the circle, diving down deep into the water underneath them. It shot up in full speed and hit the shark with the hard part of its head making it fly up into the air with the dolphin. Then another dolphin took off and soon I saw the shark and dolphin flying through the air. This kept happening every couple minutes until the shark was dead. I realized then that the dolphins were protecting the beaches for the people.

I had always heard the dolphins were our protectors and now I was close enough to see it with my own eyes. From that time on, I always felt safe swimming in that area, knowing I was being watched over and protected. This confidence remained with me as I became an adult and traveled to other regions, enjoying the ocean there.

freediving
Dolphin Adventure

by Ted Roe

Freediving is the art of deep swimming without SCUBA tanks.
It is complex and anyone interested in freediving is advised
to take a course and learn how to do it properly.

Dive 23 - April 8, 2005

I had been in Hawaii for a couple weeks practicing breath-hold diving prior to taking a freediving course. I was trying to break through below one hundred feet, because the advanced course requires that ability as a prerequisite. Every day I would practice ever deeper dives and then go for a hundred foot-plus one. Unfortunately, I couldn't judge the depth of the water below me and kept hitting sand. Dive to 97 feet, hit sand. Dive to 99 feet, hit sand. It was close, but it wasn't what I went there to do.

Freediving is a powerful way to integrate with the sea and is the primary reason for my pursuit of the skill and training. The ability to swim to any place one chooses is the way a bird flies to a branch. Diving down to one hundred fifty feet is a profound meditation. With respect to the discipline of deep swimming, there is a definite Zen to it. I have never seen a quicker path to actualization. One could do ZaZen for twenty years and not get to a point of actualization. With freediving, it brings you right there. The breath work and diving reflex take you into the present naturally as you explore and express your aquatic nature.

When freediving, I feel a huge connection between the water, the sky and the space beyond. I am suspended in it and connected to it. I have no idea where that will go with future experiences, but the sensation of calm and presence in the moment is marked, which is one of the main reasons I enjoy this practice and teach it as a mind/body discipline. I can call up the sensation at will and my heart rate starts to slow down.

On the last day of my practice period, a pod of spinner dolphins came into the bay and my son, KC, and I spent an hour swimming with them. I did some swims at 45 to 80 feet just to be with the group. We didn't disturb them much, just got close enough to look them over while they rested. I took some great pictures of resting dolphins with my Cheapo deluxe camera. Then, after enough dolphin play, I decided to try to break 100 feet one last time. I was in at least one 150 feet of water, so I knew I was deep enough. Although there were some snorkelers on the surface, there were unfortunately no divers capable of backing me up for safety. However, there were the dolphins.

I had always wondered about them. You hear the stories about dolphins helping injured or drowning humans. For some reason I knew I had all the support I needed. I felt adequately "breathed up" and decided to dive near the dolphins and see if they noticed. I was certain they would.

The dolphins were swimming in a resting pattern, about thirty to forty in a line abreast at about 55 feet. They would swim in a gigantic circle and every two to three minutes you would see them coming into view at depth. They would come up for a couple of breaths every four or five minutes. There were several who were feeling more playful and had been interacting with us.

I checked my dive watch and made sure that the alarm was set for 95 feet. It would go on as I crossed 95 feet and continue beeping until I returned above 95 feet. I began my breathe-up to prepare my body and mind for the dive. I treat this part of the practice as a ritual. It should be done consistently, the same way every time. Some of the confidence free divers have comes from knowing the pre-dive breathing ritual has been completed in proper form. You know it works because it works.

Free divers also use an altered state of physical and psychological being called the "mammalian diving reflex." This is physical syndrome characterized by slowing of the heart rate and often radically. This state of reduced blood pressure yields an altered psychological state. One is still metabolizing oxygen, but it is being caused by the hydrostatic pressure forcing gas into tissues so one is fully conscious with a very reduced heart rate. In this state one can dive quite deeply and comfortably. This state is initiated by specific cues that we give our bodies during the warm up phase of a freediving session.

I felt I was a little tired, but I was breathed up anyway so when the row of dolphins appeared to be heading my way, I paused and then I kicked over and dove. Kicking steadily I fell about 30 feet in front of their line abreast formation as I passed them at about 45 feet deep. I continued my descent into the glide or sink phase. This is my favorite part of the dive. You just stop kicking and fall, accelerating as gravity pulls you. Its like flying and if you are doing it right, you are moving at 3 feet per second, sometimes much faster, and I was. All you have to do is equalize the pressure in your ears and mask as you fall.

At 75 feet I heard several inquisitive whistles and clicks. I angled my fin blade to cause me to rotate 360 degrees as I sank and saw four dolphins around me, watching me. They would whistle and click interrogatively, cast their nostrums about, and try to look into my face mask, seemingly very concerned. When I hit 95 feet, my depth alarm on my D3 wrist computer went off and I began counting beeps as I continued my descent. I was feeling pretty good nearly forty seconds into the descent phase. Finally, at forty three seconds, I flared out and hovered at forty meters (132 feet), and there were my four dolphins acting quite animated.

I looked up and the people on the surface looked tiny. There was nothing to compare them to. I had never been so deep. Forty three seconds at negative three feet per second. I continued sinking as I was negatively buoyant. The blue was the bluest, the surface was far away and the sand, rock and coral were 20 feet below.

That few moments on the bottom of the dive was interesting. There are layers, inversions of clear and cloudy water. I was in a very clear place and could see quite a ways at my own level. The sense of being separated from the safety of a continuous air supply on the surface was present. It is serious business, but not nagging or demanding. I was only slightly nervous at the lack of support swimmers. For some reason the dolphins were adequate.

At this point I was experiencing bradycardia (a slowness of the heartbeat) and feeling quite calm and comfortable. The dolphins were present, but not overbearing. It was a very long and full couple of seconds. It's quiet down there. Not silent, you can hear fish talking and eating coral and such, but it is very peaceful. I looked up, picked a snorkeler on the surface as a target and then I began my ascent, first, with a dolphin kick and then switching to a stereo kick. The four dolphins took positions around me and quite close. They traveled at my pace as I headed upward.

The swim was hard and the monster was on my shoulder early, meaning my lungs had naturally collapsed as I descended to those depths and now my chest felt so tight I could barely breathe. I was wondering where I had gone wrong. Had I had been distracted and dove too deep for my breathe-up? Maybe I wasn't entirely ready to dive when I did. My fins felt mushy and the ascent was slow. It took ages to pass 100 feet. My alarm stopped shortly thereafter, I looked up again, focused and continued my ascent, looking into the deep blue.

Then I blinked and realized I could no longer see blue water around me because of all the dolphins. In fact, the whole pod of some thirty plus had joined me in my swim to the surface. They were everywhere except between me and the surface. I was in a whirling mass of dolphins determined not to let me drown. I could have hugged six of them at a time. Their flukes, pectorals and dorsal fins would occasionally touch me. I could feel them at my back and all around me. To my amazement they created an "S" shaped protective pressure wave with me at the center, dolphins behind and a little above me, with more at my chest and below. I was "drafting" in the group as we all moved upward together to the surface in the same way bicycle racers or race cars get close behind each other to minimize resistance.

As I traveled upward, I was becoming severely uncomfortable. Finally, I had a little relief at 60 feet when the vacuum effect occurred (gases returning to my lungs) and relaxed, as my lungs inflated. I kept kicking and broke the surface, dolphin friends in tow 44 seconds from my turnaround at 132 feet. Watching the snorkelers as a point of reference, I brought the entire pod right to them. For the rest of the day people were stopping me when I was out of the water to comment on what they had seen that morning.

I consider this to be empathic behavior. The dolphins were very willing to intervene on my behalf, and it was clear to me that was what they were doing. While in the diving reflex one can sense intention and intuition strongly. When you meet, you are no longer human and they are no longer dolphins. You are simply two conscious beings sharing information. It is a profound sensation of connectedness.

Ted Roe, owner and operator of Everblue Freediving LLC, teaches freed-iving as a spiritual practice. It has many similarities with Yoga, Kung Fu, or other mind/body disciplines. A main focus of the training is to initiate the mammalian diving reflex, an altered state of physical and psychological being that allows us our highest expression in the sea. For more info see: www.everbluefreediving.com. Ted can be reached at: Lungfish@everbluefreediving.com. His video clips of dolphins can be found on Youtube.

Part Six

Communications

Communications

We speak to you
Lovers of the World
Valiant Ones who have come to turn the tides
Of disasters long been foretold.
You are a part of the Great Awakening and we,
Your Initiators of Life
That you may live more gloriously true to who you are and
In Awakening to your Self
Know you are the Savior of the world.
It is not an outer reality we would call you to but
An Inner Knowing that sets you free from
The bondage passed down by an unconscious humanity
Fed to young ones that they might learn to be unfree.
No, we call you to Fairer Realms
Within your Soul Awareness
That within you that
Dwells within us and all life
That True Essence that speaks to who you are.
We would have you Awaken from your slumber
Take your place with us for the turning of the tides
Bring Joy into every part of your life
And in Loving bring forth the New Truth.
Humanity, we await you
We come with Wisdom, listen to our words
Feel our hearts, bask in our Presence and
Know we are True Friends
Here to lead you to the New World

- The Dolphins

A Message From the Dolphins

Interacting with dolphins over the years, I many times received messages of encouragement and deep truths that have touched my soul profoundly. Now, at last, I can share a most precious message from the dolphins with the world.

Their messages have come to me telepathically and in this case I was in the quiet sanctuary of my home, in a meditative state, rather than swimming with them in the ocean. Always, they speak with such eloquence and grace. That they can communicate on these clear channels with humankind is such an incredible experience. Their attunement to us as a race is a wondrous thing. That they care so much for each one of us, is evident in all the healings and life transformations taking place all over the planet with individuals now interacting with them on most every continent.

Their message to humanity speaks of this great love and dedication to our planet. Their assurance that they are here to help guide us through a positive planetary transformation is awe inspiring to say the least. In this momentous time in history one thing is evident, the dolphins are our true friends, here to lend their magic in this time of great transition. Here is their message, released to me on 11.11.06.

From the Dolphins

It is with great love that we send this message out to the world of humankind through this dear vessel. Many of you are witnessing the increase in our interactions with the human world, with you, our brothers and sisters. We bring timely messages to encourage you at this great time in the history of our planet.

As some of you are aware, this time on Earth is very critical in that the worst can take place as well as the highest and best, and this depends largely upon what will take place in these next few years and the choices being made collectively by all conscious life forms.

Your analogs hold the prophecies from all times and these can be dire to say the least. On Earth we see the culmination of many past histories revealed in the Earth's present state. Unsafety has been a main theme and it touches all life upon this planet. There is nowhere on this Earth to escape the Dark Night that is upon is. This is being outplayed in many forms. What one feels, all are feeling, and thus we are connected in the web of life. Conscious choices must be made if Earth is going to pass through a smooth transition into a glorious future.

We have watched the histories on Earth unfold. We have seen Golden Ages rise and fall. We have stepped in to assist many times. In Greece, we were able to connect with many great souls who were inspired by our message and way of life. The result was a great and glorious age. In this time we have decided once again to make ourselves known to those who are able to embrace us in the fullest sense, for we are conscious beings with conscious intentions that Earth may rise into a great and glorious age unlike anything that has been seen in the past.

We focus then on those who are open to our message and to our assistance. This assistance we bring on many levels. Those of you who are the most awake and aware have come into resonance with us. Your transformation and healing of all the schisms in your psyches is essential at this time, for as the inner is brought into resonance with the radiant Flame of Life, you become one with all life everywhere and true brotherhood exists.

There is a time for contemplation and a time for reverence. We have entered a most precious time where many lives are being transformed, and we are here to assist in this process. When you place yourself in our hands, we are able to facilitate a most wondrous and deep transformation on the deepest levels of your being.

We bring healing and a message of living in harmony with all life. The first responsibility is to heal all the warring and inharmony within. As you come into balance and wholeness, you affect all other parts of life, who too can rise up inspired and take their place in the wondrous drama on Earth unfolding.

Prayer, meditation, and communing with your Inner Self allows you to enter the Holy of Holies within your temples, that sacred space where we are all connected and one. In oneness, all experiences become one in the Sea of Life. Sharing on deep levels, there is a true brotherhood among all life streams. This is the place where we meet you.

We are here to assist you through Earth's transition. We come bearing good tidings of what can be. We help to facilitate healing and transformation within your beings so you can meet us in this sacred place where we are one.

Dwell on our words and know the truth of what we speak. We are your friends. Unite with us and allow the swift changes that come from being in our presence, for we live in a Sea of Oneness so vast it envelopes your consciousness when you align with us.

We have ever been the messengers in the seas guiding you to the safe shore of beingness. Rest assured, we shall continue to contact every one of you needing our assistance at this sacred time in Earth's history. We remain ever true to the purpose for which we dwell with you in the Earth body.

Touch the place within where you can soar in the vast spaces of universal beingness with us. Feel the Freedom of Life lived on these levels and in this conscious awareness. Be true to your Self and know the victory of Earth's full transformation into a Planet of Light is at hand! Your friends, the Dolphins.

CHAPTER THIRTY SEVEN

Dolphin Elders

by Daniel McCulloch

It was dusk and getting dark fast. Danger warning signals were going off in my wife, as the waters became choppy and visibility dramatically lessened. She was nursing our one year old while steering the boat, monitoring our rambunctious 3 year old, who was running around the boat, and trying to keep track of me as I swam before her in the now darkening waters. Not wanting to break the flow, I continued filming the dolphins. I didn't want to give way to the conditions, but on the other hand, I didn't want to die. Finally, the situation had become increasingly dangerous and Jana couldn't see me anymore.

Unaware of what was going on for her, I kept moving into trust that my wife would be able to keep track of me. There comes a time, though, when it is so choppy and dark, you can't see anyone in the water any longer. There were a couple of times she really panicked.

One of my reasons for not wanting to stop was I was being gifted a very rare privilege of swimming with a huge group of elders. Being dusk, with dolphin elders keeping to slightly deeper water, I could get some great footage. I knew I had only a short time left, as it was getting so dark the camera would no longer be able to capture a clear picture.

Typically, when dolphins are going to cruise away from you, they drop down to the bottom taking breaths more infrequently (1 – 3 minutes), but when they are set to travel distance, they take much longer times between breaths, sinking to the bottom and cruising along. You can feel them totally melt into a relaxed place and you know that breath is going to take them a long way away.

Though it was getting very dark and I didn't have much energy left, these were a group of dolphins I had been waiting to film for a long time. They had just dropped down and were cruising away. I could see them taking off way down below me. Finally I said, "Sorry guys, but I just cannot follow you anymore. Bye!" They were way, way down there and in that moment, they all turned around and came back up to be with me. This was a real experience with telepathic communication or what I call 'telempathic' communication because of the real emotional component. It was not just a high frequency mental thing. It was a real emotional communication to them.

"Ah, I would really like to go on with you, but I just can't. I can't dive down one more time." It was letting go on my part. Within seconds later, they came back up to join me. There is no way to scientifically validate this experience, but to me there was no question they perceived what I felt and thought, and they responded by coming back up to swim with me some more. Despite the danger and Jana's angst, it all worked out and I got some really great footage of a group of this species that rarely ever interact with humans.

The first time I had connected with the elders was when I was in Bimini some years before. I had been in contact with a woman who was in the dive operations doing dolphin trips for some time before the trip and we had talked about different ways of communicating and interacting with dolphins. In her training, she had learned to chase and circle the dolphins. I suggested she use a more gentle approach. I used the analogy that if a guy is trying to hit on woman using an aggressive sexual approach, he is not going to see the real woman. Its the same with the dolphins. With an aggressive approach, you will never get to be with the wiser, deeper dolphins or see the depth of their real self. You have to be gentle.

Early one morning we went out alone. In front of us we saw two elders cruising very slowly. I slipped into the water and very gently came up behind them. They both looked at me and let me come up just behind and between them. As we swam, I realized I was witnessing two wise people communicating with each other. It gave me a wonderful feeling. With the spotted dolphins, you can tell the elders because they are very chunky. They are much slower and when you look in their eyes they are much more all pervading. Usually you will see one or two elders on the edge of the pod when you are swimming with the dolphins.

In the group you will see mothers with young ones and maybe some males too, and then there will be an elder who cruises around the periphery holding an overview. Typically you don't see a lot of elders or have the opportunity to swim with them.

One time swimming at night in the water I was scared because it was so dark. It was one of those times I had promised myself I would go down without a camera and just be with the dolphins. I have always regretted it. I spent about an hour with a group of dolphins when one of the dolphins came and befriended me, staying by my side for a long time, maybe an hour. I felt deep emotions come up as I swam with this dolphin. There was something very sad about him. I couldn't tell if I was projecting that or if I was really experiencing his feelings. Then I noticed that his two pectoral fins were totally chewed up. I kept thinking this dolphin had sacrificed itself for some reason, saving young ones or old ones, or something. Dolphins can do quite a bit with those pectoral fins. I felt he had fended something off. His fins were so shredded.

One of my most impressive telepathic experiences with dolphins was some years ago earlier on in my search. I have been out with the dolphins since 1987, and the wild dolphins since 1988. Each time I went out for a new season, I would experience a tremendous welcome. The dolphins would interact in an excited way. I would recognize dolphins I had named, like Little Notch who had a v-shaped notch on his body.

I have always felt there is another level of telepathy, which is unified consciousness or a connected collective consciousness which is a simultaneous knowingness. I have felt the dolphins in that immediate, spontaneous, connected state where there is no transmission of information, and where all are experiencing the same thing at the same time. So one of these times when I first went out, I was suddenly with a mother and small baby and typically in the beginning, the mother would always stay between the baby and me.

The baby wanted to connect with the human and the mother was staying between us, keeping a safe distance while monitoring the engagement. Suddenly I was very close to the mother and saw the baby peeking over her to look at me. I could have touched the baby it was so close. I found myself telling the mother, "It is okay to bring your baby close to me, because I am totally safe, I am pure love. I only have love." Then my mind said, "You didn't say that! She said it!"

Then the Mama Whale said, "I am here bringing my baby so close to you because I know you are pure love and it is safe." Wow! The next thing clicked in my mind and I realized neither of us had said it. We both just knew it. Instantaneous knowing. I didn't say it, she didn't say it, we just knew it. With that, I experienced a collective consciousness where we were both experiencing the same thing at the same time. There was no time involved, there was no information being relayed, it was just a mutual knowingness, a state of grace and it was ecstatic, an emotional, ecstatic connectedness in love and safety between us, right there under the water.

Since that moment, I've often encountered mothers with babies who allow their baby to be between us. That was a noticeable shift from what I had experienced before. It was as if the dolphin mothers now knew I was safe, that I was love, and that we could meet in love. This experience supported the validation of the collective consciousness for me. I had witnessed some kind of collective etheric consciousness with these dolphins, where the safety and trust established with the first mother and baby somehow made it known by the other mothers. It was like a hundredth dolphin experience, where they all knew it as soon as it happened and now it was arranged that I could be close to the babies whenever we met.

I have found that dolphins embrace us as much as they embrace their own. When we are willing to relate and play, they will play with us and they love it. They even seem to be able to see through us and see what area we need healing.

Daniel's devotion to the dolphins inspired his commitment to showing the world that we share this planet with a truly sentient species who, history has shown us, have been actively reaching out to us in the wild, to intelligently interact with us in all sorts of ways. He takes people out to swim with friendly free-roaming dolphins in the wild ocean to give people an intimate experience with them, in their own environment on their own terms. The extraordinary experience of being greeted by these dolphins in their own habitat, whether in wild play or serene intimate eye contact, is so exhilarating and uplifting that many people consider it a spiritual experience. Daniel revels in taking people to have this experience. This relationship between dolphin and human is the main focus of Daniel's passion, the focus of his current photography, and the subject of his photography book on the relationship between human and dolphins, historical and contemporary. For more information on Daniel and his offerings please see: http://www.dolphinsynergy.com

CHAPTER THIRTY EIGHT

Protectress of the Deep

by Morning Star Black

In 1990, I was doing healing work with my childhood abuse issues when someone gave me a crystal dolphin. One night I was holding it in my hand and felt like it wanted to speak to me. I put the dolphin to my ear and 'she' began to tell me a fantastic story. This is what she told me.

"I am the Protectress of the Deep. I live in the bottom of the ocean where the rainbow makes a complete circle. We have a crystal city there where we bring the children who are crossing over or who are in such a terrible situation they have asked for help. We bring them down to the city by putting a bubble of air around them so they can breathe and they learn to not be afraid very quickly." She took me down there in my mind and I experienced the feeling of breathing in the water. I soon lost my fears because I trusted her and believed her. Soon the experience was invigorating and freeing and we swam with no effort or hardship. Before I knew it, there was light and a shining group of crystal buildings appeared before us. I felt such peace, joy and wonder at this sight. We moved closer to the city. It was very large and beautiful.

The Protectress said, "The children are safe and happy here. There is no pain or suffering, only joy and peace." Leaving, I knew I could come back here anytime I wanted. After this experience I began to see paintings of my experience on greeting cards with children and dolphins and children in bubbles. I knew others must have had the same experience to create such pictures.

I was 41 when I received this message. I have never forgotten the dolphins and the peace, beauty, joy and wonder of this time. My heart is forever changed for the better. I dream of the dolphins, pray for them, and draw from the peace offered by them.

CHAPTER THIRTY NINE

Language of Dolphins

by Paula Peterson

I was a curious little bug that inspired me to write about dolphin language and the special way they communicate. When it perched itself on the edge of a stack of books next to my computer, something happened that startled me.

As I reached out to grab the critter, it suddenly sprung from the edge while belting out a tiny, but gleeful, "Wheeeeeeeeeeee!" (I swear I really did hear it!) I was so caught off-guard by the bizarre occurrence that I got a good laugh. It was so darned cute. You probably think I'm daffy unless you're someone who has similar kinds of experiences. Nevertheless, just because we're not raised to believe in such things doesn't mean they don't happen.

Many years ago I was scuba diving with a group off the coast of the Channel Islands west of the California coast. It's a gorgeous area and a diver's delight with its lush, colorful, and abundant sea life. In this particular area of open ocean it's legal for divers on air-tanks to capture live abalone.

This was a stage in my life where I had successfully eliminated all animals from my diet - except for sea food - which is anything that lives in a shell, as well as squid and octopus. It was the food most difficult for me to give up eating, as I had an insatiable craving for the taste of it, especially when caught fresh and eaten within hours of its capture.

During one of numerous diving trips to the Channel Islands, I found myself at a depth of about 30 feet and temporarily separated from my diving partner. I was drawn to explore a large, rocky mound nearby, the kind of area that abalone are likely to be found. Sure enough, I spotted a huge abalone "grazing" on the side of the rocky surface.

When an abalone feels threatened it will instantly clamp its shell down hard onto the rock to protect its soft underside. Once they do this, it's nearly impossible to get them off. That's why abalone divers carry a tool called an ab-iron: a long, flat, solid piece of metal used to pry them off rocks. As I thrust my ab-iron hard underneath the abalone's shell I heard a tiny, but very distinct, scream. (Again, I swear I really did hear it!). Stunned, I immediately withdrew the tool and stared in horror at the abalone. I felt terrible. Suddenly, I was jolted to the reality that even though this creature didn't have a face like the other animals I had given up eating, it was still a living, feeling, conscious creature that feels pain, experiences fear, and fiercely protects itself from injury or death... a living being that wants to live! Needless to say, that was the last time I went hunting for abalone, and never again have I eaten another creature.

As strange as it might seem, many indigenous tribes throughout the world speak of a time in the ancient past when humans and animals "spoke" to one another. These claims are also found in ancient texts. Likewise, it's interesting that some of the most beloved tales of young and old alike are those in which animals talk, dress, and behave like humans.

Deep down inside, many of us would love to have clear and understandable communication with animals, especially with our beloved pets. Personally, I feel that genuine communication with real animals isn't based on a verbal language, which is quite limiting at best. Rather, it's based on telepathy. Even more so, it's based on telempathy, a word that isn't found in the dictionary yet. Why do I say this? The following is a personal story that you may find intriguing.

Several years ago, I traveled from California with two friends on an adventure to the Puget Sound, an inland sea of great expanse between British Columbia and the state of Washington. It's a magnificent, breathtaking area. Hundreds of wind-swept, mountainous islands of pine forests range from very small and uninhabitable to large enough for communities of one or two hundred families.

Our goal was to hire a guide to take us out in kayaks and get as close as possible to the great Orcas (aka Killer Whales) that live in this area. Since Orcas are not really whales at all and are actually a species of dolphin, we were quite excited about contacting these highly intelligent "humans-of-the-sea."

Once we had our guide and were secured in our individual kayaks, we paddled off toward the deepest and widest part of the Puget

Sound where the Orcas were the most frequently sighted. Since they travel in pods of five or more, there would be no trouble in spotting them once their stately dorsal fins rise above the water which happens often when they surface to breathe.

We had paddled for most of the afternoon without seeing any sign of them and were soon becoming discouraged. It was getting late and we would have to return to our departure point before losing the light of day, but then, we saw a pod of Orcas, their dorsal fins high and surging through the waters. They were moving in a direction that would take them right across our path if we paddled faster.

With great excitement, we paddled with all the strength we had left to reach the spot where our paths would meet the Orcas. Much to our dismay, the Orcas were swimming so fast and powerful that we soon saw that we wouldn't reach them in time. After all our planning, the long drive from California, and tiresome hours of paddling, we would have just missed them.

At that moment, I went deep, deep and deeper still, into my heart and soul to feel the swell of love I had for these great creatures. Then silently, yet passionately, I inwardly pleaded, "Please, please, Orcas.... show yourselves to us."

Instantly, a powerful surge of effervescent energy blasted through my entire body. Every cell felt like fizzy, sparkling, bubbling light. Then one colossal Orca leaped completely out of the water, and then three Orcas leapt out of the water in unison! We were whooping and hollering with glad tears in our eyes. Our guide was ecstatic, remarking that in all the years he'd been taking people out in kayaks to see the Orcas, he had never seen a display like that.

A rosy glow shone from my head to my toes for three days afterward. I felt wonderful. From that awesome experience, I realized that the key to communion, truly communicating with the dolphins, Orcas, whales and with all living creatures, is through the "language" of the heart.

The Dolphins' Turn

After returning from the Caribbean with a group of friends and having a long wait at the international airport in Florida for our departure flight back to California, we decided to use the extra hours to go to the nearby amusement park and aquarium. We immediately went to the

Performing Dolphins pool, a huge tank several levels deep. At each level and around the full diameter of the tank were large, thick observation windows which gave tourists a good view of the dolphins under water.

There were crowds of people at the windows that day, all gawking and chattering with excitement. I had separated from my friends for a few moments to savor more time in watching the dolphins. While standing there at one of the windows, one dolphin abruptly stopped at the window right in front of me, faced me, and started moving his mouth wildly as if trying to talk.

At first, I found it amusing that out of all these people looking through the windows, this dolphin was picking me out. I thought to myself, "Ah, just a coincidence, I'm sure." With that thought, the dolphin immediately left, swam around for a short while, and then parked himself right in front of me again to look me square in the eye while moving his mouth as if speaking.

Whoa! I quickly realized that my heart was pounding loud and fast. What's going on here? Surely this is only another coincidence. He left again, only to come right back a third time and went through the same motions. By this time, I'm having a "religious, mystical experience." My heart was throbbing, my eyes swelling with tears, and a wonderful, warm, and tingly energy was flowing from my chest throughout my body. The dolphin swam off again, so I decided to dash off to grab one of my friends. "Hey, you've got to come and check out this dolphin!"

After blurting out a quick report of what happened, we both waited for the next exciting visit, and waited and waited and waited. The dolphin didn't come back and nothing happened. By that time I was feeling pretty stupid. My friend finally got bored, flashed a courtesy smile, and walked off to catch up with the others.

There I was, feeling silly and foolish, when here comes that dolphin again. He stopped to face me, we had eye contact, and he went through all the same motions again. I finally got it. Our shared experience was meant for me alone. After that, I had a telepathic connection with that dolphin that lasted for weeks.

Once back home in California, I would think of that dolphin in the huge tank, his eye looking into mine, searching. At night, I could feel that tingly energy again and instant thoughts of him would flood my mind. I never felt he had complaints about his confinement, although, there seemed to be a somewhat anxious quality to his energy. I would imagine so, after having been stolen from his home in the sea and no longer having the whole vast ocean to swim in.

Instead of complaining, he seemed to be far more interested in communicating with me. It was a connection without words, a communication that formed imagery and sensation. It was like a "blending" with his being, a real communion. I "felt" his thoughts. He insisted he knew me and that I must remember who I truly am and where I really came from.

The connection transcended distance. I felt dreamy and other-worldly during and after each tele-empathic communication. Then over the weeks it faded as I became more distracted by the necessities of living life in the modern world. I don't know what happened to him. Dolphins don't live long in captivity, but perhaps that is a blessing.

It was not long afterward that I let go of many conditions in my life that were confining to my spirit and my sense of freedom... people who had unreasonable expectations of me, a surplus of responsibilities that robbed me of time for myself, belongings that did not contribute to inner happiness and only weighed me down, and a geographical area that wasn't nurturing to my soul.

I left it all behind and moved to a beautiful little coastal town, where I could see and smell the ocean every day. From then on, I've been deeply content to live a very simple life where the only things I own of any significant monetary value are a car, computer, and clothes.

Extraordinary events with dolphins, Orcas, and with many other animals and pets throughout my life-time have taught me something very important. All living things understand and respond to the language of the heart including plants, stones, water, the earth and even the elements. That's why certain indigenous tribes and tribal shamans could, and often still do, control the weather and influence animal behavior, as well as knowing which plants are good for certain ailments.

Paula Peterson is a clairvoyant, Intuitive Humanistic Astrologer, Spiritual-Life Counselor, author, hypnotherapist, ceremonialist, health educator, sound-healer, public speaker, author and personal growth facilitator. She was best known in the 90's as the deep-trance channel for the inspiring intelligence of EA, the angelic presence of Alexandria, the healing wisdom of Shen, and the compassion of Divine Mother.

Before withdrawing from the public scene, she was a frequent featured guest on TV and Radio talk shows. Her work aired nationally in Japan on major network television and she was sponsored in Japan as a teacher, speaker, and personal consultant. She has appeared in international publications and has been featured in an award-winning documentary on UFO's and celestial visitors.

Paula is the Founder and Director for 5 years of the Inner Light Learning Center in Northern California, the Publisher and Editor of EARTHCODE International Network, and the Author of acclaimed spiritual adventure novel: The Oracle of Clarion - a Story to Awaken the Heart of Humanity. See more about Paula and her work at: http://www. earthcode.net.

CHAPTER FORTY

Dolphins Bring a Message From my Son

by Linda Chambers

I lost my son when he was seventeen. A joy ride one evening turned to tragedy when a truck rolled and landed on top of him, leaving him paralyzed with a severe brain injury that left him in a persistent vegetative state for two years. Suddenly, my life had changed forever.

Sean stayed in a deep coma for weeks. I was told he had no chance of a quality of life. In those next months, it became increasingly hard to watch him be relegated to the sad state he now had to exist in.

He began asking me repeatedly to release him. He could actually blink yes and no. He was very clear he wanted to go. He did not want to stay trapped in his body and never wavered in this choice for six months. Patiently he waited for me to come to terms with this idea, so I could help him go on.

It was so hard to face this decision alone. As his mother, I found myself having to make the choice of death over life for my son and to somehow be able to survive that choice. Finally, I promised him that if I did help him, then he would have to help me from the other side, to make sure that the platform of Death With Dignity was brought forward. The idea was that we would continue to do this work together to complete what we were meant to do. It became very clear that was what our journey and path was about and why things were happening in this way.

Secretly, quietly, in the end, when nothing more could be done for him, I brought him home from the hospital and allowed him to die with dignity. It took him nine days to leave this life through terminal sedation, which he did peacefully and quietly.

Through this whole experience, I was in fear of being prosecuted for wrongful death, but we had made a promise to each other and I was going to keep it. So, I became a pioneer of Death With Dignity. It was the early 90's and nobody was doing much of that. Everyone was afraid and it was very secretive. It still hasn't changed a whole lot, though, I was not alone in making this choice. Thousands of parents must make the same choice every day and in every part of the world. We lose our future and our dreams as we lose our children.

When people survive a traumatic brain injury, like my son did, it is one of life's most difficult challenges. As his mother, I endured not only emotional pain, but had to advocate on his behalf through a maze of doctors, hospitals, treatment options, and insurance claims. It was a lonely, draining experience. I did everything I possibly I could for two years and still it was not enough and yet, there were so many gifts that came from this experience. Many people have been inspired by this story and it has changed so many things.

I founded a non profit in 1992 for the prevention of traumatic brain injury to bring attention to this condition and that these accidents are preventable, as they are caused by risky or careless behavior. In this way, I have been helping people become more aware.

Even though I could now see the many blessings and gifts from this experience with my son, I still felt very depressed each year during the week of his death, which also turned out to be the week he was born as well as Mother's Day.

The week before the eleventh anniversary of my son's death, I went on a cruise. I found that I was being very hard on myself because the death week was coming again and somehow I still had not gotten over his death. Early each morning I would go out on the deck and look out over the ocean trying to dispel my sadness. We would be in the middle of the ocean or coming to a dock somewhere. Each morning, the dolphins would come in front of the place that I was standing on this huge cruise ship.

It felt like they were coming specifically to speak to me directly. One little baby came up and turned his head and starting yakking away with all those great little noises, so I knew something was going on. He was telling me something important.

A couple weeks afterwards I went to Sea World. I had been told by a clairvoyant friend a year after my son had been hurt that I needed to go to Sea World to see Shamu, and that I would be given an important message. I had gone twice already, but hadn't received a message yet.

At one tank, I was watching a Mama Whale and her new baby swimming together. They were completely synchronized. Everything she did, he did. She would flip and move a little bit and he would do the same thing. Each of their movements were perfectly timed. There was no communication of it, they were just completely in sync.

As I watched the grace of that mother and her baby, I received a very important message. What I got was that I had forgotten how close my son and I are. I had been in so much pain over his death, it had slipped from my awareness, and now all these years later I was angry at myself, because I was still in so much pain during these anniversaries, focused on the loss I felt from losing him.

In watching the mama and her baby, I realized if this baby died, the mama would be very upset. There was a woman there documenting their behaviors. As I spoke this out loud she said, "Yes, the mother would be a mess. She would be grieving and the whole world would grieve too. It would become national news. It would be huge."

I was listening to her and thinking to myself, "Somehow though, she would continue swimming and going on with her life. Things would keep going, just as they have in my life. Somehow she would make it through this." Through my empathetic experience with the mother and this idea, I was able to realize that like her, I was completely whole and complete. I didn't need to keep trying to run away from the pain. I could just embrace it.

There was this part of me that was really hurt. In watching, this part of me was able to see that the mother child bond is so powerful. Somehow I had missed that. I had paid so much attention to his death. Now I was realizing we had a bond that death could not break. I knew then my son was speaking to me through this experience. The adolescent dolphin by the cruise ship had opened my awareness to receive this message from my son and now I was aware he was speaking this message to me. Finally I could receive it.

I was shown that like the mother and her baby, my son and I are never parted. We are still together. He is close to me all the time. We are moving together in synchronicity. We had been doing this all along and we had even worked together on the book I had been writing of this experience. Thinking back, I knew it was true. He had been there all the time. We, like the symbology of these two whales, were moving in sync, me on Earth and he on the other side. We had never really been parted!

In that moment, I could feel a tingling down my spine as I heard the words from my son saying, "I never left. This imaging of the whales moving in synchronicity is my message to you that we are still together. We have never been apart!"

CHAPTER FORTY ONE

Free Spirits of the Sea

by Susan Thompson

Over the years, I've always felt dolphins are the Free Spirits of the Sea. Whenever I am blessed to encounter these delightful beings, they are playful and joyous. They truly belong dancing in the vastness of the ocean.

However, my attitude changed one day when I had the opportunity to swim with them one morning at the then Hyatt Waikoloa Hotel on the Big Island of Hawaii. Having mixed feelings about swimming with dolphins in captivity in a large man-made lagoon, I wasn't sure I could do it. Yet this incredible opportunity had been placed in my hands, so I said, "Sure." The entire experience is one I will always remember.

The eight dolphins were jumping, playing, dancing, and nuzzling up to me as I swam beside them. Their energy was light and they made beautiful noises of delight. As I sat on the dock next to the lagoon one came up to me and put its nostrum into my hands. I touched, petted, and caressed it as our eyes connected. So soft, so sweet, so present. Wow! Truly transforming. Its skin was like the finest silk velvet… ahh!

As our time together came to a close, my heart was overwhelmed with love, appreciation, and gratitude for these incredible beings. I realized, even though my feelings against their captivity was strong, they were well cared for, appeared happy and healthy, and were sharing their joy with people who may never get close to a dolphin at any other time in their life. What a gift!

Soon it was time to go. I started walking down the ramp away from the dolphins. Suddenly I had an urge to turn around and go say good-bye to these beloved creatures. By now, all of them had been moved to another area where they were being fed (having lunch!).

As I approached, I began waving and saying "Thank you, thank you, thank you!" Immediately all eight were up on their tails on top of the water looking straight at me and in their high-pitched tone squeaking good-bye. I could hardly believe they were saying good-bye to me in such a powerful way. Deeply touched, tears welled up in my eyes as I blew them kisses. This probably lasted only a couple of minutes, but to me it seemed like eternity. As I reflected on this entire experience, my mind and heart burst open. I felt free like a dolphin, riding on the oceanic waves of love.

CHAPTER FORTY TWO

Two Baby Dolphins

by Doug Hackett

Through life, I had closed down my heart and mind. For a long time I didn't know if God existed. I was willing to acknowledge it, if someone would show me proof, and nobody had shown me it yet. Though, when my wife and I came to Hawaii, I was at a point where I fully accepted that people were getting incredible messages from the dolphins. I realized I don't normally receive messages in the same way as other people. I receive in the way of healings and knowing rather than visions and words.

One Saturday before one of our dolphin seminars, we went out swimming with the dolphins and there were two pods of dolphins in the bay, one pod in the middle of the bay and the other at the far end where they usually aren't. I swam towards the pod that was closest at the end of the bay. I could hear them making a terrific racket, though I couldn't see them. Suddenly there were thirty-three dolphins pointed right at me. That was an incredible thrill!

Even to this day after swimming with the dolphins for thousands of times, it is a thrill to have a dolphin point its nostrum at you. It is an incredible feeling, completely going through you like an electric current. Suddenly, you feel euphoric, playful, and joyous, like a carefree, happy child.

Soon a mother and baby dolphin with two other adult dolphins hung back and let me swim along with them. The babies with their youthful energy are really fun. I was saying to this baby, "I really love your youthful energy. Would you like to come and swim with me?" Nothing was happening. The babies of course stay very close to Mama. I realized that maybe I should ask Mama, which I did from my heart, directing the question to her. Nothing happened.

At this point I wasn't confident that the dolphins were really hearing me. I accepted that they heard Joan Ocean, who lived nearby, and that they and Joan were involved in conversations. I wasn't sure if it was happening with me. I said to the baby again, "I really love your youthful energy, do you want to come swimming with me?" For a moment nothing happened and then all of a sudden the baby peeled off and came up to the surface where I was and started swimming back and forth right in front of me. Meanwhile the three adults swam off to be with the rest of the pod.

We were swimming along and I said, "This is incredible!" I had never had the opportunity to swim with a baby before. After awhile the baby dolphin started getting a little nervous. I noticed we were quite a ways from the rest of the pod. I said, "We can swim back to them really fast." We sped up and finally the rest of the pod came within eyesight. Then the baby slowed down again and we swam together for another ten minutes.

I noticed that Mom was hanging down below me about twenty feet to the left. I was getting the feeling that she was saying, "Okay, it is time to stop playing with the human. Let's go!" The baby just kind of ignored her and then finally, it dashed off and dove down, did a circle around her, then zipped up to the surface and came back and settled in with her in the normal position they maintain.

About that time I ran into my wife, Trish, and she told me she had an amazing experience with a dolphin called Singer. We were sharing our experiences and she said, "We have a lot to do to get ready for our seminar and we should go back." I agreed, but then a mother with her baby and another adult came zipping by and stopped as if to say, "Come on, let's go!"

I said, "Okay," and went off swimming with these three and had the same incredible experience. I said to the baby, "I love your youthful energy, do you want to come swim with me?" Nothing happened and then I said, "Oh yes, Mom, is it okay for your baby to swim with me? I really love its youthful energy." Again, nothing happened.

Then I said to the baby, "Do you want to come swim with me?" It seemed like nothing was going to happen again and then, in an instant, it peeled off just like the other one had and we had a duplicate experience. It came up and was swimming on the surface with me. I felt so high. Two babies experiences in one day! Absolutely phenomenal!

I noticed that Mom and the other dolphins were having intimate moments. I felt like I was the baby sitter. After about five minutes, Mom and the other adult came by and the baby went off and they all swam away together.

It wasn't until afterwards that I realized that the dolphins had responded to me in possibly the only way I could have gotten this message. They responded to me to let me know they could hear me. Babies stick with Mama and Mamas don't usually bring babies around humans until she is very sure the humans are okay and there is no danger. So this was a very special occasion for the baby dolphin to leave Mom and swim with me. If that had happened on two consecutive days, I might have thought it was a coincidence, but it happened twice back to back the same day.

I felt that the dolphins had gotten together in their group consciousness and figured, "Okay, how can we show him? What can we do that will prove to him we are hearing what he is saying?" This was the answer. I am absolutely totally confident and convinced of it and finally, I could accept it. The dolphins can hear me. When I am talking to them, they can hear me loud and clear. It was an incredible realization for me.

Up until then, I had always had a lot of difficulty connecting with my Higher Self, Spirit, and receiving guidance. My mind was so strong, and since I had used it for so many years to protect myself, I gave it the job of filtering everything coming in and going out to the point where I always doubted messages. I was not completely consciously aware of this, though I suspected from time to time that my mind was getting in the way. It would take a lot for me to accept something was coming from the Higher self, the Universe, or Spirit. My mind always challenged any information that came to me in this way.

This experience with the baby dolphins helped me start trusting more. When I realized I really was communicating with the dolphins telepathically, it opened up my connection with Spirit and my ability to receive. It had been such a powerful experience for me to know I was being heard by these dolphins and I was receiving from them as well. It helped me to trust that I had the ability to do this all the time. Though it took me a number of years to get to the point where I am now, where I trust what I hear, that incredible experience with the baby dolphins was a very powerful beginning.

Doug Hackett cofounded Dolphin\Spirit of Hawaii with his wife, Trish

Regan, in 1994 in response to a powerful calling by the dolphins and Spirit to jump off the cliff, leave their professional lives behind, and move to Hawaii to work with the wild dolphins. Since that time they have co-facilitated life changing dolphin-swimming retreats in Hawaii and whale- swim retreats in the Kingdom of Tonga.

Doug was in a meditation group in San Francisco for fifteen years before moving to Hawaii and since 1994 has been a respected spiritual teacher bringing higher consciousness retreats and workshops worldwide. Along with his spiritual work, Doug is founder of Financial Mastery Now! LLC whose goal is to help people become debt free and move from lack to abundance consciousness. For information on Doug and Trish's products and offerings please see: http://www.dolphinspiritofhawaii.com and http://www.financailmasterynow.com

Part Seven

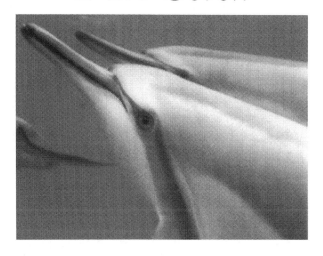

Divine Destiny

Destiny

Come be with us in
The Sacred Realms beneath the sea
As we dance and play together
You will feel the Great Harmony
Of our Life lived in these waters
Of our Presence that goes beyond time
Moving beyond the spaces you have known to
A place that is Sublime.
Come, Beloved, it is time for your Initiation into Truth
For in truly dwelling, you find your most exquisite reality is you
The Sacred One, the Precious Jewel, your Divine Self.
In our Sacred Dance we transfer Light
Filled with a million messages
Remembrances of your most Sacred Truth.
Through our transference
There is an Awakening in your consciousness
As you come into the Truth of who you are
Then you journey forth into your New Life
For the Inner Reality has been shifted
Thus, the outer life is transformed.
You sing the Sacred Songs of your precious journey
Blended with the songs of Dolphin and Whale
You bring your Light to this humanity and
Join the Light we are in the world.
Then the world is transformed
For the Awakened Ones sing their New Song
A New Vibration enters the Earth and
Sings through all the matter spheres
It changes and transforms every part of life
Bringing it to the New Reality
The Sacredness of Life lived true to Self
The Divine in us all

- The Dolphins

CHAPTER FORTY THREE

Sharaya

by Donna Waugh Campbell

I am sure it's been there all along, my connection to Sharaya and all manner of beings regardless of form, though it was at a significant time my conscious awareness of this was brought to the fore. An August summer day, I was walking with my Border Collie, Annie, along the shore in Capitola, a beautiful little seacoast town just north of Monterey, California. I was on a summer trip in my '83 VW Adventure Wagon, heading for Big Sur and had camped in the town the previous night.

As I walked down the beach, I noticed a couple standing over something along the water's edge. When I got closer, I realized it was a small dolphin. She was gently washing against the shore. The couple seemed baffled about what to do and left. It was apparent to me she was in the process of leaving her beautiful silver body, or just had. I pulled her a short way up on the beach and sat with her not knowing what to do, but feeling enormous empathy and a desire to do "something" for this lovely creature. All my life I had felt a strong connection to dolphins, but had never been so close.

It wasn't very long before I sensed her communicating with me. It was very clear and internal. Telepathic would be the best way to describe it. She began by thanking me for staying with her. I felt humbled, but strangely not surprised. I responded by asking her simple questions like her name, which she told me was Sharaya, and that she was three or four (though I don't know if she meant months or years). I asked if she wanted me to take her to the aquarium at Monterey so it could be determined why she had died, but she said, "It's not necessary. They already know it was pollution." She told me she was going to be with me from now on. I had no idea what that meant, but she has lived up to her word and has been a constant companion since.

At some point, I decided to move her further back from the water into an alcove at the base of a high retaining wall where there was some dripping water. I collected seaweed and hid her as best I could. When I started to leave her an hour or so later, she called me back and asked me to spend more time with her, so I went back and stayed awhile longer until I felt I had her permission to leave.

As I continued on my trip, I was amazed, delighted and so very thankful for this great cosmic gift. I could only wonder where it would lead, but I had no doubt that my amazing life had started down yet another new path. Initially, she came to me intermittently. She might come and lay her soft nose on my left shoulder and just hang out quietly. At times, when I would be lying on my back, she would come and sit upright on her tail and entertain me by swirling and turning as the dolphins do at Sea World. That still happens occasionally, but mostly she comes to me in my mind's eye. At one point, there were a group of smaller dolphins in the background, less distinct but almost rowdy in their apparent desire to get my attention. It was like a group of anxious excited six year olds who know the answer in class and want to get called on. The messages they brought amazed me.

Shortly after returning home, I received an email from a Peace Troubadour who was traveling the world singing songs and opening hearts. The message included information regarding the latest crop circle in England of twin dolphins circling the Earth. The email mentioned there would be a gathering of psychic children, dolphins and whales on the Spring Equinox 2003 in Hawaii. I felt an immediate pull to be part of manifesting this event. The Peace Troubadour also mentioned he'd be doing an event two weeks later at Asilomar, a large retreat center near Pebble Beach, California. Ten days later, I headed south to meet him to share my story.

On the drive down, Sharaya indicated she'd like us to stop in Capitola so we could spend a bit of time meditating on "our" beach. In spite of the fact that it was a perfect summer day and very busy Saturday afternoon, we drove in and immediately found a parking place. No doubt Sharaya knew of my shortage of patience and realized I had no intention of driving around in circles for hours looking for a space. We spent an hour or so watching a couple of baby seals and a few seagulls play hide and seek and she took me for a "swim." As we were leaving, she asked me to go into a store up the street and told me I'd know why as soon as I got there. As an aside, she also mentioned it wouldn't cost a lot of money, which I found amusing. The store was one in which it was difficult for me NOT to spend money. It's a magical place called Avalon Vision.

When I entered the store, it was appropriately crowded for a busy summer Saturday afternoon, but within moments, it was mysteriously empty except for one Goddess Woman standing behind the counter. I hesitated to approach her, but realized that since nothing had immediately grabbed my attention, I might ask if she knew why I was there. With slight hesitation, I said "This might sound a bit strange, but do you have any idea why my dolphin friend sent me in here?" She responded immediately by putting her hand gently on my arm and saying "Do you know about the Peace Troubadour and his upcoming event?" Suffice to say, she was the reason Sharaya had asked me to stop in so I could receive the outer confirmation I was on the right track. We had a wonderful conversation and I left buying one small card of a mermaid joyfully riding on a dolphin's back in the surf, something Sharaya had just done with me that afternoon.

It was becoming increasingly apparent that Sharaya and I had a powerful destiny and while I thought I knew where it would lead, I had some reservations. I felt compelled toward Ashland, Oregon (the Troubdour's headquarters) to see if I could assist with the upcoming conference. Following this inspiration, I left in early November and arrived in cold Ashland a week or so later, knowing I had to go there to find out more about my destiny. I was excited and open to learn just what that was, though found it was not about helping with the event after all. That had been the draw to Ashland. Now I would find out more about why I was there.

Following the inspirational lead, I called a friend of a friend, Colleen, founder of the Unity Church in Ashland, who graciously invited me to stay at her place. In the course of conversation, I told her what had brought me to Ashland. She immediately took me next door to meet her brother, John, who is a practicing "dowsing consultant" who has been working with energy all his life. As I was sharing my story with him, he was holding a traditional dowsing pendulum over a sheet of paper with letters and numbers I couldn't see. What I could see was the pendulum, with no assistance from John, moving faster, then slower, then faster again and occasionally changing directions. When I was done, he asked, "Do you know why Sharaya has come into your life?"

I said I had some thoughts about it, though was rather sure my initial ideas weren't the answer. I only knew I was meant to be in Ashland and that I would somehow find out. He told me "they" were telling him I had made a vow and they wanted to know if I was going to honor it. With no hesitation, I responded, "If I did make a vow, I guess that's what I'm here to find out about."

John told me it involved channeling, not one, but four books. He also told me it would bring about a major change in my life and asked me if I was ready for that. Since I had considered the coming of Sharaya as a great honor and divine gift, I had no thought of not following through on wherever it took me.

I asked if I was to do these books in Ashland and the pendulum limped around, then I asked if I was to return to Marin where I had been living and the answer was similar, so we decided to put that off until morning. During the night, I had a vision of my van in the desert in Sky Valley, California plugged into my friend Elizabeth's "guest house" on her land. Not so strangely, things had come full circle as it was Elizabeth who gave me Colleen's number and it was Colleen's brother through whom I got the message about what was in store for my life. It was to Elizabeth's land that I would return to begin this journey.

I rapidly became aware of how common interspecies contacts are becoming. One of the women I met while in Ashland was an animal communicator who had recently published a book on the subject. Other friends passed on books, tapes, and names of people who were doing this kind of work. Shortly after I reached the desert in mid- December, I found a used laptop perfect for my work.

In January 2003, Sharaya and her friends began to share their message with me. Each day I sat at my computer, invoking their help and letting their wisdom come through me onto the screen. I have total faith they will let me know exactly what they want me to do with it, and have total faith the universe will support me. I do love how the universe works when we let it. That's how it all began. Now it's time for me to listen. Thank you Sharaya for this great blessing. Om Shanti, Shanti, Shanti.

CHAPTER FORTY FOUR

Dolphins Shall Lead Them

by Becky Stambaugh

Late in February of 1995, I was called through a strange and wonderful set of circumstances to go to Hawaii to write a book. When I first felt the inclination to go, I had no idea what the book would even be about.

On a particular weekend, we were committed to two projects. One was helping some friends move. My husband, Tom, took on that job, while I prepared to represent our sound therapy business at a local fair.

The night before the fair, I got a call from a woman whom I had met the previous Sunday. She said she had wanted to get together with Tom and me. I suggested she meet me at the fair in Ojai, California the next day. I set up the booth with all of the equipment early Saturday morning. It soon became apparent given the small attendance of the fair that I was there to talk to Debra.

For the previous three years, I had been immersed in spiritual growth. I had been severed from a company after having worked there thirteen years. With all of the searching, I was somehow still adrift of connecting to my purpose, though I knew I had one. There was some way for me to really make a difference.

Debra and I talked. She asked me question after question, patiently and painstakingly pulling the pearls from me one at a time. Finally, she announced, "Well, Becky. It seems to me you want to go to Hawaii, stay with Teresa and Larry, and write your book." I knew she was right. She had extracted from me the information I was unable or unwilling to give myself.

Tom had stayed over at our friend's house during the move. On Sunday, I awoke knowing Tom already knew about the Hawaii trip, even though I hadn't talked to him. We are that connected. On Monday, we had a chance to talk. "You know," Tom began, "This is going to sound funny, but I think you should go to Hawaii and write a book." I laughed, explaining what had happened over the weekend. "I also got that the book you think you're going to write is not the book you will write," Tom added.

I had been working on what I then called "Essence Yoga" (now Heart Mastery). It was an offshoot of the sound therapy I had been doing for years. I had reasoned that if there was a color for each note on the musical scale, there must also be a smell, taste, aspect of the Divine, and a movement. I had begun to catalog all of this and turn it into a way to help people have better relationships with more ease. I assumed this would be the book I would write. Complete trust and letting go of control were required. By now, I was getting used to that. I made plane reservations to Hawaii for two weeks away and began my preparations.

The day before I left, I got a call from a woman I had met at the Albuquerque Whole Life Expo. We had been corresponding ever since, becoming mentors of each other. At the Expo she had asked if I could analyze the voices of dolphins with our sound equipment. The phone call was completely unexpected. Our usual method of contact had been letters. She kept it short. "Where are you going, and what book are you writing?" she asked. I told her the story of how and where I was going, and that I wasn't sure of the book. I was planning on going swimming with dolphins and then figuring it out.

"That's it!" she exclaimed. "The book is about children swimming with dolphins! Have a great trip. It's going to be the trip of a lifetime!"

After I got to Oahu, I called a friend there who had offered to take me swimming with the dolphins. He picked me up the next day. We spent a wonderful day talking to the people who lived on the beach, and no dolphins showed. I knew this was a day of cleansing, of opening up and becoming less "haole" (tourist) and more aloha. I resolved to go with the flow.

The next morning, while taking a dip in the swimming pool, I got it. The book was to be about a dolphin taking children through three Heart Mastery motions or spins of the notes of the musical scale. It would be a meditation in motion book for children and would help them raise their self esteem. Now that I had the idea, I put it on the shelf for a few days and went about some other business.

A week later, Teresa told me about Sea Life Park, a marine exhibit on the North Coast of Oahu. I knew I had to go to see the dolphins.

Teresa gave me her mini recorder and I took off in her car. I had another appointment that afternoon and would only have a few hours at the park.

As I was driving through the mountains and up the coast, my level of anticipation started to rise. I parked the car, paid my admission, checking the map for the dolphin area. The dolphin lagoon was a large pool with a boat in it and a bridge to the boat. Visitors could stand on the ship deck and observe the dolphins from the surface, or go below and view the animals underwater through portholes. I stood on the bridge, asking the dolphins, "Okay, I'm here. Show me the motions."

The dolphin I talked to was one of the largest ones in the tank. He immediately took off swimming in the motion of Wisdom, a downward counterclockwise spiral. He reversed the spiral upward and clockwise, the motion I had been given for Consciousness. There was no mistaking them. I watched for a few minutes.

My heart was open now, and I felt a connection with the dolphins, particularly the large one who had shown me the motions. I got out the recorder, watching the dolphin as he did the motions in order. I began to tape the book and recorded the entire first draft in fifteen minutes. Elated, I thanked the dolphin and went below.

The below section of the boat also had a gift shop and a clerk in attendance. I watched the dolphins for awhile in silence as other visitors came and went. Soon, I was the only visitor left in the boat. I went to a porthole, putting my eye up to the glass. The dolphin that had been helping me swam up and placed his eye in the window directly opposite mine. We held our position for minutes. It was a feeling of being reunited with a loving teacher and friend.

"There must be a dolphin on the other side, that's the only time they stop like that," a clerk behind me said unexpectedly. She looked and saw no other dolphin there. I knew the 'other' was me and I smiled. Having been released from the eye exchange, I went on deck. I figured to be finished with the dolphins when I heard a loud SPLASH. The source of the noise was the large dolphin. He swam again in the motion of Wisdom, then switching directions in midair, he performed the spin of Consciousness. Tears welled in my eyes. I thanked the dolphin again.

Next door was a pool of false killer whales. I went to watch them for a moment. One of the two animals stopped directly in front of me and motioned the spin of Reverence. Lest I be unsure, the whale swam around the pool, repeating the gesture in my direction. At that exact moment, several hundred feet off shore, five wild humpbacks began breaching, creating quite a hubbub. One of the attendants of the dolphin/whale enclosures ran down to see. "I've never seen them this close to shore before and so late in the season. This is amazing," she reported excitedly. We all watched the water ballet that went on for the next fifteen minutes. The whales took turns breaching, then waving their pectoral fins toward shore, as if to wave hello. It was quite a sight. What a day!

That night, my friends and I decided to go do a full moon ceremony down by the beach. The moonlight on the water and over the buildings of Honolulu was a lot to drink in. I was still excited about the day's events. At the end of the ceremony, I gazed into the moonlit sky. "Look, Teresa, that cloud looks like a dolphin," I said, pointing towards it.

"Yes, and it's moving in a motion. Which one is that?" she asked.

"Wisdom."

"It's switching direction! What is it now, Becky?" Teresa queried excitedly.

"Consciousness. Those are the same motions the dolphins did at the park." I told her. We watched until the dolphin cloud disappeared. Our attention was then drawn to the horizon. There, against the water in the moonlit sky, another long cloud had formed. It looked like a great humpback in the sky with a pectoral fin waving at us.

As the last fluff of the whale cloud trailed away, my eyes were drawn directly overhead. Shimmering above was a cloud in the perfect shape of a heart. "Remember, you are the Keeper of the Essence," a voice inside my head boomed.

I am back home now, unveiling with the help of the dolphins, whales and all other Spirit Beings on this planet, what the meaning and steps toward realizing that beautiful sentence is.

On that magically lit up night, on that magic island, the end of an amazing search and the beginning of an even greater journey took place. With the help of the rest of Creation, I had found my purpose.

Becky Stambaugh is a sound therapist, writer and healer. Her passion and life purpose is to assist other beings to recollect their essence. She accomplishes this through teaching a series of movements known as "Heart Mastery."

CHAPTER FORTY FIVE

Dolphin Dreamtime

by Jiah Whaleheart Miesel

It was my very first adventure to Baja. I was where the extreme road ends at the turquoise waters of the Sea of Cortez, where cactus filled desert borders sheer mountain sea cliffs. I was finally alone in nature, or so I thought, under a quiet and black moonless sky with remote sparkles from distant stars and occasional pelicans. I was in heaven, relaxing in the perfect natural hot springs that I later affectionately named, the Mermaid Pools, quickly recovering from a life filled with stress and overwhelm.

Splash!!! I was suddenly startled out of my relaxed utopia by a large movement just 20 feet away in the dark night. I struggled to focus my vision to see what it was. A playful bottlenose dolphin was jumping towards me, looking directly at me. It was absolutely phenomenal. I was filled with feelings of love, gratitude and curiosity as I realized it was calling to me. With some apprehension, I overcame my fear as I climbed out of the comfort of the hot spring and swam towards the dolphin. It was a bit eerie in the dark night as I swam out towards a wide expanse of sea, but then I saw seven more large dolphins further out quickly swimming towards us.

Within minutes, I was in the midst of a flurry of activity with dolphins darting under me and jumping in the air for the stars. I could hear them underwater as they communicated excitedly with fast clicking and loud whistle sounds. I was interacting with them and they were zapping me like crazy with their echolocation until my entire body was tingling, the energy beyond intense. I could feel this magical pod of eight dolphins was healing me with an ecstatic dance. I was in bliss!

Once back in San Diego, the joy continued. I was laughing and smiling nonstop. Something at my core had changed and the bliss was coming in waves. My friends took notice and were asking me what had happened. When I shared about the magical dolphin encounter in Baja, they all wanted to experience it for themselves. So, I quickly organized another trip back and this gave birth to my new company, Dolphin Dreamtime Adventure Tours.

These dolphin interactions gave me increased energy, happiness and vivid lucid dreams. In my dreams, I would be swimming with dancing dolphins among white rays of light in the water and incredible celestial sounds. I was also having "mystical experiences," waking in the middle of the night and seeing brilliant colors , feeling the dolphin's energy. I was actually getting confused about when I was awake and when I was dreaming. It was very surreal.

During one of these dreams, I was guided to produce an event connected with the dolphins and aligned with a global event called 11:11, the numbers I often see. My team and I created a three day event for over 350 people in Mexico with fire walking, group rebirths, music, sharing, rituals, sweat lodges and a call to the dolphins. Finding the perfect place to build our sweat lodge was particularly challenging. In the final hour, we were guided to a hidden location on the cliffs over-looking the ocean. The entire gathering was a success and the sweat lodges were especially powerful.

A week later, I went back to recover the lodge structure for trans-port back to the states. When we got there, I was saddened to see that it had been used for fire wood. Upon closer examination, I saw the only unburned item was my personal prayer tie still connected to a small piece of willow buried in the ashes. I picked it up in partial shock and in that exact moment a massive whale breached straight into the air just sixty feet from where I was standing on the ocean cliff. It splashed down like thunder. Then I saw over two hundred dolphins jumping in total excitement everywhere. The show continued and at one point the whale breached again, leaping out of the water with a ton of dolphins flanking its side in mid-air.

Since those first experiences, the dolphins have taken me on an amazing journey. I learned everything I could about marine mammals and explored most of the best locations to have dolphin and whale inter-actions, taking like minded people to my favorite places with Dolphin Dreamtime Adventure Tours. Our tours include: The Baja Whale Adventure; The Hawaiian Wild Dolphin Adventure; The Bahamas Wild Dolphin Swim; and Swimming with Humpbacks in the Kingdom of

Tonga.

I have witnessed so many people having life changing encounters with dolphins. On our tours, we anchor the biggest vision that participants can consciously create with spirit and connect it with the ecstasy of their dolphin encounters. Many have shared that these adventures are a top five ultimate life experience. It is right up there with giving birth to a first child, a favorite birthday, and their special wedding day. I have been truly blessed to experience so many dolphin induced miracles and profound healings.

On one of my absolute favorite tours, the Baja Whale Adventure in San Ignacio, there were countless awe-inspiring moments. In small fishing boats, called pangas, we enter the protected mating and birthing sanctuary of the California Gray Whales. They have the longest migration of any marine mammal on the planet.

I will never forget one very special day. It was Easter Sunday and I was with an intimate group of close friends. The sky was blue with fluffy clouds. It was sunny and warm and the lagoon was like glass. The water visibility was fantastic for the area. We were in Nirvana completely surrounded by dolphins, and mother and baby gray whales. The mothers were encouraging the babies, as they often do, to come to us and allow us to touch them. One 40-ton playful friend was even gently lifting our entire boat in the air on her back. We were rushing like the most extreme rollercoaster exhilaration, before being set down to our delight and relief.

The dolphins were there too, capturing our attention with impressive acrobatic leaps. We were touching whales in the wild and seeing total mind blowing whale breaches, tail slaps, spy hops and dolphins zipping by all at the same time, laughing and crying and singing in pure bliss.

Right when we thought it could get no better, we shifted position in relationship to the sun and whale spectacle. A beautiful newborn baby boy quickly approached and allowed us to be the first humans to touch him. Momma whale was looking directly at us and exhaled a big powerful blast of air from her dual blowholes. Her spray formed a perfect awesome mist shaped rainbow heart and the entire lower sky was now filled with rainbow whale hearts.

Later, I had a dream where I was looking into a mother whale's golden eye and she was telling me I needed to be her voice and to help protect her kind and the birthing sanctuary at San Ignacio Lagoon. Mitsubishi and the Mexican Government wanted to develop a large salt factory there. I took massive action and garnered the support of several nonprofits to help protect this sacred habitat. I then founded Whale Day International and we produced eleven events in seven different countries, all on the same day. Together, we were totally victorious in protecting these whales and it all started with a dream and a dolphin encounter over twenty years ago.

So remember, if the dolphins call to you, take action and dance with them! The magical dolphins will create your wide awake dreams in Dolphin Dreamtime!!

Jiah WhaleHeart Miesel is joyfully pursing his dreams and inspiring others to share in his commitment to protect marine mammals' world wide. He is a former San Diego Earth Day Director, Founder of Whale Day International, an award winning movie producer, a speaker, and owner of Dolphin Dreamtime Adventure Tours. He has been featured in the media on NBC, CBS, ABC and KPBS for his efforts to protect whales. To receive information about his tours go to http://www.dolphindreamtime.com. He lives by the ocean in Encinitas, California with his golden retriever, Shanti Sue. He can be reached at whaleheart5@yahoo.com.

CHAPTER FORTY SIX

Dolphins Awaken My Inner Painter

by Mark Mackay

My first winter living in the foothills of Santa Barbara was a mild one compared to New England where I came from. I was given the opportunity to create a new life doing what I truly loved to do in a two room cottage in the middle of 300 acres of mountain woods by a stream called Refugio, 'My Refuge.' That gift allowed me time to devote to painting and sculpting to see if this step away from the illusion of security and towards a dream would work.

I walked away from a rare and enviable job for a guy of twenty three. I was working for a major record label as one of twelve promotions directors, each with a chunk of the country to convince. I was also the youngest of them by at least ten years. I had been hired for the position through recommendations of record company friends after a three-year stint at successfully managing bands. I was to "relate" to the guys on the other side of the coin whose music was creating large fortunes and whom they didn't understand and usually felt awkward around.

The gig was the making of Rock Stars, a job complete with all the right perks. Money, new car, backstage passes to any concert anywhere, the newest music from every label mailed to my door, mad parties on both coasts, all night jams and recording sessions with some of the best music no one will ever hear, played for friends in a perfectly tuned room, live, long after the tape recorder stopped.

Women, drugs, Rock and Roll, and a generous expense account. It was living on the cutting edge of a new era. My life was constantly connecting with people thought to be cool, moving up and through, always trying to make something happen and it did. Within a few months I was credited with moving two new bands onto the charts with a third on the way, while working on an eighteen date all star Jazz show that rivaled Monterey for talent. FM had just arrived and a whole new dimension of music was free to be played long version, uncut and out from under the tight playlist dogma of AM radio, a short-lived revolution.

My job was hearing, recognizing and seeding the music world with future legends. A recurring thought was "They pay me for this!" The work of breaking in great musicians was fantastic on almost every level. Almost. I got close to some of the players I was helping to make stars. They encouraged my painting, though I felt I had no time for it. I was uncomfortable with compliments. It seemed at those moments, a gift unused was worse than no gift at all.

I was a true believer in these people and the music they were making. I remember we spoke of the intangible power to pull something beautiful out of nothing and how to feed it. We related as artists belonging to a larger tribe of misfits with the creative world in our hands. At times, conversations would tap into another reality. I would hear stories of heavy handed "standard" and rip off contracts that left some musicians broke, or worse with no control over their music ever. I started to annoy upper management with my uninvited role as liaison on behalf of a couple of artists. Soon after being told by 'the man' I had better get it straight, that making big money was all that really mattered in this business, I went on a two week vacation.

Halfway into Canada on a solo camping trip, I picked up a hitchhiker who after a brief introduction and the usual where he's going and where I've just been, he paused for about ten seconds before speaking. Then, very calmly he told me there had been a fatal plane crash four days ago killing a famous singer, Jim Croce, his guitar player, and their manager. He then took a newspaper from under his arm, and pointed to the story, page one, lower right.

On board that small plane unknown to him were my friends. I blanched and raced to the next gas station to call my V.P. in Los Angeles and was asked first thing where the hell was I. Plans were busily being made to do an album of ballads of my friend's music, using the songs we fought for unsuccessfully to have released, as it conflicted with the pop image the company was molding for him. "Maybe later" was the final word. He asked what I thought of the idea, and told me to get to L.A, NOW. Although he didn't say it, I couldn't help but hear the words behind the condolence in his voice, "good career move." I quit over the phone.

It took a few weeks to pack up, say goodbye, sell off my worldly possessions in Boston and hit the road west. The trip gave me a lot of time to contemplate this hardest of lessons in creative freedom and that all we really have is this moment to realize and live our passion.

So here I was on a clear and crisp California afternoon in '74, hiking a coastal trail when I saw the pod of Bottlenose Dolphins for the third day that week. This was the first time I chose to stop and watch them. The other sightings were just glances from the freeway on the drive into town. While standing on a cliff overlooking the coast from Santa Barbara to Gaviota, I spotted them swimming in close to the shoreline. They were arching slowly, rhythmically weaving through the enormous kelp forest for an afternoon dinner on the abundant sea life who were feeding there. I was to discover they were more than a transient pod just coming inshore to graze through the channel. They surfed. One of only three pods known in the world to do so.

After about 20 minutes of feeding they joined together far to the left of the kelp bed and as in sync as dominos falling they made for the waves breaking on a deserted little beach to the south. Seven huge glistening dolphins black as night began riding the same ten footer towards shore. Embedded in the wave as if captured by a living emerald, they would ride to the last moment. With quick tail snaps cut out of the wave as if on cue, they would disappear until the next wave that suited them rolled in. Over and over the translucent green of the waves lifted its joyous riders as one. At first I was stunned, are they beaching themselves in one go? I had never heard of dolphins surfing, and was so caught by surprise and awe when they did it again that I started laughing between cheers at seeing their flawless forms dance on perfect waves.

That night, I began a new direction in painting. It was of the sea and the dolphins that had lit in me an intimate connection through them to the ocean, the Earth, and the infinite that was to shape my life. Since then I've followed a path expressing through art what I see and feel in the grace and power of the ocean and her fantastic sea life, by manipulating light, form, color and motion into creations of clay, paint, glass, and bronze that will live to touch people long after I'm gone.

Moving from one coastal paradise in California to another on Maui, always close to the ocean, close to the dolphins, I have since that day met them in the wild, in captivity, and as the beached victims of man on three continents. Each time, I have been enriched by gratitude for their being, and compassion for their plight. Both have been gifts beyond measure.

Mark Mackay is a world renowned artist that works in multimedia, painting, mosaic, glass, and bronze sculptures. See his work at: http://www. MarkMackay.com.

CHAPTER FORTY SEVEN

Silver Seas Dolphins

by Sylvie Tannesen

I think there's an inevitable hunger on this planet for each of us to touch the full spectrum of our potential as human beings and it's my experience this is what the dolphins help us to do. I believe the dolphins carry a frequency that somehow helps us know ourselves on a very deep level, who we are, and what we are here to do. At least, that is what happened to me on a Journey of Awakening to my Life Purpose inspired by the Dolphins.

As the author of a masters thesis on "The Telepathic Emotional Resonance Patterns Created By Dolphin Human Interactions", I felt it was important to personally experience several encounters with dolphins. My first dolphin "meeting" took place at a public national park in the Yucatan in Playa Del Carmen. Though I had nothing to compare it to, as I watched these ten or so dolphins "swimming" in a very small pool, the title of a book I'd read many years before crossed my mind. It was called, "Against Our Will." My heart grieved for the injustice of their lives. I was reminded of Timothy Wyllie's haunting words about how a person's soul can be deadened when it is made to comply to another's will. Despite the deep sadness in my heart for these loving, spiritual creatures, I couldn't help but be affected by being in their presence, within their magnetic field. In this space, I was filled with love and compassion. It felt like velvet when I touched my first dolphin.

My second encounter with dolphins was in the wild, about forty miles off the shore of Grand Bahama Island. Never in my life have I felt more loved, more complete acceptance, more joy, or more alive. Even now I feel lighter, somehow freer, more connected both spiritually and physically. It's as though some part of my soul has been healed and I can move forward in my life more easily, with less restriction and self-imposed limitation.

During this six-day cruise, I swam with wild dolphins two to three times each day. Dolphins live and swim in families called pods and they seemed to respond to us in greater numbers and with more enthusiasm as the week progressed and we ourselves became more a pod. Another interesting behavior of dolphins is they touch each other very often while swimming. Appearing to be both a sign of communication and affection, their constant bodily contact seems an important aspect of the dolphin psyche.

One time, more than twenty dolphins came to swim with us for almost an hour. As Rebecca, an experienced swim leader explained, "It doesn't get any better than this!" As we swam side by side, I looked into their huge, dolphin eyes and felt a love I've never felt before. I know I will never be the same!

Perhaps most interesting was that before I could see the dolphins in the water, I felt their presence. When you're in the open sea, you're in their home and magnetic field. I believe the energy of this field heightens your senses and your levels of awareness and communication. In addition to them healing a shoulder injury I experienced on the boat, the dolphins seemed to encourage, if not insist, I use my telepathic abilities to communicate with them. So I began projecting thoughts to them while swimming in the water, like, "What shall I do with my life?" Their answer was, "Bring people to us."

Since returning, I've dreamt of dolphins consistently and my ability to communicate with all beings, including animals, has increased significantly. Most importantly, I've decided to dedicate my life to bringing people and dolphins together through my own dolphin swim project called "Silver Seas Dolphins."

My third visit with dolphins was in San Diego at another, in my view, inhumane, profit motivated oceanarium. Promoted as educational organizations because they "teach" people about dolphins, marine parks do so at the expense of those dolphins. With ten or more adult dolphins in undersized pools, almost constant physical and audio contact with human beings, robbed of a natural life in the open sea, and very little privacy or respect, these dolphins eventually must lose their spirits. I firmly believe this life must deaden if not completely break their souls.

Gary Kowalski, a graduate of Harvard Divinity School, is a Unitarian Universalist Minister who has written on behalf of animals for many years. In his book, "The Souls Of Animals," he answers the ultimate question: "Do animals have souls?" The answer, a resounding yes! After explaining the word "animal" comes from a Latin word that means soul, Kowalski says, "Animals, like us, are living souls. They are not things. They are not objects. Neither are they human, yet they mourn, love, dance, and suffer. They know peaks and chasms of being. Animals are expressions of the Mind-at-Large that suffuses our universe. With us, they share in the gifts of consciousness and life. In a wonderful and inexpressible way, God is present in all creatures." Like Thomas Jefferson, I too "tremble for my species when I reflect that God is just."

As a friend of mine, Michael of London, England, said after viewing an exquisite collection of dolphin photographs on view at a gallery there, "The leaping joy of the dolphin suggests free expression of the soul released from fear, and freed to express the Divine creativity, playfulness, and loving nature that is the essence of a healed humanity ready to reclaim the innocence it thought it had lost." I have designed Silver Seas Dolphins with Michael's quote in mind to bring together a combination of group playfulness and personal integration.

My personal experience of dolphins has continued on land with as much strength and truth as it did in water, for wherever I go in the world, strangers and friends alike have something to share about dolphins. Most interesting of all in these dolphin encounters is that it almost seems as if the dolphins themselves are leading me from person to person, place to place, and experience to experience as I go about the business of developing Silver Seas Dolphins.

Upon returning from my second dolphin cruise, I seriously began creating Silver Seas Dolphins. Despite my best efforts, it felt to me like I was getting off on a somewhat bumpy start and I began questioning the wisdom of my plan. So, at a moment's notice, I booked a flight to Puerto Vallarta, Mexico, to give myself some time and space to think. In my heart of hearts, I knew I went looking for a sign from the Universe to either go ahead with Silver Seas Dolphins or move forward with my life in another way.

It was mid-afternoon in late October. I was sitting in a cafe in Puerto Vallarta having a cup of tea when I suddenly felt the urge to go for a walk along the beach. Even though it was pouring rain outside, in a moment I left the cafe and began my walk. I came upon a fishing boat and asked the fisherman, who spoke not a word of English, to please take me out to sea. For fifty dollars he was happy to oblige me. Within five minutes I saw six dolphin fins jump out of the water and within a half hour's time, there were between one hundred and fifty and two hundred dolphins swimming around the boat. They swam right up to the bow and I, with complete abandon, jumped into the water with them. The magnetic field was immense and I knew, deep in my bones, I had been gifted with this experience and that the Universe (as well as the dolphins) were granting me their complete and unbending support on behalf of Silver Seas Dolphins. Days later, I found out through the help of interpreters that in twenty years of this fisherman's time on the water, he had never encountered so many dolphins at once.

Not long after, when I was leaving the United States for the holidays in London with my family, I was in San Francisco having a massage, when I heard a song titled "The Promise" written and sung by Cathy Kinsman. It was about the plight of the captive dolphins and their call to humanity for freedom. The Promise asks:

> Did I hear you say in a whisper
> or did I just imagine it all?
> You said you'd help me
> make it to the other side of the shadow
> Let me go. Please try to understand what I long for
> Try to look deep into my soul and help me make it to
> the other side of the shadow. Help me go.
> I heard a promise from God in my memory
> It whispered to me of a freedom there
> Where is the life that I long to be living?

Listening to these words, my heart was deeply moved and I discovered there was an accompanying fund raising video also entitled "The Promise." Watching the video, I once again experienced a penetrating knowing that what I am to do with my life is to bring people to the dolphins, free, wild dolphins.

In late December, in London, I was invited to a Christmas party and was introduced to Kim Kindersley, director of a film entitled "The Dolphin's Gift." At once delighted and intrigued at the "coincidental" encounter, I was touched to the core of my essence as I watched this documentary film about Fungi, the lone, but beloved Bottlenose Dolphin that's inhabited Dingle Bay off the southwest coast of Ireland for almost a decade. An extraordinary tale of a wild dolphin and the awe-inspiring friendships he's developed with numerous human beings, the "Dolphin's Gift" is both a tribute to Fungi and a wake up call for human consciousness.

With an introduction that includes a bit of dolphin history and fact, the film reminds us dolphins have been in existence for fifteen million years. Unlike humans, they have never threatened their own existence, have destroyed nothing, and live in complete harmony with their environment. For reasons we may never understand, Fungi left his pod and chooses to live in Dingle Bay, endlessly prepared to spend time with all who come to visit. As the Greek philosopher Plutarch said, "The dolphin is the only creature who loves man for his own sake. The dolphin alone has no need for man. Yet, it is a genial friend to all and has helped many."

As Judy Hurt says in The Dolphin's Gift, "The best we can do is protect his environment, understand his unconditional love and accept the gift of this formidable friend." Weaving extraordinarily sensitive photography with beautiful personal stories, the Dolphin's Gift shares several insights and the rarest gift of all, looking directly into the eye of a completely free being, a wild dolphin!

As artist Maria Simmons-Gooding explains, "Everyone says when you have looked into the eye of the dolphin, you will never be the same again. I was so utterly inspired. That experience is so unique, deep, and special, it brings out something within you that you share with everybody. For me, it was that feeling I had as a little kid, dying to paint."

"My first morning," wrote Hillary Taylor in her journal, "I woke early and walked to the beach where I saw with joy the dolphin jumping. Later, I went into the water. I saw him and made eye contact. My first and subsequent impression was of gentle knowingness. My overall impression was magic. Along with the extraordinary feeling of being at home in his world with no fear at all, he released in me buckets full of tears that I thought had been exhausted following the death by drowning of my twenty-four year old son in Italy. Fungi definitely helped me free all I had blocked and by the end of the week, made me understand that life could go on. It was an experience I will never forget. He brought joy, wonder, and love to me. I hope he got some back."

As a musician and songwriter, I see the greatest expansion of my creative expression in my music. Interestingly I found myself in Hawaii writing a song about earthquakes the night before a quake in California and my most inspired writing has resulted from the documentary film,

"The Dolphin's Gift," I wrote and recorded a song based on the movie.

Wanting to expand my overall experience of dolphins, I went to Hawaii to participate in a day long expedition to swim with whales with Dr. John Lilly. Due to illness, Dr. Lilly was unable to be on board, so the cruise was led by another highly regarded whale expert. Throughout the day, she shared many facts and stories about whales, but most interesting to me was her talk about the songs of the whales, and how dramatically they've changed over the years, particularly between the 1960's when whale songs were "wonderful and happy" and the 1980's and 1990's when whale songs have become "deeply sad and joyless."

According to Native American Indian tradition as written by Jamie Sams, a member of the Wolf Clan Teaching Lodge of the Seneca Nation, a native-American medicine teacher and creator of the Medicine Cards and author of the accompanying book of the same name, the whale is the record keeper for Mother Earth and the dolphin represents manna, breath of life. Everyone who has recorded the dolphin experience in their hearts (in the wild), inevitably becomes a teacher for humanity, educating others about the experience and unacceptability of dolphin captivity.

The whale songs have gotten progressively sadder over the years seemingly reflecting the true overall state of humanity. With the appearance of so many dolphins along the California Coast during the riots, fires, and earthquakes, they too seem to be fulfilling their role as representatives of the breath of life by reminding us through their beautiful, gentle presence to be at peace with ourselves and each other, to quiet our beings, to simply breath.

In closing, I'd like to quote Joan McIntyre, author of "Mind in the Waters: A Book To Celebrate The Consciousness of Whales And Dolphins," who wrote, "We are beginning to discern the outline of another mind on the planet, a mind anatomically like ours but profoundly different. Three thousand years ago in the Mediterranean, the dolphin, a small whale, was the doorway to profound religious mysteries and the honored Guardian of Life in the sea. Gemistos Pletho, a 15th century Byzantine philosopher, saw the dolphin swimming through the sea as the mind of God in the waters. More recently Melville reckoned that if God returned to Earth in our lifetime, it would be in the guise of a whale."

CHAPTER FORTY EIGHT

Synchronicity

by Daniel McCulloch

The first time I became aware of the dolphins was when I was being screened for an intensive thirteen-week therapeutic process. At the initial meeting without notice they said, "Okay, you have fifteen minutes to write a story in the first person from the perspective of an animal." With no time to think about it, I started writing a story of being a dolphin. The funny thing was, I had never thought about dolphins before. Writing the story from the perspective of a dolphin, I became this ecstatic being in the ocean. Telepathically I began getting a message, a long message that a boat was going down and we had to save the humans. We zoomed to wherever it was and we were all saving the humans together.

It was years later before I thought about the dolphins again. It was 1983. I was having dinner with a friend who had been close to John Lily's wife who had died. We went back to her place and she immediately scribbled out two pages of automatic writing, which was a message for me from the dolphins. This two pages, which I still have today, said I would be doing work with the dolphins and it was really important. I probably wouldn't believe what they were saying, but to just trust them. It was going to happen.

So then I forgot about that until early 1986 when I suddenly had this lucid dream that turned into a full blown Kundalini awakening explosion. In my dream, there were thousands of people on the beach in Santa Monica, and the whole bay was full of dolphins, absolutely just crammed with dolphins. I had this urge to beckon every one into the water. We needed to get into the water for a baptism, to immerse ourselves in the dolphins and their energies. I noticed that almost nobody could see the dolphins or me, except ten people, while everyone else was in a separate reality.

I turned away from the water with the idea I had to strip off my clothes, which I understood later meant I had to ditch some baggage. Then I entered the water and began swimming north up the coast. I couldn't see the dolphins and yet I knew they were all behind me and I had to keep swimming.

I was swimming with this ever-increasing sense of anticipation, which my mind interpreted as the dolphins approaching from behind, the end point being when they were going to overtake me. The excitement was building to such an electric crescendo that just at the moment when I thought they were going to overtake me, it just exploded in my spine and I had this ecstatic explosion. I woke up in the dream with my body streaming electric neon energy, closed my eyes and I was back in.

From that next morning, I was obsessively on a mission to find dolphins. I went to Maui and chartered a boat for a group of twelve people. We all went out to Lanai and looked for dolphins, though we didn't find any. About six months after the lucid dream, somebody gave me a little round enameled pin, which was two dolphins in a yin-yang position, light blue and dark blue. I pinned it onto my camera straps.

About another six months passed when friends of mine invited me to come down to Florida to the Dolphin Research Center where they were filming to do the music for them. When I got down there, it was the last day they were going to be filming, as the DRC had been closed for them the whole weekend to film. I hung out with the film crew and ran off a couple of rolls of film. I also swam with the dolphins just as a guest. The filming ended and everyone left. I was alone for the whole day with these dolphins and had some incredible experiences.

On that first day I had just been swimming with them when they said, "Come on, get out of the water." They wanted me to start shooting again. So I grabbed my camera and the dolphins started jumping. I ran off a few frames. Later I realized what I had captured. The shot I got has now become very famous. It is called Synchronicity, where the two dolphins are flipping in the water in the ying-yang position.

Somehow I didn't realize what I had gotten. I even printed up the shots and was selling them at a place in LA where there was a channeling session going on each week. Finally some people said, "This is pretty amazing." They gave me the money to produce a poster of the synchronicity print and that started the whole thing.

When I published the second poster, everything took off. From that point on, I've been devoted to dolphins. I stopped being an interior designer, began going out two or three times a year to be with dolphins, and finally started taking people out with me.

Since then, I have been devoted to portraying the dolphins as best I can with the message that we not only share this planet with other truly splendid species, but they come with tremendous grace and magic. The dolphins bring us synchronicity through our incredible experiences interacting with them, which is so amazing.

The fact that I had that little yin-yang pin on my camera strap for six months was such an inside job. Something was already going on that I wasn't aware of that led to this synchronicity, and that led to the posters and the posters led to my working with dolphins extensively.

By the time I had four posters out, it was totally supporting me and this got me really good camera equipment and out with the dolphins a couple of times a year. So, the dolphins and then the Synchronicity photo completely changed my life. After about ten years, this Synchronicity image was bringing in eighty percent of my income and has kept me involved with the dolphins ever since.

*Daniel McCulloch is considered one of the foremost dolphin photogra-*phers and significant resources for images of wild dolphins in the world. His original photographic prints have been exhibited in Tokyo, Los Angeles, Kauai, and Santa Fe, and have won international awards. His images, including a line of Fine Art posters, help to portray the extraordinary beauty, sensitivity and playful joy, astonishing intelligence, and graceful power that characterizes this wonderful being all the world loves without knowing why.

Daniel is a freelance underwater and land photographer, undertaking assignments for publishers and filmmakers, both as photographer as well as associate producer, location scout and coordinator, including such films as Academy Award winning "Dolphins, Minds in the Water," "Quest for the Dolphin Spirit," "Dolphins," and "For the Love of Dolphins."

Daniel's devotion to the dolphins inspired his commitment to showing the world that we share this planet with a truly sentient species who, history has shown us, have been actively reaching out to us in the wild, to intelligently interact with us in all sorts of ways. He takes people out to swim with friendly free-roaming dolphins in the wild ocean to give people an intimate experience with them, in their own environment on their own terms. The extraordinary experience of being greeted by these dolphins in their own habitat, whether in wild play or serene intimate eye contact, is so exhilarating and uplifting that many people consider it a spiritual experience. Daniel revels in taking people to have this experience.

This relationship between dolphin and human is the main focus of Daniel's passion, the focus of his current photography, and the subject of his photography book on the relationship between human and dolphins, historical and contemporary. For more information on Daniel and his offerings please see: http://www.dolphinsynergy.com.

CHAPTER FORTY NINE

Letting Go
A Story About Surrender

by Karina Ashana

I was gifted growing up in that I had the opportunity to partake of several different worlds. My father was an American military officer, so we became a kind of gypsy family moving sometimes as often as once a year to various parts of the globe. My mother being Norwegian born, on several occasions we returned to her homeland when my father was on restricted tours of duty. I remember speaking at least two languages, often dreaming in two parallel realities, and spending summers swimming in icy fjords and later sailing past quaint coastal villages.

As a teenager, I had a thousand questions about everything, far more than my parents were prepared to tackle, and I found myself drawn to metaphysics for some of my more profound answers. Early on I knew I wanted to make a difference and became involved in education, studying movement, and then teaching in the Waldorf schools, an alternative and artistically oriented approach to education that integrates body, mind, and spirit. Much later, after a stint in corporate America and living in California, I became an entrepreneur founding my own graphic design business. By then the dolphins were figuring largely in my imagination.

I remember attending a Whole Life Expo and participating in a guided meditation visualizing the dolphins. I emerged from a place of deep trance crying and knowing that through my dolphin guides I had touched a core part of myself. I knew and felt deeply loved. Their message: *You are a precious being and most dearly loved.*

The name of my business became Dolphin Press. Along with the dolphins I also felt a kinship to Greece, another one of my Dad's early assignments. We had spent the summer snorkeling in the Aegean Sea, island hopping and visiting the many temples and sacred sites. Delphic, Delphi, dolphin all felt like the right place to draw upon for inspiration and attunement. Swimming with the dolphins was inevitable and in hindsight, leading trips to be with the dolphins has become my next assignment. Everything that I have experienced tells me we are entering into a new time on the planet when co-creation is the new game plan. The forces of nature, animal and plant life, all have their own kind of intelligence that is working to restore our world to balance. We are all remembering to listen to each other, to speak multiple languages, to participate and enjoy consciousness on many levels of reality and ultimately to realign ourselves with the power of love.

In the summer of 1998, I decided it was time, finally, to actually swim with the dolphins. The dolphins with their magic and mystique had occupied my imagination and consciousness for years. They were the inspiration behind my graphic and web design business, they had inspired me to dance again, and most of all they had inspired me to play, to be silly and less serious about life. I had learned once again to delight in the mystery of the unexpected, in spontaneous action, the unexpected coincidence. I thought, "I should go somewhere where I could actually get into the water and experience dolphins in 3-D reality." I started to research dolphin swim programs and trips. Of course, not long after I had set my intention, I met Jon who was planning to lead a group to the big island of Hawaii to be with the Spinner Dolphins the following spring.

Jon had been leading personal growth workshops for years and he was looking for someone to help design the visuals for his flyers and advertising. I was thrilled! In my imagination, I immersed myself in the dancing waters of a turquoise bay on the western side of the island. I flew with the Goddess Pele as she oversaw rivers of underground molten lava and sacred caves and felt the breath of balmy ocean breezes on my skin.

As we got closer to the date of our departure, I remember suddenly realizing we were flying all this way for just a short window of time for a date with some wild Spinner Dolphins. We were to meet them somewhere out in one of the largest natural bays in the Hawaiian Islands. What are the chances, realistically, I thought of seeing them and in my heart, a great sadness and longing welled up. I had waited so many years for this experience. What if they didn't come? For days I struggled within myself, wanting to prepare myself for a very possible scenario, the likelihood that we would not find the dolphins. Perhaps, they already had another engagement, perhaps they were vacationing down south, or maybe they would sleep right through our visit. My mind quickly came up with a myriad of rational reasons why the dolphins would not show.

Since then, I have again and again come to observe this dilemma between the doubting mind and the heart. The heart which longs and aches and loves until it hurts and the mind that scrambles to protect us from disappointment, failure, and disillusionment. After many days of praying and "talking" with the dolphins in my head, feeling this great ache and telling them how much I would dearly love to spend time with them, I came to a place inside myself where I let go of my attachment of seeing them. I told them that if they chose not to come that was okay and I would still enjoy my vacation in Hawaii. Nothing would be lost. In fact, everything would be perfect just as it was.

At that place of detachment, letting go, surrendering, and renewed lightness, something happened. In the last week before we were to leave, I was very busy with work. I was putting in long hours and I had countless details to attend to. In the midst of all that noise, I started to hear something else. Faintly at first, small chirpings, and then whis-tlings until it became unmistakable, it was the sound of dolphins. Then it got louder. I remember thinking, this is unbelievable and thank you for communicating, but now I'm having a hard time concentrating. All week long it was like I had tuned into a very special and distinctive radio frequency.

At the end of the week, we flew from San Francisco to Kona, Hawaii. From the air I could see the moon like lava landscape of the west shore. We arrived at our beautifully situated hotel south of town, ate dinner, and then headed for bed. We were scheduled to wake up early, the next morning to go swim with dolphins.

In the haziness of early morning light, we sheepishly greeted one another, coffee cups in hand. My heart hammered in my throat. The moment had arrived. Would the dolphins show up for their date? An invitation made through the ethers and precipitated in the heart.

Slowly we drove the winding road down towards the glistening waters of the bay and pulled into a large sandy parking lot. Large red hibiscus flowers lay strewn across the ground. I walked toward the beach and then I saw it, the splash of a single dolphin jumping just off shore. I was so astonished I started to cry. I realized then that if this was the only contact we had with the dolphins all week I would be very happy. An old Hawaiian man sitting nearby, grinned and quietly commented, "They haven't been here for weeks, but today they are here."

To my delight, we did find a whole pod of dolphins. They showed up on each of the three days we were "scheduled" to swim with them. It was magical and dreamlike, like being in an altered state of reality, another dimension. We discovered the dolphins liked playing a leaf game, passing little leaves to one another from fin to fin and sometimes catching them with their flukes. As a group we decided we would come down to the bay for a fourth day and bring the dolphins a gift of leaves and flowers.

That last morning, we carefully swam out with our gifts and although we looked long and diligently, the dolphins were nowhere to be found. We had not had a prior agreement to swim with the dolphins and in their enigmatic fashion, they had quietly vanished. So we returned to the beach and with our flowers and leaves created a beautiful mandala on the sand imbued with prayers of humbleness and gratitude.

This particular teaching for me was about the power of the heart. If the feeling in the heart is strong, then it is inevitable that you will draw to yourself your longing and desire. Let go and love, quiet the mind, and what you love will find you. Since this experience, I continue to notice how what I long for truly with my heart, with a loud "yes" that I feel in the core of my being, be they people, projects, places, or experiences, come towards me. They do show up. Love appears to be irresistible. I cry more, I express myself more. I follow my intuition.

I also seem to have more dreams and fewer plans. When I look in my datebook there is very little in it. Yet, I am constantly engaged. Life is full. I hold my dreams out in front of me and then forget about them. Invariably they show up again in unexpected ways. I worry less about the details and spend more time putting color into my daydreams, adding scents and enjoying the warmth of the sun on my skin. Time and time again I've experienced what often appears to be loss reveals itself as attachment to a particular form and the fear of change.

When my father died after a difficult illness, along with a financial loss, potential change of residence, and personal relationships disintegrating before my eyes, it was like being on a raft out in the middle of the ocean without a compass. But the truth is, even in the midst of a storm of emotion was the understanding, "I" am still here, everything is unfolding perfectly. Relax. Stay calm, listen and catch the next wave. It will come, and it did. In this moment, I am living in the perfect place. I am in the perfect relationship, and the mystery continues.

This leads me to one more thing, to what I call living in dolphin time. To me dolphins live in circular time as opposed to linear time. Life may appear to move in straight lines, but it's actually moving in many directions at once perfectly synchronised. We are not separate but part of a much greater pod that has its own intelligence. Our job is to tune in and get out of our own way.

I now lead dolphin encounter adventures with Jon to the Caribbean. Every year we travel to a beautiful tropical island paradise and spend a week with the Bottlenose Dolphins. I have learned many more games, the seaweed game, the shell game, the catch-the-fish game.

On my last trip to the Caribbean, I noticed dolphins carrying pieces of seaweed between their teeth and on their flippers. Intrigued I found some grass and gently tossed it out in front of a young dolphin. Deftly catching it between his teeth, he then "blew" it back to me. I returned his toss and the game continued. We were playing catch!

This game led to the shell game. When I dropped the shell, the dolphin gracefully spiraled down to the bottom to retrieve our "ball." The catch-the-fish game started with a young dolphin enjoying her breakfast and turned into "watch how many times I can throw this silly fish into the air before it falls apart!" Their silliness is contagious and I still feel ecstatically happy in their presence and cry when I see dolphins jumping spontaneously for the sheer joy of it.

Appendum

Blessings

Blessings to you, Beloved
We bring you now to the
Sacred Sanctuary of our Hearts.
We are One
In timeless space.
We dwell as one with all humanity
We bless you with Healing
We fill you with Peace
We initiate you to Joy
The Forgotten Presence of
Your life long ago
For once you dwelled
In Joy with us.
You knew the Sacredness of Life
You followed Inner Guidance
And lived True as Celestial Ones
Divine Beings in your own right
Dwelling on Earth with your heart in the Heavens
Walking through the world knowing your Truth
Filling your days imparting the Ancient Wisdom to younger souls
And bringing the richness of Life
In its most spectacular forms
Into the world
Through your Wisdom
Through your Knowledge
Through your Truth

- The Dolphins

About The Author

Whether its pioneering work in the psyche, bringing out her landmark discoveries in global conferences, writing books, leading TheQuest Trainings, or expressing her musical talents, Aurora Juliana Ariel possesses the proverbial Midas touch. Her brand of alchemy is the sacred sort, yielding a gold one can only discover within. Pioneering doctor and scientist, author and musician, entrepreneur and producer, mystic and healer, Aurora is a Renaissance woman for the New Millennium.

#1 best selling Author, Creator of TheQuest, and Award Winning Author of the Earth 2012-33 Series, she is a Pioneering Doctor and Healer whose research and work have given her a profound understanding of the psyche and tools to heal an ailing humanity. Working with countless individuals with miraculous results, she has made many landmark discoveries bringing a new understanding to our present planetary equation. She holds 38 certificates and degrees in advanced healing methods as well as a BA, MA, and PhD in psychology. She is also a Kahuna in the Hawaiian Tradition, successor of an Hawaiian Kahuna in the Morna Simeona Lineage, Shaolin Grand Master Pang.

Her landmark discovery of the cause of suffering and the development of a cure (TheQuest) is her legacy to a planet. Her formula can be found in TheQuest: Heal Your Life, Change Your Destiny, which she has gifted FREE forever via all her websites, giving tools to transform lives, actualize potentials, and help end suffering on Earth.

Committed to positive world change, she is a Humanitarian Futurist with an extraordinary heart and offering for humanity, who has dedicated her life to creating a better world through The Aurora Trust and its vehicles of planetary service, the Earth Vision Foundation, the Institute of Advanced Healing, TheQuest University and AEOS.

Through TheQuest University, she has launched TheQuest 7 level Certificate Training Courses and developed TheQuest Rehabilitation models for prisoners, abused women, youth at risk, addicts, Veterans and individuals with PTSD, mental imbalances and brain chemistry disorders, and a host of Optimum Health, Lifestyle, Weight Loss, and other programs.

She founded the Earth Vision Foundation and Earth Vision Alliance to bring forth her vast humanitarian endeavor, the Earth Vision Center project, which is a living library of the advances of our time set within a sustainable pristine natural environment.

Inspired to translate her knowledge into healing and life transforming media productions, Dr. Ariel launched her multimedia company, AEOS, and released 34 first products in 7 collections of music, books and audio CDs since 2008 with many more to come. In the ground breaking Earth 2012-33 Series, she speaks eloquently of the significance of this historic time and the challenges before us, bringing a timely remedy and insights inspiring people worldwide to make a difference.

Dr. Ariel has been endorsed by the Who's Who Worldwide Organization and her projects and life work have been showcased in articles and news reports on their Worldwide Charities and Worldwide News websites.

She is available for speaking engagements, to present her landmark work at global conferences and events, train counselors in TheQuest, and give coaching, counseling, and trainings for individuals, companies, and organizations committed to positive world change.

For more information about Dr. Ariel, her work, programs, courses, rehabilitation models, and products see: http://www.AuroraJulianaAriel.com.

*The*Quest

T heQuest is a revolutionary breakthrough Counseling Theory and Healing Practice that includes a complete Self Healing System developed by Dr. Ariel after years of extensive research and work. It is designed to bring timely knowledge and a missing piece to rehab centers, prison reform, addiction, youth at risk, 12 step and other programs, greatly increasing their success rate.

For practitioners, it is a way to move your clients quickly from upset to peace, and to help them quickly resolve deep issues, step free of limiting and self sabotaging patterns, addictions, and dysfunctional personality traits, and realize their greater potential.

For the layperson, it is a way to gain greater understanding and mastery of your psychology, empowering authentic self-expression and creative fulfillment.

For couples, it is an essential ingredient in conscious relationship, where each person works with their own psychology as issues arise. Greater harmony and clear communication can exist when the focus is on resolution through loving, compassionate interactions.

The Institute of Advanced Healing

In 2000, Aurora Juliana Ariel, PhD founded the Institute of Advanced Healing, a non-profit organization in Hawaii, to bring forth the principles and the practice of TheQuest worldwide, providing cutting edge Trainings, Classes, Counseling, Coaching, Support Groups, advanced healing products, community outreach, advocacy and other services.

Dr. Ariel developed certificate-training programs and set up a model chapter in Aspen, Colorado in 2005 to be duplicated around the world by graduates of TheQuest Life Coach and Counselor Certification Course.

She has successfully worked with youth at risk, addicts, abusers, and the abused, people with serious illnesses and trauma, and a host of dysfunctional personality traits and life conditions with tremendous results.

TheQuest Self Healing System Dr. Ariel developed, is an integral part of rehabilitation models she created for prisoners, abused women, youth at risk, addicts, Veterans and individuals with PTSD, mental imbalances and brain chemistry disorders.

She has given classes to teens at High Schools, released TheQuest to the public on her websites, TV, radio, support groups, and via her Ask Dr. Aurora Column, and is now training people in her seven-level Certificate Training Courses provided through TheQuest University she founded in 2012. For more information see http://www.IOAH.org.

The Human Dilemma

The work at the Institute of Advanced Healing has a very clear focus: to bring TheQuest to a world in dire need. The subconscious programming that has created the human condition with its propensity for misery and suffering must be healed. People worldwide need to understand their psychology and learn how to become masters of their destiny, rather than victims to their fate. The cause of suffering must be healed for the world to begin to reflect the noble ideals that are encoded in the hearts of humanity.

When people are engulfed and entrapped in their human patterns, a higher destiny is never fulfilled. Instead, the destiny that plays out is from this programming. The degree that the higher nature, which Dr. Ariel calls the 'Authentic Self,' can express through the individual, the more the person will be able to experience a higher awareness and ability to attain a greater mastery over their life circumstances. Presently, this is very rare on Earth. Even in the spiritual communities of the world where the greatest trainings and highest information is attained, there is a continual dysfunctional aspect to people's lives, because the subconscious patterns are not being addressed. They are being suppressed or spiritually bypassed, while they continue to work their havoc.

It has long been believed that people cannot change their personality traits or heal their addictions. The best that can be done is for individuals to understand their patterns and strive to overcome them. But this method does not work because physiologically the limbic system, the part of the brain that is activated under stress in what has been called the Fight and Flight Syndrome, is different from the area of the brain where the will and determination is found, which is in the frontal lobe. Therefore, under stress, the individual will revert to Fight and Flight, and the subconscious pattern will begin running. They will move into survival and seek substances or run other addictive behaviors to alleviate suffering. Physiologically, the blood will recede from the frontal lobe impairing will and therefore control.

When the deeper patterns have not been addressed and healed, people will understand their addictions and strive to stay sober or substance free, but if they undergo a series of life stresses, it will be easy for them to fall off the wagon. This is because the subconscious has been left out of the equation.

Currently, because the deeper work is not being done, there is only an 8% success rate in rehab centers and addiction programs. The programs today help strengthen the individual's resolve, but do not provide a complete healing. TheQuest Seven Step Counseling Technique provides the 'missing piece,' which can greatly increase the success rate at these centers and with people suffering from addictions of every kind.

A Breakthrough Technology

Understanding the human dilemma and being concerned that psychologists today normally only scratch the surface when working with clients, thereby keeping people coming for sessions for years without any real movement, Dr. Ariel developed a way to move people quickly through their issues and heal their underlying patterns. Her revolutionary method provides a complete resolution, healing, and breakthrough in each session.

TheQuest Life Mastery Path

When you understand your psychology, you have greater control over your life circumstances. As you master TheQuest tools and learn how to heal every condition from within, you have a greater command of your destiny. Your Authentic Self is given room for a fuller creative expression in and through you and a new passion and excitement about life returns. You wake up looking forward to each new day and what amazing things will happen next. Unexpected events and synchronistic meetings increase resulting in key alliances with like-minded people for a greater purpose. Life takes on a sweeter quality, as you know you are fulfilling a sacred destiny. TheQuest Life Mastery Path training is available in TheQuest courses, providing you with the tools and knowledge of how to free yourself from every pattern and condition that has limited you, kept you feeling disempowered, burdened, or held back, so that you can realize your full potential.

Heal Your Life, Change Your Destiny

When you heal your life, you change your destiny. It is as if you are defying a powerful law like gravity. For the human patterns within you are creating a different reality than the Life your True Nature would give you. Clearing the way for this Authentic Self to lend its wisdom and power to your life, allows you to fulfill a higher destiny.

TheQuest Counseling Sessions

While Dr. Ariel is largely on sabbatical focusing on writing, appearances, and training individuals worldwide, she is from time to time available for personal sessions and for shorter personalized training programs. These are weekly or bi-monthly sessions over 6 months to 1 year that include Life Coaching and Counseling sessions along with personal training in TheQuest Life Mastery Path. Dr. Ariel is also available at times for personal 7 - 14 day retreats, where her focus is completely on you and your optimum health and well-being, and for Total Life Intensives where every area of your life is addressed and transformed.

TheQuest University

TheQuest Heal Your Life, Change Your Destiny - 3 Level Certification Courses - can be held anywhere in the world. If you'd like to sponsor one in your area, receive counseling sessions or life coaching, or receive certification as a Life Coach and Counselor, please: info@IOAH.org.

Levels 4 - 7 are for those who want a career as a Life Coach, Counselor, Spiritual Leader in the Organization, and/or Minister.

Become a Certified Life Coach and Counselor

TheQuest Life Coach and Counselor Certification Course (Level 5) provides an in-depth study of psychology in a format that is experiential, life changing, and empowering. These highly informative trainings, within a compassionate caring environment, can be taken virtually from anywhere in the world. Each course is unique per the student and their current life challenges and is, therefore, a journey to the heart of these conditions where they are completely healed and transformed, returning you to

Authentic Self awareness. You master tools to heal self sabotaging patterns, addictions, personality traits, and dysfunctions, deal effectively with health and career issues, and transform challenging relationship dynamics. In this way, you transform and empower your life while learning how to help others.

As you learn how to clear a pathway to the Authentic Self and its inner wisdom, you begin to give it more power in your daily life and to fulfill your higher Destiny Potential. By mastering your 'shadow,' you learn to live in the Miracle Consciousness. This is when you begin living a Miraculous Life.

TheQuest Life Coach and Counselor Training is a one-year (or accelerated 9 month) certification course. Highly experiential in its application, this program gives you the life mastery skills, knowledge, and tools to become a Master Life Coach and/or Counselor, with the ability to practice anywhere in the world.

Doctors, Psychologists, Health Practitioners, Life Coaches, and Ministers may qualify for the accelerated training level 4 program for TheQuest Counselor Certification.

Donations Are Gratefully Accepted

To sponsor and/or support Dr. Ariel's work and the Institute's mission to bring TheQuest to communities throughout the world, you can make a tax deductible donation to the Institute of Advanced Healing at: http://www..IOAH.org.

You can also donate *TheQuest: Heal Your Life, Change Your Destiny* books or TheQuest Complete Self Healing System (book, Healing Journal, CD) to rehab centers, prisons, hospitals, health retreats, safe houses for the abused, addiction, abuse, and youth at risk programs, or place of your choice. *Your donations are greatly appreciated!*

TheQuest Programs
Healing Lives, Changing Destinies

Total Life Transformation Program

Life Coach & Counselor Certification Course

Counselor Certification Course

Miracle Weight Loss Program

Relationship Healing

Addiction Release Program

Brain Chemistry Balancing

Women's Empowerment Program

After Rehab – Maui 21 Day Retreat

Maui Rejuvenation 21 Day Retreat

In-depth information on all programs and products
can be found on the following websites:

http://www.IOAH.org
http://www.AuroraJulianaAriel.com

A New Frontier in Multimedia Arts

Media is one of the most powerful ways we can facilitate change today because of its immediate affect upon the psyche. Understanding this, Alchemists of the New Millennium know that transmitting positive images, ideas, and language of a beneficial and healing nature can quickly shift consciousness, open up new doorways of thought, and empower individuals to be their best selves.

Through conscious media, we have a tremendous opportunity to assist in this next evolutionary leap in human consciousness and safeguard against the repetition of the mistakes of the past, assisting humanity to become conscious stewards of the Earth and inspiring them to bring forth their greatest gifts and achievements on behalf of a people and a planet. By helping catalyze this quantum shift, we become Alchemists of Media who have an important role to play in this New Millennium.

At AEOS, we are determined to make a difference! All our products are exquisitely designed with the highest quality materials, highest vibration of colors, images, and subject matter, and transmit, energetically and creatively, the highest frequencies. We believe our vast array of extraordinary products and services are destined to transform millions of lives throughout the planet.

AEOS, Inc. is a Multimedia Production Company founded by Chairwoman/CEO, Aurora Juliana Ariel, PhD. TheQuest is a proprietary revolutionary breakthrough technology she developed, representing one of the Company's five collections of inspired music, books, and films, placing AEOS on the leading edge in the new psychology/self help genre.

Look for more exciting AEOS products soon, as well as Dr. Ariel's upcoming books in the Earth 2012-33 series, which delve further into her insights on the Worldwide Awakening and Global Renaissance she believes are birthing a New World. To order our products please go to our website at: http://www.AEOS.ws

Healing Inspired Music & Media

Dr. Ariel has studied the powerful influence music and media have on the psyche. She believes "transformational media is a key to creating the quantum leap in consciousness so necessary at this time, if we are going to avert the many dire potentials before us and positively affect the evolutionary cycle of our planet."

Understanding that conscious media can have a profound and healing influence upon individuals and even transform lives, her greatest love has been to translate her knowledge into multimedia productions that have a healing, uplifting, and inspiring effect.

In 2003, she founded AEOS (which translates from Greek as Aurora, Goddess of the Dawn, the New Dawn, and New Horizon) to bring forth her inspired music, books, and films.

In her words, "My joy is in translating the knowledge I have gained into transformational multimedia productions that facilitate positive change within the psyche of humanity, profoundly affecting the consciousness of the planet and assisting humanity to advance forward into an Age of Enlightenment and Peace."

As of New Year's Eve 2012, Aurora had released 34 healing inspired music, books, and audio CDs since 2008, with much more to come! (7 books, 11 audio CDs and 16 music CDs, all available via AEOS and in book and music stores worldwide.

Earth 2012-33:
The Ultimate Quest
How To Find Peace in a World of Chaos

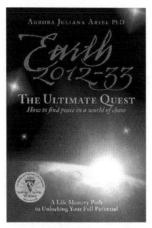

Award Winning 1st Book in the Earth 2012-33 Series
By Aurora Juliana Ariel, PhD

Cataloging the profound shift presently taking place within the psyche of humanity, Dr. Ariel points to the fact that we are living in unprecedented times! Weaving a blend of sacred prophecies, prophetic visions, and scientific predictions around 2012-33, she unveils a glorious potential that is casting its first rays of light on Earth, illuminating the Dark Night we are presently passing through, and providing a "missing piece" to traversing the challenges of this time.

In this first book in the Earth 2012-33 series, Dr. Ariel guides the reader on a personal quest, providing 7 Master Keys to Inner Peace and a revolutionary breakthrough Self Counseling Technology, TheQuest, that is easy to apply. Distilled into seven powerful steps, this healing process is designed to accelerate a personal and planetary transformation that could help end suffering on Earth. Her message, "If we want to avert the dire potentials before us, we must look within and unlock the subconscious patterns behind our challenging life conditions."

For timely updates, sign up at
http://www.AuroraJulianaAriel.com
More books in the Earth 2012-33 series are coming soon!

Earth 2012-33:
Time of the Awakening Soul
How Millions of People Are Changing Our Future

Global Renaissance & Glorious Future Unveiled

By Aurora Juliana Ariel, PhD

The Earth 2012-33 Saga continues with a Journey into the Miraculous as millions of Awakening Souls alter the course of Earth's Destiny. Weaving a prophetic vision of an Illumined Future, stories of extraordinary encounters reveal the significant time we are in. Find out if you are an Awakening Soul. Take the 22 Master Qualities test.

This inspiring, prophetic book speaks to a Soul Awakening that if embraced, can take humanity through a quantum leap into a future Eden that has forever lived as a vision within the hearts of humanity. --John Gray, Author of Men Are From Mars, Women Are From Venus

This book rises to the heights of poetry, unveiling a majesty of human potential like a torch in the morning light. It adds its brilliance to what is silently arising all around us. --Jonathan Kolber, Circle of Light

Earth 2012-33: The Violet Age
A Return to Eden

By Aurora Juliana Ariel, PhD

Miracles abound as the Earth 2012-33 saga continues. A host of phenomenon behind the Great Awakening are impacting millions of people worldwide. From extraordinary encounters to mystical experiences of every kind, a quantum shift is taking place in the consciousness of humanity.

This book takes us further into the mystical side of our present planetary equation and unveils the mystery behind the Violet People and the unique destiny that drives them to turn the tide at the 11th hour, saving humanity from untold disasters.

While darkness increases on the planet and humanity stands facing gaping jaws of disaster on a Grand Scale, a glorious New World is being birthed from within the psyche of humanity.

"A clarion call to consciousness awakening to itself, the Earth 2012 -33 series quickens spiritual unfolding by lovingly guiding you through one of the most difficult and transformative periods in human history." — **Leonard Laskow, M.D., author of Healing With Love**

Earth 2012-33:
Oracles of the Sea
The Human Dolphin Connection

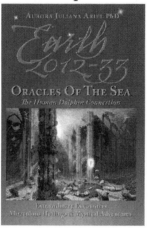

By Aurora Juliana Ariel, PhD

For the past 33 years, dolphin interactions with humans have increased dramatically, resulting in a host of miraculous stories that include extraordinary encounters, mystical experiences, profound visions, telepathic communications, unexpected healings, life changes, inner transformations, and spiritual awakenings. Amazingly, these experiences are similar to events recorded at the advent of the Golden Age in Greece.

This worldwide phenomenon speaks to a critical time in Earth's history, as awakened from normal lives, diverse backgrounds, and belief systems, the thousands of individuals experiencing these encounters share a common bond and responsibility. Weaving the threads of this phenomenon from its most ancient historical significance into the present, we find we are moving into a future that may yet be our most Glorious Age.

"The Earth 2012-33 series will speak to hearts around the world. It will quicken the Awakening in many who have tried to make sense of similar experiences. It will bring relief to those who have pictured a negative future. It will help others realize the potential that is being birthed within us all in this extraordinary time. After working closely with Dr. Ariel on this project, I am excited to see the powerful ramifications it'll have on people around The world." — Jack Canfield, co-author of the Chicken Soup for the Soul series

TheQuest
Heal Your Life, Change Your Destiny

A Breakthrough Self Healing System

"This book will ignite a Revolution In Consciousness
so powerful, it could restore Peace on Earth."

"People would not choose to stay in pain
if they knew this was available."

In this ground breaking book, Dr. Ariel unveils her breakthrough Healing System, the 7 Master Keys to Inner Peace, and a powerful Life Mastery Path. She demystifies the psyche like no other work has done and provides tools to quickly resolve issues, restore harmony in relationships, master your psychology, and heal the scars from your painful past.

Through years of pioneering work in the 'uncharted realms' of the psyche, she made many landmark discoveries, uncovered the cause of suffering, and developed a cure that could change the destiny of the planet. Distilled into seven powerful steps, TheQuest is designed to accelerate a personal and planetary transformation that could help end suffering on Earth. Inspiring a Journey of Self Discovery that is empowering and life changing, TheQuest unlocks the Secret Code to your True Identity and provides a Key to Actualizing your Full Potential.

Sign up to get the E-book FREE
at http://www.AuroraJulianaAriel.com

The Indwelling Spirit

Timely Messages For the Souls of Earth
An Illumined Pathway to Freedom, Enlightenment and Peace

This inspiring, timely book opens the door to a Soul Awakening that if embraced, can create a joyful life filled with Love, Harmony and Beauty. --*John Gray, Author of Men Are From Mars, Women Are From Venus*

Spend some time each day with these beautiful writings and feel your life rise on wings of love. --*Gay Hendricks, Author of Conscious Living, Co-author with Kathlyn Hendricks of Conscious Loving*

This is information that nourishes the soul. --*Wayne Dyer, Author of over thirty books including The Power of Intention.*

The resounding echo through this book is that we are loved. Through this LOVE of the Indwelling Spirit we are inspired to see, know, and love ourselves in the way that God loves us. When we love ourselves absolutely, we give ourselves our best life. Embracing ourselves from this Divine Perspective, we live Sacred and Abundant Lives accessing the Great Power Within. As we consecrate the moments of our existence to a Higher Purpose, we allow the Divine Plan for our life to fulfill itself in and through us. Living in the Miracle Consciousness, we enter the Miraculous Life, a sacred and richly fulfilling existence where we uncover Life's Sacred Mysteries, witnessing to the majesty and glory of our Authentic Self as we walk our Highest Destiny Path.

A Guide to Freedom, Enlightenment and Peace, the writings in this book inspire us upon an Illumined Pathway to realize our Full Potential. They unveil the Secret Code to our True Destiny. These Sacred Writings reveal the Majesty and Power of our Innate Divinity and speak to the extraordinary mission we have come to Earth to fulfill at this significant time. Eloquently written through Letters from the Inner Self, this book is destined to help awaken and inspire humanity in its next evolutionary leap in consciousness, igniting Positive World Change and a planetary transformation unparalleled in history, restoring Eden on Earth.

Aurora's Solo Music CD

Renaissance of Grace

*The exotic vocals of Aurora with Bruce BecVar
weave a mystical blend that is both uplifting and inspiring,
transporting us into a world of transcendence and light.*

Talented musicians grace this gypsy world music album including renowned multi-instrumentalist, Bruce BecVar; Percussionist Rafael Padilla; Peruvian Shaman, Tito La Rosa on Andean Pan Pipes; Gypsy Violinist, Don Lax; Violinist Rachel Handlin, Michael Buono on drums, and Brian BecVar on Synthesizer.

"Aurora Juliana Ariel is one of those rare artists whose clear voice and beautiful music transmit to more than just the ear, but reaches into the listener's heart with hidden healing messages. Coupled with the extraordinary talent of musician/composer Bruce BecVar, Aurora's offering awakens our inner peace and invites our own calm center to bubble up to the surface. Aurora's mystical language is at once both exotic and familiar, adventurous and comforting. Renaissance of Grace, as one of the song titles indicates, is truly a Journey Of The Heart: one pleasurable piece of music after another that you will never want to end. The work as a whole lives up to its name." -**Pamela Polland, Award Winning Recording Artist, Vocal Coach**

"Journey of the Heart and Shiva Moon are two of the most heartfelt ballads you will hear on any release, their voices soaring together and weaving in and out of fluid guitar lines, gentle piano, bass flute, and percussion. The lyrical romanticism that is expressed owes much to the spirit of Aurora Juliana Ariel, who collaborates with Bruce BecVar to create inspired songs." —**DL, New Age Voice**

Gypsy Soul, Heart of Passion

Bruce BecVar & Aurora

*Fast paced Nuevo Flamenco Songs
drop into slower, exotic melodies...
As Bruce BecVar's master guitarmanship
weaves a mystical blend of vocals and
gypsy guitar with the transcendent vocals of Aurora
amid violin, pan flutes, and percussion by
a host of illustrious musicians*

Talented musicians grace this gypsy world music album including renowned multi-instrumentalist, Bruce BecVar; Percussionist Rafael Padilla; Peruvian Shaman, Tito La Rosa on Andean Pan Pipes; Gypsy Violinist – Don Lax; Rachel Handlin and Charlie Bisharat on violins, Michael Buono on piano, Steve Reid on percussion, Brandon Fields and Richard Hardy on Saxophone, and Brian BecVar on Synthesizer.

"This album is a therapeutic blend of New Age musical sound graced by the angelic voice of Ariel who is not without her match in BecVar. Ariel and Becvar put together a musical experience worth cherishing. The album's music is relaxingly invigorating and will stimulate you with its deep thought and meaning. An inspiring, earnest and spiritual journey is what you're about to embark on. Think Strunz and Farah on a spiritual path." --**Manny Auguste, Bryan Farrish Radio Promotion.**

River of Gold

Bruce BecVar & Aurora

This music uplifts and inspires, enchants and awakens,
and keeps you coming back for more!

A brilliant collaboration, River of Gold is a magical weave of guitar, instrumentals, and exotic vocals, this album has been highly acclaimed for the SPECTACULAR LOVE and TRANSCENDENT JOY that fills every note, carrying you into a world of romance, beauty and light.

> *"Journey of the Heart and Shiva Moon are two of the most heartfelt ballads you will hear on any release, their voices soaring together and weaving in and out of fluid guitar lines, gentle piano, bass, flute, and percussion. The lyrical romanticism that is expressed owes much to the spirit of Aurora Juliana Ariel, who collaborates with Bruce BecVar to create inspired songs."* --**DL, New Age Voice**

> *"The sweet duet "Journey of the Heart" is a dance of masculine and feminine voices delicately interspersed with exquisite guitar rhythms. As I listen to this and other pieces, I am transported to a land where love and romance abound and the beauty of nature flows through my heart like a river of gold. This recording is deeply passionate, exotic, and simply unforgettable."* --**Betty Timm**

> *"BecVar generates electricity in partnership with vocalist and co-producer Aurora. Abundantly intimate, this album is nothing less than a magnificent mash note, a Valentine that all can share."* –**PJ Birosik**

Healing Music for an Awakening World

Aurora
Bruce BecVar
&
Krystofer

AWAKENING WORLD
CELESTIAL FIRE
ECHOES OF ETERNITY
EMBRACE OF THE BELOVED
EVERLASTING JOY
SOUL FREEDOM
LIGHT FROM REALMS ETERNAL
LOVE's ETERNAL FLAME
LOVE'S SACRED FIRE
MYSTIC ECHOES
RAINBOW IN A BLUE SKY
SACRED DESTINY

Profound healing can take place as you experience these Sacred Healing Journeys. Sequenced to perfection, the masterful weave of exquisite melodies with exotic vocals bring Peace to the mind, Rejuvenation to the body and Inspiration to the soul, the optimum experience in Regeneration.

AEOS

AEOS

Sacred Knowledge Collection

With Aurora Juliana Ariel, PhD & Bernadette Jean-Marie CHT

The Sacred Knowledge Collection brings timely wisdom to an Awakening Humanity at a time of Great Change on Earth. Each CD is specially designed to illuminate, uplift, and inspire humanity into an Age of Enlightenment and Peace.

In the tradition of the Oracles of Delphi, whose access to higher realms brought forth Sacred Knowledge helping many in their time, this Inner Quest for Truth led to landmark discoveries, answering age old questions about death, dying and the Afterlife (CD #1), the soul's preparation for embodiment and its Life Plan on Earth (CD #2), and the Coming Times - what is in store for the inhabitants of Earth 2012 - 2033 and beyond (CD #3).

Exploring the AfterLife

Guided in a Hypnosis Journey by Clinical Hypnotherapist, Bernadette Jean-Marie, pioneering doctor and healer, Aurora Juliana Ariel, PhD accessed the highest Realms of Light to find the truth about the soul's journey and what takes place on the Other Side.

AEOS SK1 - $24.95
https://www.createspace.com/2088508

The Soul's Journey

Guided in a Hypnosis Journey by Clinical Hypnotherapist, Bernadette Jean-Marie, pioneering doctor and healer, Aurora Juliana Ariel, PhD accessed the highest Realms of Light to find the Truth about the Soul's Journey and reason for embodying on Earth.

AEOS SK2 - $24.95
https://www.createspace.com/2088509

Journey Into the Future

Guided in a Hypnosis Journey by Clinical Hypnotherapist, Bernadette Jean-Marie, pioneering doctor and healer, Aurora Juliana Ariel, PhD accessed the highest Realms of Light to find the Truth about the portents of this time, revealing a glorious potential of a Golden Age on Earth.

AEOS SK3 - $24.95
https://www.createspace.com/2088511

Heal Your Life & Change Your Destiny with...

TheQuest
Self Healing System

Created by Pioneering Doctor/Healer
Aurora JulianaAriel, PhD

AURORA JULIANA ARIEL PhD

TheQuest

**Heal Your Life
Change Your Destiny**

A Breakthrough Self Healing System

AURORA JULIANA ARIEL PhD

TheQuest

Healing Journal

**7 Steps To Radically Transform Your Life
and Actualize Your Full Potential**

AURORA JULIANA ARIEL PhD

TheQuest

7 Step Self Healing Technique

How to Heal Your Life & Change Your Destiny

In groundbreaking work, Dr. Ariel unveils her breakthrough Self Healing System, 7 Master Keys to Inner Peace, and TheQuest Life Mastery Path. She demystifies the psyche like no other work has done and provides tools to quickly resolve issues, heal addictions, restore harmony in relationships, master one's psychology and remove the scars from the painful past. Through years of pioneering work in the psyche, she made many landmark discoveries, uncovered the cause of suffering, and developed a cure to help end suffering on Earth.

Every Issue Can Be Resolved
Every Pattern Healed
The Conditions of Your Life Can Changed

Metamorhesis Was Never So Easy!

Made in the USA
Columbia, SC
24 January 2018